Adventures with Emilie

Taking on Te Araroa trail in 138 life-changing days

Victoria Bruce

PENGUIN BOOKS

Map of Aotearoa

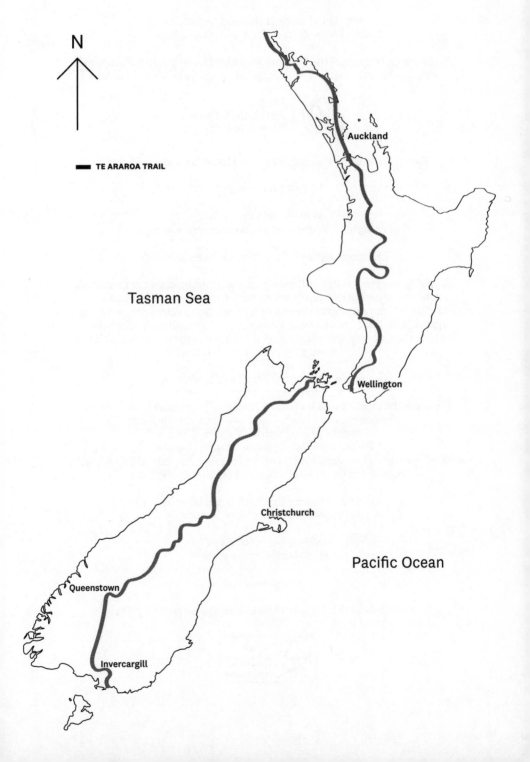

N

TE ARAROA TRAIL

Auckland

Tasman Sea

Wellington

Christchurch

Pacific Ocean

Queenstown

Invercargill

PENGUIN

UK | USA | Canada | Ireland | Australia
India | New Zealand | South Africa | China

Penguin is an imprint of the Penguin Random House group of companies,
whose addresses can be found at global.penguinrandomhouse.com

Penguin
Random House
New Zealand

First published by Penguin Random House New Zealand, 2023

13 5 7 9 10 8 6 4 2

Design and illustrations by Carla Sy © Penguin
Random House New Zealand
Photographs on front and back cover, pages 6–7 (Isthmus Peak traverse,
overlooking Lake Hāwea) and page 8 by Danilo Hegg
Author photograph by Victoria Bruce
Prepress by Soar Communications Group
Printed and bound in Australia by Griffin Press, an Accredited ISO AS/NZS
14001 Environmental Management Systems Printer

A catalogue record for this book is available from the
National Library of New Zealand.

ISBN 978-1-77695-047-8
eISBN 978-1-77695-373-8

penguin.co.nz

Some names in this book have been changed to protect privacy.

MIX
Paper | Supporting
responsible forestry
FSC® C018684

'Into the forest I go, to lose my
mind and find my soul.'

— often attributed to John Muir

Contents

Prologue

Te Araroa
Day 106

THE WIND IS SILENT UNTIL it encounters objects. And then it can command an orchestra of sound that drowns out all other noise, plucking the harp strings of branches and banging the drums of rocks, building up intensity until it transforms peaceful landscapes into terrifying infernos of energy in motion.

Wind over land flows like water over rocks, picking up speed, increasing in energy with everything it touches. Unchecked and insatiable, it runs around corners, gallops through gaps, contorts across cliff faces, rolls around bluffs and tears through tussock, pummelling everything in its path in a deafening, all-consuming roar.

I'm lying in my sleeping bag, holding my seven-year-old daughter tight in my arms, the thin fabric of our ultralight tent pressed against my face, waiting for the next gust to rip the roof off our flimsy shelter and suck us out into the night sky. We're camping at 950 metres' elevation in a valley encircled by dark craggy peaks; a high mountain pass is behind us and ahead, a narrow funnel of a creek that eventually opens into the icy blue expanse of Lake Hāwea.

A front is moving swiftly across the Southern Alps and we're in the middle of it. The previously rain-swollen clouds have run up against the rock wall of the mountains and dumped their load on the jungles of the West Coast. Now jubilantly free of burden, they've risen over the mountains and are descending upon us.

Sheltered valleys can turn into wind tunnels, and with nowhere to go, the wind rolls around, increasing in pressure and speed, packing a punch that will rip off branches, knock over dead trees and throw a 100-kilogram human off their feet.

That's why they say the only thing that will kill you in the New Zealand backcountry is the weather, and here I am, huddling with my little daughter, 1500 kilometres and 106 days into the longest walk of my life.

Each powerful gust swoops down from the craggy ridgeline and rolls around the basin, picking up speed, filling our terrified ears with its banshee roar.

It rips through the tiny grove of beech trees I'd hoped would offer us some protection and is upon us, bending poles and flattening the tent against my chest, so I must turn my head to not choke on a mouthful of material. How can the poles withstand such rough treatment? How much longer will the rocks I placed over those tiny red pegs keep them in the ground? This tent weighs less than 1.5 kilograms, yet with the force of each gust pressing down on me, it could weigh a tonne.

Minutes stretch into eternity while I wait for our prostrate bodies to be exposed to the full wrath of this storm. These moments of claustrophobic terror feel eternal as I force myself to lie still and keep breathing, when all my body wants to do is fight free of this fabric tomb and run, screaming, to safety.

But I can't breathe anymore, and my head is ringing with the roar of the raging wind and flapping tent, and I can't believe Emilie isn't screaming her head off, because right now I'm so fucking close to completely losing my shit.

I use my free arm to push the tent off my face, again, and miraculously, it just bounces back up, again. I turn to reassure Emilie only to find her nestled into the crook of my shoulder, all wrapped up in her bright yellow sleeping bag like a little doll, snoring peacefully through rosebud lips.

Somehow, I've transcended from the turmoil of fear and panic to a quiet sense of calm. I'm not really losing my shit. I'm brave and strong. I am a warrior woman, wahine toa with my little one sheltering safely by my side. The wind will eventually blow itself out over the eastern plains, dawn is just beyond the horizon, and once there's enough light in the sky we'll pack up and start walking again. Four hundred and sixty-six kilometres to go. Just another day on the crazy adventure of Te Araroa.

Mystery Lake in Hakatere Conservation Park with the snowy tops of Two Thumb Range in the distance. DANILO HEGG

Chapter 1

One big project

I'D NEVER HEARD OF NEW Zealand's 3000-kilometre long-distance walking trail, Te Araroa, until my daughter Emilie and I had a chance encounter with a giant Frenchman in a tiny historic hut. We were getting ready for bed at the end of a long day's tramp when a very tall, heavily bearded man knocked on the door and asked if there were any bunks left for the night.

We indicated the third sagging-wire bunk was free then sat and watched with interest as he gathered the crumbs from his various half-empty Ziploc bags to create his evening meal. He was the first person we'd seen for days, as we were spending our school holidays surrounded by mountains and rivers on a 66-kilometre multi-day tramp on the St James Walkway in Canterbury's Lewis Pass.

Emilie interrogated him with all the sweetness of a gap-toothed six-year-old — what was his name, where had he come from, where was he going? We were astounded to hear he'd been walking for several months on a path called Te Araroa, having commenced his colossal trek at the very top of the North Island and with another 1000 kilometres ahead of him. He'd walked over 40 kilometres that day, scaling a high mountain pass that bordered the nearby Nelson Lakes National Park before dropping into this valley and arriving at the rusted tin shed of Rokeby Hut.

Pierre was one of several other trail walkers we met over the course of that summer, as many of the tracks we followed on our weekend and multi-day tramping adventures also formed part of Te Araroa.

After we parted ways, I kept thinking about the freedom that surrounded him as he walked through an ever-changing landscape with only his food supplies to worry about. As a novice tramper, I was fascinated to think that all these different tracks could join up with each other, linking our national parks and wild places with farmland and towns, and that one could just keep on walking for the entire length of New Zealand.

I could only dream of doing something like that. But I was a busy, 36-year-old single mother with a new mortgage funded by a stressful full-time job with local government.

So, I got caught up with the whirlwind of life and forgot all about Te Araroa.

That was until a breakdown saw me craving the sanctuary of our wild places.

It's post-traumatic stress disorder, the psychiatrist said. The psychologist explained that it was my body's way of responding to repressed memories of traumatic events. They talked about concepts such as hypervigilance, a dysregulated nervous system, damaged neural pathways, altered perception, dissociation and major depressive disorder. All I knew was that I was sinking deeper into a black hole from which there seemed no escape.

There was no time, not even time to think. The darkness grew from a low rumble to a roar. Every cell in my body seemed to be screaming. I had nightmares. Panic attacks. Anxiety. Depression.

It wasn't always this way. Once upon a time, I was just like Emilie, a bubbly kid full of potential.

Born in New Zealand to Scottish parents with their own dreams and demons, I was barely old enough to say kia ora when we emigrated to Australia, our small family taking up residence in a corrugated tin shed on a three-acre bush block with no running water, electricity or flush toilet. While my parents sweated and swore as they slowly built our second home with their bare hands and a handsaw, my older brother Robert and I relished the freedom of a life played outdoors.

Our block was located down a long dirt road outside of the rural locality of Glenwood, some 30 kilometres from the town of Gympie, and with no neighbours for several kilometres, we kids made our own fun. While my parents worked on the house, we roamed the boundaries of our bush block, beating the long grass with sticks to scare away the snakes, our blue heeler dog Penny always nearby. We would escape the relentless Queensland heat by playing in the dam, smearing our naked bodies black with mud and clay, then build forts under the shade of the eucalyptus trees, our heads ringing with cicada song. One of my favourite pastimes was sneaking up quietly on the many skinks and blue-tongued lizards as they lay in the burning sun, trying to get close enough to catch one of these lithe and beautiful creatures in my chubby hands to examine them more closely.

By the time I was six years old, a year younger than Emilie is now, I knew I wanted to become an entomologist, or a zoologist like my hero Sir David Attenborough, or a marine biologist, or maybe even a veterinarian like my favourite childhood storyteller, James Herriot — anything to do with animals, preferably wild animals, and nothing to do with people.

I grew up gregarious, a voracious learner with a vivid imagination and a headstrong disposition. Home-schooled until age nine with the Australian bush as my playground, I was wise beyond my years and maybe a little wild.

I eventually went to school where I was the youngest in my class, skipping two grades as the teachers struggled to place me in a year group that matched my academic abilities. But none of that really mattered as I dropped out of school when I was 14.

My parents' relationship was plagued by broken dreams and domestic violence, and they separated when I was 10. My life as I knew it quickly fell apart. My family, who up until that point had been my whole world, became bitter strangers to one another. At age 14, I returned to New Zealand and was placed into the care of Child, Youth and Family, the government agency tasked with the care of vulnerable young people.

After surviving some of the darkest years of my life, I was declared a legal adult at age 16 and left to fend for myself in a dangerous and uncaring world.

I returned to Australia, where, teetering on the edge of what had become an increasingly shaky existence, I succumbed to a lethal drug addiction that wiped almost a year off my life and left long-lasting scars.

The darkness grew much darker until years later I somehow clawed my way through my high school certificate and into a diploma of nursing, and, after a few false starts, a bachelor's degree in journalism at the prestigious University of Queensland. Despite my childhood ambitions, this qualification had little to do with animals and everything to do with people, but it enabled me to travel overseas and work as a journalist before I became pregnant with my daughter. And yet even with the immense joy and sense of purpose little Emilie brought into my life, the darkness remained, gnawing at my soul and haunting me.

Now back in New Zealand, I tried to push through it. After maternity leave, I took a series of roles in strategic communications, bringing my experience in media, journalism and writing to non-profit organisations before moving on to local government. These well-paid, fast-paced positions helped me buy my first house. Emilie started school. Finally, I felt like I was doing everything right, everything society expected of me, but inside I was dying.

I wanted to get away from my pain and I wanted to confront it head-on, shining my head torch into every corner of my being to understand what was hurting me so badly. If not for me, then for my daughter, my beautiful, bright and bubbly Emilie, who deserved a happy life with a loving mother, not one who waited for her daughter to go to bed so she could cry herself to sleep.

I caught glimpses of that woman whenever we went tramping. I'd find her singing loudly on our way up a mountain, rolling around giggling in her sleeping bag inside a hut or our tent, calling Emilie to marvel at the sight of a native bird or beautiful flowering plant.

But at the beginning of each working week I heard her screaming in pain, and felt her slowly dying away as I rushed to pack Emilie's lunch box and drop her at before-school care, then hurry to my workplace for another stressful day with stressful people, then rush to collect Emilie from after-school care before returning home to our old house and my huge mortgage.

I felt stretched, strung out, overwhelmed and so very alone. Like a piece of rope that had frayed right down to its very last thread, I knew I was at breaking point.

The next time I took Emilie on a multi-day tramp, it hit me.

I didn't want to go back home. Even though my back and legs were aching with the effort of climbing up and over a mountain pass, my head was clear. The static and darkness and paralysing feelings of dread had been left behind, as though I'd somehow transcended myself on the way up the mountain. As crazy as it sounded, going back home felt all wrong and being out here felt completely right. Maybe if I stayed out here in the wild, I could give myself the space and time I needed to have a good rest before daring to venture deep inside my memory warehouse, sort shit out and begin to heal. Six months would do it. Enough time to rent out my house, pull Emilie out of school, tell my work that I was done. But where would we go? What track would be long enough? Then I remembered Te Araroa.

After the vision of walking Te Araroa flashed into my mind on that mountain pass, it became all I could think about. Officially opened in 2011, Te Araroa is New Zealand's equivalent of the Appalachian Trail — a long-distance tramping trail comprising multiple walking tracks and trails across public and private land. It was also my salvation, my exit strategy, the answer to everything I had sought and failed to find. It helped me get up in the morning and drag myself to work and back home again, writing lists and spreadsheets to help me understand how I'd walk 3000 kilometres across New Zealand's North and South islands.

I weighed up my finances, got a rental appraisal, and realised with a combination of fear and glee that the rental returns would be just enough to cover my mortgage, rates and insurance. I could keep my house, as long as I didn't live in it! I spoke to Emilie's school and received the blessing from her principal. She agreed this would be the trip of a lifetime for Emilie, whose school year had been badly disrupted by various Covid-19 lockdowns.

The Te Araroa website told me that a person walking an average of 25 kilometres a day would take 120 days (four months) to complete the entire length of the trail across the North and South islands. I decided we'd be lucky to average 15 kilometres a day, and with regular zero days to rest and resupply at the end of each leg, our journey should take around six months to complete.

I wandered around my three-bedroom house feeling lost and overwhelmed, wondering how the hell I would pack up all our worldly possessions and fit just the essentials into a 50-litre backpack.

How do you pack for a six-month trip anyway? There were so many different climates, different terrains. Would we need our light-weight down jackets for the tropical far north? How many pairs of socks should I take? Medications? Sunscreen? Insect repellent? How would I supply Emilie with enough sketch books and reading material to keep her from chewing my ear off?

I borrowed scales from a friend and weighed all our gear, then wrote more lists of the new lightweight equipment we'd need to buy. I emailed our local outdoor stores, asking for sponsorship. The weight of our pile of gear kept growing. And then there was the biggest question — was I really capable of carrying one to two weeks' worth of food, with only a couple of days' rest at the end of each section, before loading up and walking on again?

You might be wondering what the hell a stressed-out mother was doing taking her seven-year-old kid into the wilderness alone, but at the time, it felt like the right thing to do.

I've never been a trail walker, but I do love tramping and have been taking Emilie with me into the bush, alone and often for multiple days, since she was four years old. I knew what to carry in my backpack, how to read a basic map and follow a trail marker. I also knew that, for whatever reason, being in nature helped me feel safe and calm, strong and peaceful. Don't get me wrong, I often feel scared out there in the mountains, but there's a big difference between healthy fear and the unhealthy, insidious dread that accompanies my mental health condition.

There's that feeling of excitement and anticipation when you are setting off on a tramp, carrying everything you need to be self-contained upon your back. The way your heart races when you're scrambling up high, every muscle awake and your body strong and alert as you place one foot in front of the other, grasping for rocks and roots as you pull yourself up. There's the deep satisfaction when you finally pop above the tree line and see the views, or arrive at your destination after a long, hard day of navigating rough terrain, fallen trees and flowing streams. Then there are those quiet moments of peace when all your thoughts have blown away in the breeze and you're simply present, you, your breath, your body and the bush all around you.

That's why tramping makes me feel like a badass. After a few days out in the mountains, I feel strong and confident, in awe of the unpredictability of my environment. When I feel fear, it's the real deal, because of something that's actually happening in front of me, whether it's a slip or tumble, a fallen tree or heinous weather. But most of the time I feel awake and alert, present but also incredibly peaceful. Just like there's no room in my pack for surplus gear that I have no use for, there's no space in my mind for unhelpful thoughts.

And maybe, if I spent enough time out there, the rush of adrenaline and cortisol released from my dysregulated nervous system would simply help me walk faster, climb higher, see further and listen deeper, to be more in tune with my mind, my body and my natural world. I hoped it would, anyway, because nothing else seemed to be working.

So, I ploughed on, swinging from moments of euphoric excitement to ones of worry and despair. Secretly, I knew this was crazy, but I couldn't back down. Not now. Once Te Araroa had taken over my mind, it was as though I was already caught up in a trajectory that only led forwards. And, for some strange reason, everything seemed to be working out.

A local outdoor store offered us brand-new ultralight sleeping bags at cost price; another store gave us two brand-new backpacks. The real estate agent found someone to rent our house for the six months we were planning to be away. We were loaned a fancy InReach GPS satellite device to summon help in case of any mishaps in the backcountry.

I set up a Givealittle page to raise funds for two worthy organisations, the Mental Health Foundation and Federated Mountain Clubs of New Zealand, the latter of which would be hosting a blog of our journey. I also created Instagram and Facebook accounts through which I would share our story and encourage people to donate. Then a journalist from Stuff reached out to me, and a reporter from *Seven Sharp*. It felt surreal to be in front of the camera, and even more so to see ourselves on prime-time television. But the media were interested and people in the outdoor community were supportive — if they all thought we could do it, then maybe we could.

I decided to stop trying to look at Te Araroa as one big project and, instead, focused on preparing for individual sections. It would be just like a series of multi-day tramps, with time in between to wash our clothes, refill our food bags and check the map to remind myself where we were going next.

In several places, particularly in the South Island, Te Araroa winds its way through remote locations and tiny settlements, places where I could post myself a resupply box but could not expect to find a supermarket with a wide variety of lightweight and nutritious meals. So, I made a list of all the resupply points, then visited our local PAK'nSAVE supermarket to bulk-buy breakfast oats, packets of biscuits and bags of nuts, dried fruit, pasta, potato flakes, dried peas, vegetable protein and milk powder. I also cooked and dehydrated a range of bean and beef mince-based meals.

Emilie and I worked morning and night to package up food supplies into resealable plastic bags, me carefully spooning the correct amount into each bag and she drawing pictures or writing instructions in permanent marker on each bag. We then packed post-paid boxes with our supplies. Our kitchen was transformed into a heaving factory of dry goods and Ziploc bags.

Planning a six-month trip with only a seven-year-old for help was a frustrating, if not maddening, experience. Emilie was initially excited about our 'big adventure', especially when I explained in detail about the beaches we'd walk along, the rivers we could swim in and all the little old huts we'd visit, but when it came to the practical side of packing up our house and condensing everything into our backpacks, the cat was more helpful than she was!

Look, Mummy, the Sylvanians are having a bath in the porridge oats! she announced with glee, bouncing on a kitchen stool with a toy bunny figurine in each hand. I was mixing up a huge bowl of rolled oats with a cup of brown sugar, a heaped tablespoon of cinnamon, one bag of slivered almonds and another of painfully expensive freeze-dried raspberries.

I'd asked her — and the Sylvanians — to stir the bowl then place two cupfuls into each Ziploc bag, as I was busy smearing portions of lentil and vegetable stew across the trays of my dehydrator.

There was only so much clowning around Mummy could tolerate before I turned into that monster from *It* and got my growly voice on. After all, it was already late July and in just over two months we would need to hand over the keys to our lovely home and start our new life as trail walkers. Right now, we needed to focus on packing our stuff up, not strewing it all over the house.

Those Sylvanian Families better scuttle off and make a new home in the garage, because they won't be coming on Te Araroa, I warned Emilie.

Awww! But I want to take them! she exclaimed, before bouncing off into the garden to play with Felix, the four-year-old son of my good friend, Fabio, who was renting a self-contained studio at the rear of my Christchurch property.

Fabio came inside with a couple of cold beers and helped me stir my lentils.

Whoaa Victoria, this looks amazing! You're so organised!

With his big grin and laid-back Brazilian approach to life, Fabio always cheered me up. He was staying on to live in the studio while we were away, and Jiji, our cat, would stay out there with him and Felix. Fabio had also volunteered to post my resupply boxes, provided I packed them all up with postage paid and addresses clearly marked.

I drank my beer and tried to relax as I added more frozen spinach to the pot — additional vitamins for the trail.

At least the stew smelled better than it looked, and I desperately hoped it would taste okay when we rehydrated it for dinner over the coming months. But my heart sank as each batch emerged from its dehydrator tray as a cluster of brittle brown crumbs. Once soaked in water, would this really rehydrate into a palatable meal and fill our bellies at the end of a long day?

The dehydrator hummed non-stop, but I was only managing to dry six double-serve meal portions every 12 hours.

It started to feel like a race against time before we'd even left home. The ideal trail-walking 'season' runs from October, when the dark grip of winter has released its hold on our mountains and forests, to April.

By August, I realised two things, or rather, my body did. I was having a mental breakdown, and if I didn't pull my shit together with one last mammoth effort, I wouldn't have the energy to pack up our house and finish preparing for Te Araroa.

You're very, very stressed, my GP observed after I broke down in tears on yet another visit to her office. *Have you considered taking a period of time off work to focus on your wellbeing so you can get better again?*

The shitty thing about post-traumatic stress disorder (PTSD), which I'd been diagnosed with some years earlier, is that there's no medication and no simple cure. The feelings of panic and terror are caused by your overactive nervous system pumping you full of adrenaline and cortisol, screaming at you to fight, freeze or flee. There's no medication that can isolate these important hormones, and anyway, in normal doses these chemicals are imperative to your body's everyday functioning. The fact that traumatic childhood experiences had resulted in a recalibration of my brain's alarm system, compelling my body to secrete huge doses of stress hormones at completely inappropriate and unhelpful moments, was simply too bad.

Other than antidepressants and the occasional sedative, there really wasn't much else my GP could prescribe me. An extended period of time off work, on the other hand, had a certain appeal. I had recently received a letter from my employer rejecting my application for six months' unpaid leave, and another refusing my request to work from home once a week so I could get a grip on my mental health. My doctor recommended I resign immediately. Maybe it was finally time to walk up to the edge of the cliff then let go in a glorious freefall.

I took the medical certificate and handed in my resignation the next day. Two weeks later, after a rushed handover and a farewell morning tea, I rode my bike out of the Christchurch City Council building on Hereford Street for the last time, officially unemployed and feeling as though I was floating on air. From then on, I focused full-time on Te Araroa. With Emilie at school during the day I could concentrate on emptying our house and packing all our precious things away in the double garage. I finished the food preparation and labelled boxes of dry goods for Fabio to post to me — food supplies for five days, some for seven and a couple for 10.

As a mum, I wanted things to be as easy for us as possible. I knew that walking out of a long section on the trail to collect a box of pre-packed food would be better than having to hitchhike to the local shops with a whining, hungry kid in tow, then wasting money buying overpriced groceries that might not be suitable for carrying in our packs.

I selected two sets of clothing — colourful quick-dry shorts and T-shirts for the day and lightweight merino thermals to wear at night, two pairs of merino socks each and two pairs of merino underwear.

I'd spent hours trawling the internet for child-sized underwear and finally ordered Emilie some extra-small Icebreaker knickers at nearly $50 a pair, which she ungratefully told me were itchy and not beautiful at all. I had to agree with her, since the only options had been stripy blue, olive green or black and grey, with no pink butterflies or unicorns in sight.

For myself, I settled for a couple of black thongs, and a pair of boyleg pants to wear when that time of the month came around. I'd also recently procured a menstrual cup and successfully trialled it over a long weekend tramp, enjoying the sensation of free bleeding without needing to deal with used tampons or smelly pads. Now my menstrual blood could be buried under the leaf litter, returning to Mother Nature, and I would no longer have to wrap my used products in toilet paper and carry them with me until the end of a tramp.

I bought us both lightweight, expensive raincoats and waterproof over trousers. I was unsure about the trousers as usually I preferred wet, bare legs to being hot, sticky and eventually damp, but Emilie doesn't do well when wet and cold, so I threw both pairs into the pile. I also splashed out on some UPF 50+ sunhats with cheek flaps to protect us from the harsh New Zealand sun.

I stuffed our clothing into a compression sack, next to the sleeping bags, thermal liners, inflatable mats, tent, electronics, first aid kit, cooker, pot and fuel canisters.

My new backpack was a 50-litre roll-top made from a light,

canvas-like material with a simple harness. It was a test pack, not available on the market yet, designed by Macpac and generously donated to us to trial over our long journey. It wasn't the lightest of lightweight packs, but I liked the durable feel of the fabric and the surprisingly spacious single compartment and one elasticated front pocket. With a little practice, I found I could fit our gear inside, even the tent, packed down hard until every little pocket of air had been squeezed out or filled with something useful. Then I arranged my bags of food and held my breath until I'd forced the top of the pack over at least one turn and squeezed the clip together for that satisfying click. And there it was, one black brick of a backpack, consisting of around 11 kilograms 'base weight' (all our tramping gear), plus up to eight kilograms of food and water to last us to the next resupply point. Twenty kilograms was heavy — heavier than any pack I'd carried before — but it was solid and, best of all, I had everything I needed right there on my back.

Emilie also had a new pack, a real *big kids' pack* as she called it, a 30-litre Macpac Torlesse, that fitted her little body perfectly. I was loath to load her up for such a long distance, so she just carried what she'd usually carry on our weekend tramps — her own lightweight sleeping bag and sleeping mat, weighing around a kilogram, her sleeping-bag liner, raincoat, drink bottle and snacks, a tramping diary and a handful of coloured pencils.

After a whirlwind of packing and repacking, we handed over our house keys to the real estate agent, hugged our friends goodbye and caught two flights and a long ride to Cape Reinga at the very top of New Zealand's North Island, where an orange trail marker pointed south.

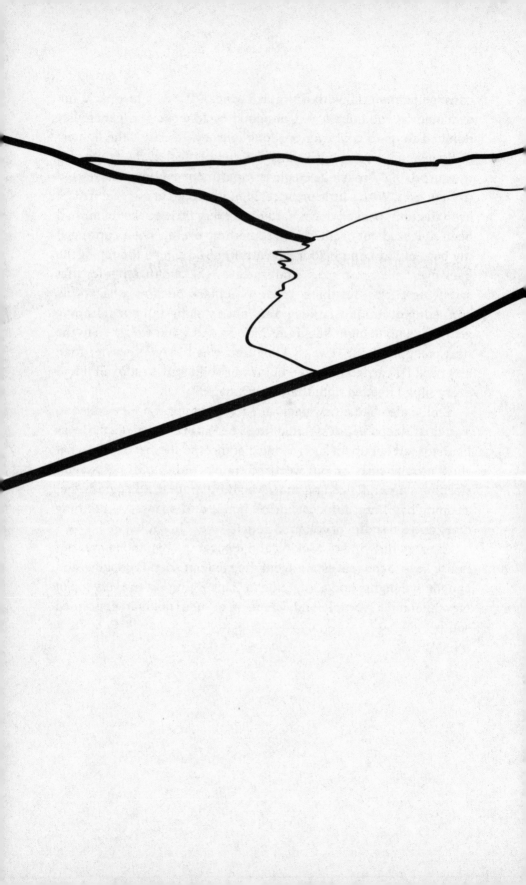

Chapter 2

Cape Reinga

Te Araroa
Day 1

CAPE REINGA, ALSO KNOWN AS Te Rerenga Wairua (the leaping place of the spirits), is a remote and windswept sanctuary at the very top of New Zealand's North Island. Out here, the Tasman Sea meets the Pacific Ocean in a spectacular swirl of currents and waves crash against dark and rugged cliffs.

In Māori legend, it is the place where the spirits of the dead gather in an ancient pōhutukawa tree before leaping into the ocean to return to their ancestral homeland of Hawaiki.

Every year, hundreds of Te Araroa trail walkers start their long-distance journey south from this point, picking their way through a colourful kaleidoscope of stunted coastal vegetation to begin the 100 kilometres of beach walking along this wild coastline that will take them to the closest town.

The trail notes say the hardest part of the Te-Oneroa-a-Tōhē / Ninety Mile Beach section is the amount of water you need to carry, as the few side streams marked on the map are unreliable over summer and some days you need to walk 25 kilometres between campsites.

So there I was, fully loaded with three litres of water to last us until the next water source, already wilting in the intense heat of the Northland sun.

I was also carrying six days' worth of food, all crammed into the pack on top of our two-person tent, sleeping bags, inflatable mats, spare clothes, satellite phone and spare battery, and holding my little daughter's hand as we wandered along a windswept beach.

We picked our way down a narrow pathway between stunted

bushes and shrubs, past fragile pink and white mānuka blossoms and reddish-orange flax. Despite their soft colours, these native plants are wiry and strong, designed to thrive in this wild, exposed setting, alternately baked dry by the hot sun or lashed by the salt-smeared wind and rain.

Our ears were filled with the roar of waves pounding the jagged rocks below as we dropped onto Te Werahi Beach, where we celebrated our first five kilometres with a quick and exhilarating skinny dip in the freshwater stream before clambering up and over the peach and pink-coloured sand dunes, past the turnoff to Cape Maria van Diemen and onto Twilight Beach.

There's something about a golden sandy beach on a sunshiny day that fills the soul with joy. Childhood memories of running down sand dunes, beachcombing, swimming and digging moats to reinforce gaudily decorated sandcastles against the incoming tide come to mind.

Strange and wonderful treasures dotted the high-tide line — cream and orange crab carapaces, a string of Neptune's necklace, bedraggled feathers, and a large, white, ball-shaped object that stank of dead fish, much to Emilie's disgust. We later learned it was a type of sea sponge.

By early afternoon, we'd arrived at the Twilight Beach campground. There we dropped our packs and charged into the surprisingly warm water. Apart from a lone trail walker, who set up her tent behind the dunes, we were alone in the campground.

I kept a stern lookout for the resident possum mentioned in the intentions book, that ubiquitous green and gold tome supplied by the Department of Conservation (DOC) for trampers and trail walkers to record their passage and share useful information. From the book, I learned that one of Peter the Possum's favourite tricks was to sneak under a tent fly and steal scroggin out of backpacks while their unsuspecting owners were asleep. After setting up our tent, I ensured our bulging food bag was secured safely inside.

That evening, sticky from swimming in the sea, Emilie and I sat shoulder to shoulder eating rehydrated lamb bolognaise with mashed potato flakes while watching the evening light paint the waves soft hues of pink. Once the sun dipped behind the headland, the rumble of the incoming tide soon lulled us to sleep, and when I woke for a pee a few hours later, stars lit up every corner of the sky.

Dawn brought warm winds and tangerine skies before grey clouds marched in. Everything I'd taken out of my pack the previous night fitted back inside it perfectly, minus yesterday's dinner and our breakfast of porridge oats. I made sure to fill all our water bottles from the tank, as we were unlikely to refill again until tomorrow evening, another 30 kilometres down the beach. That night we planned to wild camp in the sand dunes of Ninety Mile Beach, and I didn't want to rely on finding drinkable fresh water.

We descended the steep stairs onto Ninety Mile Beach with glee, only to be met with a gusty offshore breeze that stirred up the sand into thin tendrils that stung our bare legs. We were walking parallel to an amazing natural phenomenon, the 10-kilometre-long by one-kilometre-wide coastal strip of 150-metre-high, ever-changing Te Paki sand dunes. The strange and beautiful dance of the wind-whipped sand turned to monotony very quickly as we trudged down the beach, glad for the protection of our oversized hats and sunglasses, our spirits boosted with the occasional boiled lolly.

If this was typical of Ninety Mile Beach, then no wonder people attempt to boost through this section as fast as possible. Unfortunately, we two little wāhine would have to grin (or whine) and bear it, as the vastly sweeping coastline, flat as a highway, disappeared into the horizon with no sign of respite from the unforgiving elements.

Beach walking can be slow and arduous as the weight of your pack forces your feet to sink into the sand with each step, but the low tide was on our side, so we stuck to the hard-packed sand at the water's edge, playing with the ebb and flow of the waves.

An hour or so after descending onto Ninety Mile Beach — three hours from leaving the campsite — I dragged Emilie off the beach and made her some lunch, salami and cheese on pita bread with as much sand as you like, which we ate huddled together behind clumps of flax beside the shallow trickle of Te Paki Stream.

Maybe we can camp here, Mummy, Emilie said hopefully, and I wished we could too, but it was barely past noon and we'd only been walking for three hours. My Te Araroa notes recommend a 28-kilometre stint along the beach from Twilight Beach to The

Bluff campground, and in my mind, we needed to cover at least 15 kilometres before we found somewhere to wild camp amongst the dunes.

The fine-grained sand was everywhere, in our eyes, our noses, even my ears were full of it. The sunscreen I'd lavishly applied to our arms and legs earlier that morning was now coated with a thin layer of sand. But there was no point hiding in the flax bushes, as the wind had already tracked us down and kept throwing more sand our way. We changed into our waterproof pants and rain jackets in an attempt to block out the worst of it.

We felt much more comfortable for another six kilometres until our aching feet drew us back to the sand dunes. It was as though Papatūānuku, the Earth Mother herself had called us here, because behind the giant flax and tussocks was a clump of dense, windswept pine trees, blown together in a thick windbreak, and underneath, a flat green space just big enough for our tent.

We sat gasping for breath and massaging our swollen feet when the first droplets of rain blew through, sending us scrambling for shelter and tent pegs. It was only 3pm but I didn't think we'd go any further that day.

Once camp was set up, we grabbed our rain jackets and staggered back to play on the beach, the warm rain kissing our bare legs and the cool saltwater swirling around our feet. I grabbed Emilie's hands and we did a crazy rain dance in the shallows, fat raindrops pelting into the surf breaking around us.

It felt so good. Our water play was observed by half a dozen giant black-backed gulls and a pair of variable oystercatchers, their bright orange beaks the only colour against the backdrop of miles of empty windswept beach.

Snug in our tent, we listened to the gentle boom of the incoming tide while fat raindrops plopped on the roof. Emilie drew pictures of us dancing in the rain in her hut journal, accompanied by loopy seven-year-old handwriting. My hair was damp and full of sand and her twin plaits looked like frayed golden-brown rope, but she was smiling and happy and that was all that mattered.

The forecast was for more rain, but the following day we planned to make it further down the beach, and in a couple more days we would reach Ahipara and the chance of a hot shower and some fresh food before continuing on the next section of Te Araroa.

We'd made it all the way to Northland and onto Ninety Mile Beach. It was scary and surreal and I had no idea what was coming next, but I didn't care because I was so happy to be there, snuggled up in our warm sleeping bags, giggling together.

Tiny white blips on the endless grey beach transformed into a flock of seabirds, and as we came closer, I saw it was a group of terns, the striking black caps on their heads a stark contrast to their pale bodies.

They regarded us through inky black eyes until we were too close for comfort, then the small group launched unanimously into the air, coming to rest a few hundred metres down the beach.

On land, the stumpy legs of the white-fronted tern (*Sterna striata*) seemed too small for their sleek shape, but as they rose effortlessly and wheeled away into the sky, their delicate forked tails looked just like a swallow's tail, which is why they are also known as the swallowtail or sea swallow.

Closely related to one of New Zealand's most endangered seabirds — the fairy tern (*Sternula nereis davisae*), which was once widespread along these northern beaches — the larger white-fronted tern can be found on beaches and braided rivers around the country, sometimes in flocks of many hundreds or even thousands of birds.

Here there were maybe 30 birds, and we entertained ourselves trying to count the little white bodies as we kept pace with each other — another way of passing time on the monotony of Northland's Ninety Mile Beach. It was our third day of beach walking and, apart from the birds and blips in the sand that turned out to be mounds of dried seaweed, shells, pieces of flotsam and jetsam or the occasional shy fur seal, the landscape appeared unchanging, just an endless curve of flat beach flanked by a high bank of sand dunes on one side and lapped by greyish blue waves that melted into the horizon on the other.

The hard-packed sand was as unforgiving as wet concrete, and a sharp pain shot up the front of my shins with every step. That morning, I'd reinforced a hot spot on my heel with Compeed patches, hoping the fleshy gel plasters would prevent blisters from forming on my skin. I'd read enough reports from other trail walkers to know that most emerged from this 100-kilometre stint with bloody and torn feet, and quietly hoped my own feet, already calloused from tramping in boots, would survive this section without erupting into painful blisters.

Emilie pointed and I saw a pair of Southern black-backed gulls towering amidst the tiny terns, their dark wing feathers and noble heads making them appear as Goliaths beside their petite companions. While the terns fluttered and strutted, the gulls ignored our passing, their handsome heads with curved yellow bill and distinctive red spot focused on the horizon, perhaps on the lookout for something to eat.

New Zealand's largest seabird, the Southern black-backed gull or karoro (*Larus dominicanus*) is known to be an opportunistic scavenger, preferring to devour whatever it finds dead or dying than catch its own prey. You'll often see them around coastal towns, hanging out at the local refuse station or wandering around farmland in search of an easy meal. While they also enjoy the company of large colonies, breeding pairs often go it alone, sharing the task of incubating and raising their chicks with all the dedication of a monogamous married couple.

Oh, to be a seagull, a creature that mates for life and rarely divorces, living freely on the wing and reconnecting with its partner each breeding season. I think of the naivety of my 27-year-old self, consoling myself from the shock of my pregnancy with daydreams of raising a child with a devoted partner by my side, sharing the joy of each developmental milestone as our babe began to crawl, then walk, talk and transform into a little person.

Emilie's father didn't share these dreams. Instead, I was confronted with the painful reality of being a single mother and the shock arrival of a tiny, mewling, newborn Emilie, wrestled from my open-cut belly after many hours of labour and placed in my arms. There was the sinking realisation of reality as the following days, weeks, then months turned into a blur of sleepless nights and the monotonous routine of changing nappies, feeding schedules and endless nap times. While I spent many hours high on the hormone-induced euphoria of gazing at my tiny daughter, these quiet moments of joy were constantly darkened by chronic feelings of inadequacy, anxiety and fear.

I suppose some degree of fear was understandable. As a brand-new mum with little in the way of a support network or savings, my aspiring international journalism career cut short by an unplanned pregnancy, I had good reason to worry about my — our — future, the future I was supposed to provide for Emilie on my own. But this was deeper, darker, all-pervading, and I would wake in the night gasping in terror, my breasts swollen with milk that I swore was becoming infused with fear.

Every morning I woke in dread at the thought of stumbling through another day with only the echo of the frenzied thoughts inside my head for company, alone with a baby whose cries penetrated my very soul. Instead of the calm, nurturing mother I thought I'd somehow naturally be, I was panicking on the inside and full of self-doubt and loathing.

Sometimes I felt like days passed without hearing the sound of another human voice, because the cries and gurgles of a roly-poly baby didn't count. By 27, I was accustomed to being a bit of a loner, but now the feelings of being a social outcast, unwanted and unlovable, were amplified from a low hum in the back of my mind to an unbearable frequency. Something was undeniably wrong with me, I just didn't know what it was.

I used to cling to the idea that I'd had a happy childhood, home-schooled with my big brother as my best friend and the Australian bush as our backyard. But maybe my brother and I spent long days playing outside just to avoid the bumps and whimpers at home.

If inheriting my mother's high cortisol levels then spending my formative years fearing one of my primary caregivers wasn't enough to ensure some long-lasting trauma, then the 18 months I spent in foster care under the faceless entity of Child, Youth and Family surely added some marks to my emotional tally board.

By the time I was a legal adult, I was blind with rage and indignation, channelling all of my hurt and pain into these war-like emotions. But maybe 16 was too young to be considered a legal adult and left without the mental or emotional resilience to cope with the world. Just imagine, the government considers you old enough to live on your own, but not old enough to vote or buy yourself a beer at the bottle shop. Maybe my trauma was compounded by the ensuing years of drug addiction and uncaring casual sex and anything else I could get inside of me to fill the terrifying black hole in the pit of my soul. Abortion, attempted suicide, a fractured spine, a few failed attempts at university . . . finally I got into an undergraduate course in journalism that held me, shakily, to task and revived one of my childhood passions: to write.

For a while, the intellectual side of my brain thrived, and I slowly built myself a new life as part of the society that I felt had once judged and shunned me. As long as I kept performing professionally, channelling the chronic, restless energy brought on by trauma into something creative, no one could guess the darkness I was trying so hard to leave behind.

However, my negative self-image left me feeling permanently damaged, broken and worthless, even after completing university, working overseas, giving birth to my beautiful daughter and developing professionally as a journalist and communications advisor.

I tried to forget those traumatic events, but past hurts left unaddressed have a way of welling up from deep inside of you, like water from deep underground. You get to a stage in your life where you realise that to go forward, you need to address your past.

When Emilie came into my life and became my whole world, she made me want to be the best version of myself, the best mum, capable of loving her just as much as a mother and father combined. Perhaps she was the miracle I'd been waiting for my whole life. I'd never experienced such feelings of love, infatuation or tenderness for anything or anyone before I met my daughter.

Even though she brought such joy and purpose to my life, a sense of worthlessness, hopelessness and the nagging feeling of being permanently damaged still prevailed. These dark shadows, combined with sleep deprivation and the complete overwhelm of being a new mother to a tiny, vulnerable human who was utterly dependent on me, meant my bucket felt chronically empty. I didn't dare share these thoughts with anyone, and became increasingly convinced that, deep down, I was a terrible, unlovable and potentially crazy person who didn't deserve the gift of my beautiful daughter.

I had to do something. Late one night, after six-month-old Emilie had finally settled to sleep, I decided to contact a counsellor and try to make sense of what was going on inside my head.

We'll start with some basic family history, she said. *Tell me about your parents, about your childhood.*

I screwed up my face, then began my familiar narrative, how I'd been home-schooled until my parents divorced when I was 10, how I'd hung out with my dad for a few years before he became too much, then moved to my mum, her new partner and my brother for a brief period before coming across to New Zealand and ending up in foster care.

I see, she nodded, although I wanted to tell her she didn't. *And have you ever been sexually abused?*

I was raped when I was fourteen, I whispered, the soft rug on the floor of her office swimming before my suddenly tear-filled eyes.

My relationship, if I could call it that, with Emilie's father had ended when I announced I was pregnant for a second time and determined to keep the baby this time. Staying on in the rogue Southeast Asian nation of Myanmar (formerly Burma), where I'd spent the past 18 months working as a journalist and trying to win his heart, didn't seem a viable option. So, with little in the way of personal savings and no useful assets except my laptop and a string of by-lines in local and international publications, the welfare state of Australia became my destination.

After arriving, downcast, in Sydney, I found my old life and friends hadn't changed much in the time I'd been away, but with a 24-week baby belly, I couldn't exactly re-join them in the work-hard, play-hard corporate lifestyle that I'd enjoyed in my twenties. Instead, I fronted the humiliation of the Department of Human Services' new applications queue, and found myself explaining my circumstances to a bored clerk who was probably the same age as me.

I'd like to apply for the sole parent benefit, I explained, *just for a while until I can get back on my feet.*

Where's your child? she asked, and I patted my bulging belly, explaining I was due mid-April.

Well, you can't get a benefit until March, six weeks before the baby is born and we'll need a certificate from your obstetrician to confirm that due date, she retorted, as I burned quietly in shame.

My options, she continued in the same mechanical tone, were to go get a job myself, or sign up to their Job Seeker programme and actively look for work as a condition of my unemployment benefit.

I explained that I was actually a qualified journalist with local and international media experience on my CV, however I didn't feel that the local *Sydney Morning Herald* would take me on in my current condition.

That doesn't matter, she said. *You don't have to work as a journalist. You could . . . wash dishes or something.*

I didn't tell her that I'd done my time washing dishes in nursing homes and cafés while I was struggling my way through my high school certificate, or that I'd fought to keep my depression, drug addictions and suicidal tendencies on the backburner as I worked night shifts in hospitals for three and a half years to gain a university qualification.

I didn't mention the countless hours of unpaid work experience I'd clocked up on all the news and media internships I could get my hands on, before scoring myself a paid gig as a cadet journalist.

I didn't bother to explain that I'd just returned from almost two years living and working in a corrupt, dirty and heart-wrenchingly beautiful developing country, one I'd journeyed to with a backpack containing some clothes, my laptop, my life's savings of AU$2000 and the address of an Australian editor whom I'd met once and from whom I planned on begging for a job. I said nothing of the humiliating relationship breakdown I'd recently endured and how I'd spent my last $10 commuting to the Department of Inhuman Services office, or how the only thing keeping me from jumping off the Sydney Harbour Bridge was the little jellybean growing inside me.

Instead, I slunk away and wept with rage and self-pity, then emailed my mother to berate her for what I felt was her heartless and completely selfish decision to backtrack on an offer for me to stay in a self-contained cottage out the back of her and my stepfather's house near Maleny, several hours north of Brisbane.

We plan to offer our tenant the studio on a one-year lease, she wrote back. *She really wants to stay in the cottage, has a job nearby and loves the block. You could stay in our spare room, but it's not available until March. Totally get that you want a nest now, but we don't have that to offer.*

Her words were drowned out by a roaring sensation inside my head that swept through my whole body. To me, it was just another example of how, since divorcing my father, her relationship with my stepfather always took priority over my brother and me. Whenever I really needed my mother, she just wasn't there.

Anyway, it was January 2014 and Emilie was due in three months. I needed to get my nest in order, wherever it might be, so I flew across the ditch to my grandparents, back to my birth country and the place where I'd done time in foster care some 17 years earlier.

Several hours after my best friend Greg carried my suitcases onto the early-morning train to Sydney International Airport, doing his best to cheer me up with silly jokes, I stepped off a plane onto the Central Plateau, the wind from the tiny turbo-prop aircraft whipping my long blonde hair across my face.

There were my grandparents, so much smaller and frailer than I'd ever seen them before, the wind also playing havoc with Poppa's wispy white hair. Together, we wrestled my two suitcases into the car and drove to their fussy little cottage with its English roses, ornaments, family portraits and hokey pokey ice cream in the freezer, just as I'd always remembered it.

I'd flown from Australia to Taupō in the centre of New Zealand's

North Island to be closer to my maternal grandparents, partly because my grandmother seemed like the only member of my family who was excited about me having a baby, and she'd said they had a spare car I could use and an old house they were trying to sell, some 35 kilometres from town.

That spare car Nanny promised proved a blessing, and the local social services department welcomed me with open, judgement-free and surprisingly empathetic arms. It appeared that little Taupō, with its shiny lakefront tourist attractions hiding the raggedy lower socio-economic suburbs on the hills behind, was the perfect place for an unemployed single mother to pick up the pieces of her broken dreams.

The old house in the countryside was far too isolated, so I rented a cute little one-bedroom bach closer to town, walking distance from the brilliant blue expanse of Lake Taupō. My baby bump and I took long drives in the countryside behind the wheel of an old 1970s Datsun station wagon, discovering local gems including Maunga Kākaramea (formerly known as Rainbow Mountain) and the Kerosene Creek natural hot pools, as well as Mount Tauhara on the outskirts of Taupō.

Mount Tauhara became a frequent place of refuge, as I found comfort in the sad story of how this particular maunga came to be. Once a mighty warrior, Tauhara was deeply in love with the beautiful Pīhanga, a mountain standing above the township of Tūrangi at the southern end of Lake Taupō. But several other warriors also coveted Pīhanga's heart. They waged a mighty battle and a warrior named Tongariro emerged victorious. Enraged and humiliated, the other warriors fled under the cover of darkness. But Tauhara was sad, and his heavy heart weighed down his footsteps, so when dawn came, he had only reached the north-eastern shore of Lake Taupō. He was turned to stone at first light and stands to this day, looking mournfully across the lake towards his lost love, Pīhanga.

I found the story of lost love fitting for my personal situation and climbed to the summit of Tauhara several times during my pregnancy, pulling myself up the lush, overgrown track on roots and branches, puffing and blowing, knees high on either side of my huge belly. I even straddled him at 38 weeks pregnant after my midwife suggested that in lieu of sexual intercourse, strenuous exercise could help kickstart my body into labour.

When I couldn't climb any higher, I lay in Tauhara's arms and grieved as tiny birds flitted in the green canopy above my head.

Once Emilie was born my exercise routine slowed down a bit, but I quickly realised the only way to distract myself from my dark thoughts was to get out of the house, strap my little baby into my front pack and walk for hours along the many tracks surrounding our hometown.

These wanderings took me through ancient, native forests, along the shores of rivers and lakes and into the foothills of mountains where I lost myself in the soothing colours and sounds of nature while Emilie slept, her head on my chest, lulled by the rhythm of my steps.

I had no idea that a long-distance walking trail passed less than an hour's drive from my house, but back then I'd never worn tramping boots or trail shoes and knew nothing about sleeping bags or backpacks, topographic maps or freeze-dried meals. I just knew that I craved the solace of being outdoors.

I certainly never thought that six years later I'd be wandering through the country where I was born but didn't grow up, my daughter by my side and everything we needed crammed into a pack on my back: our lightweight gear, high-calorie food and the essential water that we needed to make it to our next resupply point, 50 kilometres away.

In the days after those bitter, sand-flinging winds had passed, the weather was calm and warm, and we continued trudging slowly down the flat, packed sand, our eyes searching for landmarks to help break up the monotony of sand and sea. Although the beach is officially a public highway, we only saw a handful of vehicles over the first few days. For the most part, it was just us, the seagulls, the ocean and the broad, grey sweep of horizon.

Despite our sore feet and struggles, the six days we spent wandering down the seemingly eternal coastline of Ninety Mile Beach was tinged with a warm nostalgia from my own childhood.

I showed Emilie how to climb up the sides of the sand dunes, and we played an exhilarating game of leaping down the steep slopes, the shifting sand carrying us swiftly to the base, before climbing up again. This was a game I'd played with my brother when I was maybe five years old and he was seven, pretending to be Storm Boy and Storm Girl as we ran wild around a block of untamed land on a few acres of rolling sand dunes near Nine Mile Beach outside of Swansea on the eastern coast of Tasmania, another dream procured by my parents. They spent most of their time at the block digging out our 'humpy', a rustic tin shelter, which was constantly at risk of being buried under the shifting sands.

My brother and I roamed those sand dunes together, either butt naked or wearing handmade belts of woven tussock grass, depending on whatever game we were playing. Amongst the dips and hollows of the foredunes grew spreading clumps of coast wattle and banksia, and we loved to slide down under the shelter of the foliage where the soft, golden sand was shady and cool. Sometimes large beetles would get stuck down there and we'd watch them, six mechanical legs in action as they attempted to trundle up the steep sides, eventually triggering a miniature landslide as the tension of sand broke. Clutching futilely at fine grains, the beetles would slide back down again. We would watch their progress for a while then eventually help them escape or place them into the tree, because our parents had taught us to love and care for all living creatures.

Deep in memory, I watched Emilie rescuing a bright green chafer beetle that had found itself blown out of the mānuka scrub behind the dunes and dangerously close to where the waves were lapping the shore.

But there's another memory from my early beach-roaming years that isn't so pleasant. It's of my brother and me emerging over the crest of yet another rolling sand dune to find ourselves face to face with a tribe of strange children, completely clothed with hats, shoes and everything. I vividly remember my own realisation of my nakedness and my differentness, a wild-haired bush girl confronted by a group of townies. Maybe it was my first memory of self-awareness, of the realisation that other people see you in a completely different mirror to that in which you view yourself. To them, you are the minority, the outcast, the stranger.

Every time we stopped for a break, Emilie headed for the waves and I joined her. We dropped our packs beside a clump of dried kelp at the high-tide line and she stripped off, her little golden-brown bottom wiggling its way towards the water. I undressed but hesitated, scanning the horizon in case a convoy of four-wheel-drives might be heading our way, then threw my sweaty knickers on top of hers and ran, gloriously naked, across the wide, flat sand and into the sea.

Oh, the delight of being one with the ocean. There are few sensations more exhilarating than swimming naked in cold, wild water, your entire body coming alive as energy from every single nerve ending awakens under the encouraging caress of your surroundings.

I ducked my head under an incoming wavelet and gasped with the pleasure of cold water washing over me. While Emilie splashed in the shallows, I lay back and floated effortlessly, all sound muffled except the rhythm of my breath, the echo of my heartbeat and the deep humming of the ocean. I felt safe, as though held tight by a lover, rocked in the bosom of the sea. I closed my eyes and imagined the kiss of Tangaroa, Māori god of the sea, drifting over every part of my body — and then Emilie emerged beside me and dripped water onto my face.

Te Werahi Beach with the headland of Tarawamaomao Point in the background.

Chapter 3

Tongariro Forest

Te Araroa
Day 10

I'M CROUCHED BESIDE A RIVER watching a whio, which is standing on one leg on the far bank, returning my gaze with a bright yellow eye. Emilie has paused her rock-hopping game to stand quietly beside me as we admire this beautiful native bird, his bluish-grey feathers cleverly camouflaging him against the wet rocks.

We're deep in the Tongariro Forest, a 20,000-hectare sanctuary of lush native bush in the central North Island, located to the northwest of Mount Ruapehu. Above our heads tower giant podocarp trees, rimu, kahikatea, mataī and miro, speckled with the white and yellow flowers of the native clematis vine. We're now deep in the realm of Tāne-mahuta, who in Māori mythology is the god of forests and of birds, lizards, insects and all other living creatures who dwell in this green realm.

It was hard to believe that a week ago we'd staggered into the Ahipara Holiday Park around 9pm, scurrying down back streets in the dying light, fuelled by the excitement of finishing the first 100 kilometres of Te Araroa.

Thanks to some frenzied messaging to the support team at TrackMe, who were sponsoring my InReach satellite communication device, the holiday park staff knew we were coming and guaranteed us a bed for the night. That was all it took to convince Emilie to keep walking down the rain-soaked beach for nine long hours, the dark hump of Tauroa Point to the west of Ahipara growing steadily closer with every tired step we took.

I'd never seen her so determined. Thirty kilometres is a bloody long way for a little girl. I asked her a few times if she'd rather stop and camp in the sand dunes, and we'd get to the holiday park the next morning, but she said no, she wanted to get an ice cream and sleep in a real bed.

So, we kept walking, even when the clouds blew over the ocean and soaked us through with loud, heavy raindrops, even when our quick-dry shorts mingled with salt and sand to turn the skin on the insides of our tired legs red and raw.

A few drivers slowed down and asked us if we'd like a lift, but we said no, even though our bodies begged us to say yes. It would have been bittersweet, to come so far and not finish the entire length of Ninety Mile Beach under our own, diminutive girl power.

The sun dipped out of sight and eventually darkness absorbed the remaining colours of dusk. Then we stopped for a while, me slumped on the sand using my pack as a backrest and my courageous little daughter snuggled between my legs. I could see the lights of houses against the dark mound of the headland and the first of the evening stars twinkling in the bluish-purple sky. I fumbled for my head torch, and we shared a couple of muesli bars and the last of the chocolate.

I'm so tired, sweetheart, and I bet you are too, I said to Emilie. *Are you sure you wouldn't like Mummy to set up the tent?*

She was silent, munching, her warm body slumped against mine. *How much further is it, Mummy?*

My GPS says it's three kilometres.

And how far have we walked since Cape Reinga?

Ninety-seven kilometres.

I want to keep walking, Mummy.

Okay, my love. I'm so proud of you. You're doing a great job.

I strapped our hiking poles to my pack so we could hold hands while we stumbled through the cold, loose sand on the outskirts of town. Suddenly, the arrow on my InReach navigation was pointing away from the beach, onto unknown backstreets, past brightly lit houses with people inside. A dog barked and ran out of a driveway, and we growled back at it, adrenaline driving us all the way to the reception desk of the holiday park.

I staggered in, sandy and dishevelled, and tried to say something coherent.

Emilie beat me to it, skipping up to the desk with a smile as wide as the coastline itself. *We've just walked Ninety Mile Beach! Do you have any ice cream left?*

After a good wash and a sleep between clean sheets, everything felt better. I was excited to move on to the notorious Northland forests, partly because I wanted to see how the warm, wild bush of the Far North compared with the monoculture of the colder South Island beech forests, and partly because people had told me this was one of the hardest parts of Te Araroa and I wanted to know why.

If you can get through Ninety Mile Beach and the Northland forests, you can get through the rest of Te Araroa, one trail veteran had told me, and since we had Ninety Mile Beach in the bag without so much as a blister (although I had a nasty chafing rash on my inner thigh from walking hours in wet shorts), I was looking forward to proving, at least to myself, that Emilie and I were completely capable of this challenge.

There were other trail walkers staying at the holiday park, and the next day we joined them for a drive into Kaitaia to buy fresh food and made plans to walk through the forests together. My resupply box of oats, crackers and dehydrated meals was already waiting for me at the Ahipara Holiday Park, but after six days of the same fare, I was keen to add some extra goodies to our food bags, and Emilie was delighted to have new people to entertain.

But everything changed at 6pm that evening when our then Covid-19 Response Minister Chris Hipkins announced that Northland would go into Level 3 lockdown at midnight. Travel was restricted and everyone except essential workers was to stay home. For us, this meant no more trail walking. Our plans to head into the Northland forests were on hold indefinitely.

Perhaps my tendency to be optimistic and take (often slightly blinded) leaps of faith in whatever direction I set my sights on had led to this oversight. With our nation still struggling through almost two years of Covid-19 pandemic-related disruption and our borders closed to overseas visitors, maybe this wasn't the best time to be attempting New Zealand's long-distance walking trail. But with my house rented out for the next six months and no job to return to, there wasn't much else to do now but keep walking.

After spending several days in panicky limbo, we called the government hotlines for advice, then got out of Northland. We flew to Wellington, then caught a bus north to a town called Taumarunui to pick up the trail again.

With Auckland and Waikato also in lockdown, the 42 Traverse was the northernmost section of the trail available to us, so here we were, trying to get back into our thru-hiking groove.

Apparently one of the best attributes a long-distance trail walker can have is the ability to be flexible, to meet adversity with ingenuity. I hadn't planned to fast-forward 900 kilometres of our walk after only completing 100 kilometres, but then I hadn't planned on being caught in another Covid lockdown

I was gutted to have missed out on such a significant chunk of Te Araroa and to have left the beauty of the Far North so quickly. Here, in the heart of King Country, the landscape was anything but wild, just artificially bright green rolling hills dotted with cattle and sheep. It was as pretty as an English painting, but it was not the nature immersion I was craving, and the narrow country backroad we found ourselves on was the furthest thing from a tramping track.

I knew Te Araroa involved a significant amount of road walking, but I wasn't ready to leave the beach and the bush just yet. My feet, which survived 100 kilometres from Cape Reinga to Ahipara without so much as a blister, were aching against the asphalt and my fully loaded pack was crushing me into the ground.

Still, Emilie was happy and chattering away. She'd enjoyed the aeroplane, the bus trip and a tiki-tour around Wellington. Now, having spotted a paddock with a huge Shire horse and several handsome mares, she'd made a beeline for the fence to offer them handfuls of juicy grass. I clucked my tongue and they plodded over, blowing warm air out of soft noses in greeting. A large grey mare reminded me of my grandfather's old horse, Lady. When I was a toddler, Poppa used to sit me up on her broad back while he worked in the gardens, Lady cropping calmly at his side. He loved working with horses, and he would have been delighted to meet this group, especially the big Shire stallion.

Back in my day, there were hundreds of these big fellows all across the countryside, and before they had tractors, they'd use horses to help plough

the farms, I could imagine him telling me. *I used to work with these horses, look after their feet and tend to their harnesses. There was this one horse . . .*

When I was younger, I'd listen with rapture to his wild stories, but as I grew older his repetitiveness irritated me. *You've told me that, Poppa,* I'd say instead, cutting him off short when I should have been encouraging him to talk long. *Keep telling me, Poppa, tell me all of it, enrich me with your history because all too soon, you'll be gone.* He's been dead three years now and it still hurts.

The initial distress of not being in full control of our rapidly changing plans slowly dissipated as we left the farms and fields and entered the deep green canopy of the Tongariro Forest Conservation Area. There was something about this forest that was deeply magical — and all the trees seemed super-sized, from the towering rimu, kahikatea and mataī to the giant tree ferns. Kererū flapped lazily about in the lower branches and tūī chortled and gurgled somewhere in the under-canopy. It was bliss, and best of all, it was warm.

Named after the former State Forest 42, which it crosses, the 42 Traverse track is an old logging road that runs from the town of Ōwhango, some 20 kilometres from Taumarunui, to the outskirts of the World Heritage-listed Tongariro National Park in the centre of the North Island. Although the DOC signage shows a gruelling series of descents and climbs as the track winds its way through a deep valley amidst a sea of regenerating native bush, the wide multi-use track was an easy walk, and we were soon happily absorbed in our surroundings.

It's hard to believe that such an ecological wonderland, humming with insects and echoing with birdsong, was once at risk of being chopped down and transformed into a dull, dead forestry plantation. Yet in its heyday between 1903 and 1978, State Forest 42 supported as many as 43 timber mills as man, beast and machine sweated and slaved to fell thousands of beautiful old-growth trees and transform them into timber for houses, fencing and firewood.

Many older New Zealand houses are built from the bones of our old-growth forests. Even my 1950s house in Christchurch revealed rimu floorboards that gleamed warm and golden once I'd ripped up the disgusting old linoleum.

The early European settlers' need for building materials has caused irreversible damage to so many of New Zealand's native forests. When it was realised that, even under the management of the former New Zealand Forest Service, our slow-growing native forests were not regenerating at the rate required to produce much-needed timber for our rapidly expanding population, these special areas were burned, bulldozed and converted to farmland and fast-growing pine plantations. The Tongariro Forest narrowly escaped such a fate in the 1970s and 1980s, when local community groups and conservationists fought back against these controversial government plans. Instead, all remaining native forest was transferred to DOC and allowed to regenerate to its current glory.

Wandering through a warm, sweet-smelling tunnel of greenery, I reflected on the resilience of our natural world and its quiet determination to thrive. I could see the tall, skinny stems of juvenile lancewoods jockeying for position amongst the older trees, fighting for a place in the sun where they could grow. I wondered about my own resilience, and whether I could master the art of managing whatever curveball would come next on the journey of Te Araroa with the same quiet grace as the trees around me.

On our first day in the Tongariro Forest, we took a side trip up a muddy track in search of a hut where we planned to stay the night. It was a few kilometres off the main Te Araroa trail on what started out as a wide four-wheel-drive track but eventually shrivelled into an overgrown trail and disappeared into deep, muddy pools in places. We gave up skirting our way around the edges and ploughed right in, up to our knees in muddy water as thick as chocolate mousse, the discomfort of the squelching sensation between our toes offset by the marvellous spectacle of huge dragonflies hovering overhead.

Eventually, we arrived at the dilapidated form of Ten Man Hut, its green tin roof baking quietly in the hot sun. Alone, as we had been for the past four days since leaving the township of Taumarunui, we washed off the mud and sweat of the day in the nearby stream before setting up for the night inside this old hunter's hut.

Except we were not really alone, because once a gloomy dusk settled over the hut, its other inhabitants started to stir. I was horrified to see the outline of a huge rat cruising around in the rafters. Emilie didn't seem to care — to her a rat was just a little less cute than our cat back home, but it took me all my nerve not to dash outside screaming and set up my tent on the grass.

Pulling myself together, I called a truce, and after thumping the walls and top bunk in a meaningful way to show the rat I meant business, I nestled deep in my sleeping bag with my liner pulled up over my face and fell into a fitful sleep, ready to wake up fighting the moment I sensed intrusion by little clawed feet.

Rattus rattus kept a polite distance, however, and I hoped to make up for lost sleep, with an absence of rats, the following night. Also known as ship rats, these opportunistic omnivores have a major impact on New Zealand's fragile biodiversity, eating everything from baby chicks, eggs, lizards, large insects such as wētā, as well as fruits and flowers. They are prolific breeders, and while they happily nest in forests, they're not averse to making their homes in backcountry huts, sleeping in holes in the roof or wall cavity and emerging at night to terrorise unwitting trampers and gnaw on their food bags.

The next day, after six hours of walking, we took an unmarked side track down to the riverbank, hoping to find somewhere flat to pitch our tent. After fighting our way through blackberry vines to refill our water bottles from this fresh, clear source, we spotted the whio.

New Zealand's endangered whio or blue duck lives on remote, fast-flowing rivers and streams, boasting an agility that outdoes even the most intrepid white-water rafter. Its name, whio, means whistle in Māori, which is the sound the male duck makes when he calls. Rarer than some species of kiwi, this taonga (treasure) has suffered greatly from loss of its natural habitat and predation by introduced mammals, such as stoats and rats.

Unlike many of our shy native birds, the whio is staunch. Despite casting one bright yellow eye in our direction, he stayed put on his perch, standing on one large, webbed foot on a pile of river stones, his other leg tucked neatly underneath. With his sleek blue-grey plumage, he looked just like a small, dark rock, completely camouflaged as the brisk, clear waters flowed past him.

It was a thrill to have spotted one in the wild, and we quietly retreated to leave him in peace.

After arriving at the National Park campground to learn that our resupply box was being held several miles away at the rural post office, we improvised again, standing with our thumbs out on the side of the empty highway until we could catch a ride to the nearest town to buy food from the supermarket. Emilie stood with her little thumb out and a big smile plastered across her face, so it didn't take long before an SUV pulled over and gave us a ride into Tūrangi.

Emilie burbled away about our journey and our lost food box and how hungry we were, and next minute the driver was rummaging around and pressing muesli bars and apples into our hands.

After two weeks of tramping, we were ravenous and sick of our carefully rationed trail food, so we sat in central Tūrangi devouring meat pies and ice cream, balanced with fresh broccoli and handfuls of blueberries.

When we reclaimed our resupply box from the post office, we realised another hurdle was blowing our way — a forecasted spring storm was bringing fresh snow, freezing winds and low visibility. From the outskirts of the national park, Te Araroa walkers follow the Tongariro Crossing, across 20 kilometres of exposed track over the volcanic alpine landscape of Mount Tongariro. Without an ice axe, crampons or the skills to use them, we had no chance, even once the storm blew over.

It was another setback forcing us off the prescribed Te Araroa trail and, again, the dark tendrils of anxiety squeezed my stomach and lungs in their vice grip. As a mother, I knew it would be foolhardy and negligent to take Emilie over the crossing, but the budding trail walker in me was frustrated and guilty to be missing out on yet another key part of the trail. Did this mean we were not 'real' trail walkers? We'd already missed out on 900 kilometres because of lockdowns. Had I failed Te Araroa before I'd even really started?

We couldn't even go forwards through Whanganui National Park because the storm had brought a deluge of rain that had swollen the Whanganui River beyond safe levels, and we were supposed to paddle down it in a canoe — another challenge I was forcing myself not to panic about just yet.

There on the outskirts of Tongariro National Park, we were offered a blank canvas of beautiful wilderness where we could paint our own journey. We spent a couple of days in luxury, resting, eating and cleaning our tramping gear after a kind soul, who was following our journey on Instagram, sent me a private message to offer us the keys to their empty holiday home. I felt humbled to receive such generosity and support for our cause and buoyed to think that, out there, people were cheering us on.

While a warm, clean Emilie played and watched cartoons, I pored over the detailed NZtopo50 map on my phone and sketched out a longer, lower-altitude route that would take us around the flanks of Mount Ruapehu to re-join Te Araroa at National Park Village.

The 75-kilometre Round the Mountain track is described as a *challenging and undulating multi-day track that circles Mount Ruapehu on New Zealand's North Island, traversing a mix of desert and forest landscapes,* and with a range of well-built huts to choose from, it sounded like the perfect way to experience the beauty of Tongariro and make up for some of our missing kilometres.

It was early in the season, and once we were on the track we had the huts to ourselves, spending our days wandering through strange and beautiful wonderlands of volcanic lava flows interspersed with ice-fed rivers and delicate alpine plants.

It felt good not to rush. After all we were already way further south than I'd planned to be at this time of year, where the volatile spring weather could still dump fresh snow at high altitude.

Several days later, I watched a naked forest nymph hold court on a rock, her long plaits dangling almost to the water as she peered down into her realm. A halo of sunshine backlit her head and the ripples glowed with patches of broken gold. All around us were warm, earthy tones of red, orange, yellow and brown, as though Papatūānuku herself had set a colour palette for all the plants to imitate. Beyond the mosaic of tussock, hebe, Dracophyllum and other alpine plants rose the dark blue flanks of real mountains — the craggy peaks of Mount Ruapehu.

Since leaving the lush green of Tongariro Forest and the 42 Traverse track, we had climbed onto the alpine plateau of Tongariro National Park, watching the landscape transform beneath our feet.

Tiny alpine flowers bloomed between giant red and gold tussocks, and the towering podocarp trees were replaced by stunted mountain beech. We were slowly circumnavigating Mount Ruapehu, one of three commanding mountains including Mount Tongariro and Mount Ngāuruhoe (Mount Doom in *The Lord of the Rings*) that make up this World Heritage-listed national park.

I lay back against a lichen-encrusted rock with the warm sun on my face and watched the forest nymph at play. I was beside one of the many small streams carrying melted snow down off the mountain, with bright sunlight on one side and heavy grey cloud on the other.

My body was sore after a long day of slipping and sliding through volcanic mud on the rough and rocky track, and I was looking forward to crawling into my sleeping bag beside Emilie that evening.

From my resting place beside the stream, I could see the heavy cloud had called in reinforcements. Together, they lurked at the edges of the sky, casting dark blue shadows over the lower flanks of the mountain and obscuring his gleaming snow-covered tops.

I called to Emilie, disrupting her play, and gestured for her to follow me into the sturdy wooden hut where we were staying the night. Once she'd dressed in her matching pink thermal long johns, I plopped a bowl of snacks in front of her — broken crackers with slices of cheese, a handful of nuts and dates and a little piece of chocolate. I'd boil water to prepare dinner in another hour or so, but for the moment I just wanted to chill on my bunk and paint a watercolour of the dramatic landscape outside the window while Emilie drew pictures in her tramping diary. I was carrying a little pocket set of watercolours and a notepad for quiet moments like this, although they didn't come very often.

When I was a kid I loved to paint and draw and write myself away into other, happier worlds inside my head. Art was a way of escaping the undertones of anger that seemed to pervade throughout our home, the rippling waves of discontent that constantly emanated from the patriarch of the house.

The best way to avoid his wrath was to hide away quietly with my sketchbook and colouring pencils, or to get out of there completely and take off into the wild bush that was our backyard, where my brother and I could indulge in our noisy play without fear of retribution.

Back then my name was Lulu. Lulu Bruce. My big brother was Robbie Bruce. Wearing gumboots, muddy knees and a stubborn scowl under my white-blonde pigtails, I was armed with my imagination and the unwavering support of my older sibling. Together we could fight back against anything in the world and slip away, victorious, into the Australian bush that was our home.

We spent countless hours playing and exploring our natural world, visited by our friends the magpies, kookaburras, fantails, frogs, skinks and cicadas, building forts out of fallen branches, cushions from moss, swimming holes in creeks. I guess somewhere back then my body decided that nature was a safe place, away from the volatile simmering anger of my father and the quiet fear of my mother.

No one was there to yell at us, to make us feel scared, small, powerless or humiliated. Lost in our own worlds, worlds we created out of the power of our imagination, we could be anyone and anything, the king and queen of our peaceful green realm. Rocky outcrops were transformed into watch towers. The tallest rock was the castle, a carefully curated collection of leaves, rocks and petals our treasure. The entrance was a hidden tunnel between towering tussock grass guarded by forest fairies.

Maybe that's why nature has always evoked such fantasy and magic for me — my body remembers the joy to be discovered in wild places. It's a place to soothe, to heal, comforted by the indifference of tangled branches and leaves, the gentle swaying of towering trees.

It breaks my heart to revisit these tender scenes and think we were really just two scared kids escaping the trauma of a homelife tainted by domestic violence.

I'm sure my parents didn't plan for things to turn out this way.

After all, they'd experienced their own difficult upbringings within Scottish families who emigrated to New Zealand when my parents were teenagers. They were foreigners in a country where being Scottish meant they were tarred as land-grabbing Pākehā by local Māori and jeered at for their thick accents by the local white New Zealand population.

After meeting as children, my parents later fell in love and planned a life of travel and adventure. I'm sketchy on the details of my parents' early years, as it's not a time they spoke of freely. They lived in political squats, bought an old yacht that later sank in a storm, and rode bicycles around Morocco and Egypt long before cycle-touring became a thing.

Somewhere, I have a photo of them tinged in sepia from their wedding at the registry office. My mother is beautiful with her kind eyes and soft face framed by strawberry-blonde hair curling down to the shoulders of her brown skirt suit, her nicely turned calves in low-heeled shoes. I imagine she dreamed of a fairy-tale wedding in a flowing dress that hugged her slender figure, but after emancipating themselves from the chains of the church and with no money or family to help them celebrate, the registry office was a practical alternative.

My father is wearing a dark brown suit, his thick black hair matching the dark expression behind his glasses. He could be so charming when he tried, with his quick wit and black humour. But more often he was dark, probably fighting the demons that seemed constantly present inside his head and drove him to lash out in violent rages.

I suppose it was hard work growing up Scottish, the poor cousin to the mighty England, our lands ripped from us in a series of bloody and brutal conflicts, our fathers and grandfathers forced to take part in wars that weren't really ours. I've never been to Scotland, although I've often wondered if my toes would tingle as I wandered across my own ancestral soil.

Scottish people possess a great affinity with the natural world, and I've read that the Scottish Gaelic letters were named after trees because their original shapes resembled trees and branches. There are many words to describe landscape features, including different types of hills according to their size, shape and even the vegetation that grows upon them. There's even a phrase — 'Cò leis thu?' — meaning 'Who do you belong to?', which mirrors the Māori worldview of genealogy as a combination of people and place.

My family comes from the densely populated industrial centres of Glasgow and Coatbridge, and if we had claim to any lochs, isles or hills, these are now long gone. I was born in an Auckland hospital without my father's presence, because, true to form, my parents had a huge, violent argument in the days leading up to my birth and my mother left our home on Waiheke Island to give birth to me in peace.

Maybe my trauma started in the womb. My mother once told me that my father convinced her to climb up a ladder and help him fix the roof when she was nine months pregnant with me. Then, up on the galvanised steel roof of our Waiheke Island bach, they had a fight and he got down and took the ladder away, leaving her there terrified and upset.

During my own pregnancy, I remember the midwife lecturing us expectant mothers to take it easy and avoid unnecessary stress as it was bad for our bodies and our unborn babies.

What the midwife didn't explain was that mothers who produced too much of the stress hormone, cortisol, could poison their babies with this toxic chemical while still in the womb and potentially give them life-long mental health problems. No one ever told me that a traumatised mother could pass on altered genetic material to her child. And I don't suppose my parents had never heard of the terms epigenetics or intergenerational trauma.

Maybe if they'd been enlightened with this information, my father wouldn't have left her up there on the roof for several hours before eventually letting her back down so he could lay into her with his fists. Or maybe my mother would have had the confirmation she needed to leave my father right then and there, instead of spending another 10 years working up the courage to flee, taking my brother but leaving me behind.

I don't know why she went back to him once I was born — except I do, because back in 1980s New Zealand, knocking your wife around was an acceptable part of family dynamics that police didn't want to get involved in. My mother didn't have a phone, or a car, or her own bank account, and my 18-month-old brother was back on Waiheke with my dad. Plus, my mother was probably used to being hit. Her mother had had a temper and took it out on my mother and her siblings, and so had her father. Back in the depths of cold, dark Scotland, it was standard practice for teachers to use the cane to discipline students, as did the pastors at Sunday school. The Scottish people are Olympic-grade experts at enduring suffering, that's why they're referred to as 'stoic Scots'. Stoicism is practically a Scottish cultural phenomenon. A Gaelic verb, 'tae thole', is loosely translated as 'to tolerate' or 'to endure', but really, it's much deeper than that. The verb has been summarised as a 'profound sense of dignified silence and patience in heavy sorrow, of moral and spiritual stoicism and fortitude'.

I suppose you'd need to explore more of their individual family histories to understand the events that shaped the many scars my parents wore, causing them to oscillate between suffering in silence or screaming in pain and rage, but the oral history from either side of my Scottish heritage is scant.

My maternal grandmother, a stoic Scotswoman who has always retained her soft Scottish lilt, painted a picture of her own childhood as the youngest child of 11, or maybe it was nine, walking to school in the snow or being carried on her elder brother's back. *But we always had enough to eat and nice clothes to wear*, she made sure to tell me.

My grandfather's story was darker. He came from a different class, where his father would be away working at sea and his mother left at home alone to tend to him and his many siblings.

Every time he came home, he knocked her up, he once commented, recalling the coldness of their dark, cramped lodgings and his angry, grieving mother who, ravaged by alcohol, chose to spend her last pennies on a bottle of gin instead of potatoes for their supper. Genetically, Poppa's traumas shouldn't have had too much impact on my mother or myself, as he was my grandmother's second husband, a loving stepfather to my mother and her siblings. My real grandfather died before I was born, committing suicide in front of my parents by jumping off the little yacht they owned and swimming away into the dark night. My mother was eight months pregnant with my brother or she would have gone in after him.

I'm glad she didn't because a few days later, his body was recovered from the barren coastline.

As Emilie grew older, she and I ventured further on our excursions, exploring much of New Zealand's front country in Nanny's old car, which later towed a series of retro caravans bought for a song.

I'd travelled Rangipo's Desert Road south from Taupō many times, Emilie tucked in her baby cradle in the back of the old white station wagon, towing the equally old orange caravan, trying to escape my loneliness with yet another road trip.

I'd admired the snow-capped peak of Ruapehu while driving through this vast stretch of inhospitable land, but I'd never guessed that one day I'd be gazing down at State Highway 1 from a perch high on the mountainside.

From its position at almost 1600 metres on the eastern flanks of Ruapehu, Rangipo Hut has a commanding view of the Rangipo Desert and Kaimanawa Range, but the trade-off for these sweeping views means the hut is exposed to the full wrath of the weather.

Soaking up the morning sun on the hut's wide wooden deck, it was hard to believe we'd spent the previous night huddling, freezing cold in damp sleeping bags, after trying and failing to coax a fire to spring to life in the woodstove.

Somewhere between Mangaehuehu Hut and the Wahianoa River, the weather had closed in around us, and, instead of turning back, we'd kept going, scuttling helplessly across the barren desert landscape of Mount Ruapehu's eastern flanks, its volcanic rock and wind-sculptured sands devoid of all shelter.

We had emerged from the stunted beech forest and mounted a ridge before the wind turned, unleashing its full wrath upon us. The savageness took our breath away. The darkened sky hurled a million tiny, icy raindrops at us, sharp as nails upon our bare skin. Freezing damp mist swirled around like smoke from a dragon's breath. The moss-blackened rocks and red earth appeared scorched from ancient fiery battles of long ago.

I had never felt such cold and it took all my internal fortitude to keep going. At that stage, it felt like the best thing we could do was to keep moving, keep our bodies warm and cover the remaining three kilometres to the hut as fast as we could manage.

Time feels eternal when you're slogging through desert sands, dried-up lahar flows and volcanic rubble, pummelled by icy gusts of wind and lashed with rain. But eventually, the solid shape of Rangipo Hut loomed out of the mist and we scrambled up the steps like a pair of drowned rats, coaxing warmth back into frozen fingers and wringing water out of soggy socks.

I tried, and tried again, to coax the damp firewood to light, snapping a match between numb fingers, my eyes filling with tears and angry at myself for being so stupid to keep going into the storm, for dragging Emilie all this way, for risking her catching hypothermia or worse.

For a moment, emotion flooded over me and I sank to the floor sobbing as my breath rose around me like mist inside the cold hut. Stupid, rookie, not even a good tramper, can't read the weather, bad mother, failure, loser . . . all of these thoughts thundered inside my head until Emilie chirruped, *Don't worry, Mummy, I've got our sleeping bags all set up now!*

I looked up to see that she'd shaken them out of their compression sacks and was busy stuffing our thermal liners inside, a vision in her bright pink pyjamas and messy curls.

It was all I could do to drag myself up off the floor, change into my dry thermals and climb in beside her. My toes were frozen in my merino socks, but inside I was warm with a deep love and appreciation for my beautiful, brave little daughter.

There were the faintest colours of a rainbow in the spray of the waterfall, and I shifted in my seat to watch it as we floated by. Beyond these sheer cliffs were sharp ridges cloaked in dense green vegetation and water running straight down to form hundreds of little waterfalls, from fairy-size trickles to deep flows, all feeding into the Whanganui River. Giant tree ferns leaned over the steep riverbanks and the narrow gorge echoed with birdsong. The green canopy of this broadleaf-podocarp forest gave off an almost tropical feel reminiscent of Southeast Asia, and after hearing the eerie cry of a peacock, I almost expected to see a troop of monkeys swinging through the trees.

Instead of monkeys, there was the torpedo shape of a kererū and the outstretched wings of a harrier hawk, turning and gliding across river and bush in search of its next meal, probably the carcass of one of the feral goats that, like the peacocks, have infiltrated and thrive in the warm climate of Whanganui National Park.

We were paddling our way down the mighty Whanganui River, our gear packed in large plastic drums that were carefully strapped inside our big Canadian canoes.

Before I clambered into the leaky craft that would become my home for the next week, I had mixed feelings about taking a canoe trip down the second-longest river in the North Island. Around 150 kilometres of the river forms the iconic Whanganui River Journey, one of New Zealand's Great Walks.

One of the highlights of Te Araroa, she — for this special river has its own legal status as a person — offers tired trail walkers the opportunity to swap hiking poles for paddles to cover, in six days, what would have taken Emilie and me around two weeks of solid walking.

We'd booked our canoe hire from a Taumarunui-based tour company, who delivered the boats to Blue Duck Station at Whakahoro on the banks of the Whanganui and Retaruke rivers, some two full days' walk from National Park. The hire company had been reluctant to loan a single Canadian canoe to me when they realised I was to be the only adult paddler. Instead, they teamed us up with a handful of other trail walkers for the six days it would take us to reach the town of Whanganui.

I felt like I knew how to paddle a canoe — after all we'd mucked around in homemade canoes as kids and I had an inflatable paddleboard stored in my garage at home. But that had all been on flat water, not the swift, deep waters of the Whanganui with her treacherous rapids and submerged tree trunks threatening to snag and tangle you before tipping you out of your canoe and pinning you underwater.

Somehow, I climbed into that canoe and, somehow, I even volunteered to be the navigator, claiming the seat at the rear of the vessel from which the steering would be done.

Emilie sat in the middle of the huge boat, all trussed up in a brightly coloured life vest, and up the front was Erin, a fellow trail walker who we'd teamed up with after leaving National Park.

In separate vessels but also part of our river convoy were a Dutch couple, Tom and Hilijana, and a young British vet named Stew. Between the six of us, we commanded two large Canadian canoes and one smaller kayak, our gear distributed between the boats. We were under strict instruction from the hire company to stick together and not to let go of our paddles if we fell out.

Although I'd watched the safety video at the hire company office in Taumarunui and had a rudimentary idea of how to navigate through the rapids, my brain had already pushed the panic button well before we floated down the side stream to join the steady flow of the Whanganui.

The problem with PTSD is that your hyper-vigilant body releases massive amounts of adrenaline and cortisol in an attempt to 'keep you safe' from threats, and right here on the river, with the unresponsive canoe spinning slowly into the current, my frontal cortex had all but shut down and I was really freaking out. Sadly, bar throwing myself overboard, bailing out was not an option, so I clenched my jaw and paddled as hard as I could, steering the boat downstream through the rapids and hating every fucking minute of it.

The toxic cocktail of stress hormones ate at my stomach and eroded my self-esteem, sending me spiralling into a silent self-loathing shame. I guess it had been building up for days, slinking along behind me on the long, dusty back roads between National Park and Whakahoro as Emilie chattered away to Erin.

After the solitude of Mount Ruapehu and the northern beaches, the sudden coming together with new people had triggered a surge of anxiety, mixed with a liberal dash of resentment at having other humans invade my quiet nature immersion.

As long as I can remember, I've felt as though I'm different from other people, and I often struggle to relate or connect with people. While others chat about where they grew up and went to school, I am painfully reminded of my own dysfunctional upbringing and years spent in foster care.

I've learned to go to great lengths not to share these details of my history with anyone, in order to avoid blank stares and awkward silences, or worse, pity. I worry that the panic and anxiety I feel will show on my face and cause people to misunderstand me or judge me as being unfriendly, damaged, broken. Not as good as them. Over the years, I've simply started avoiding social situations, especially if I must interact with groups of people I don't know. Professionally, I can perform just fine, but personally, I often feel lost in the company of others.

I've always wanted to be one of those people who can casually wander into a group, crack a joke and suddenly be the centre of attention. Instead, I feel so socially awkward and shy that I wish the ground would open and swallow me whole. Emilie, on the other hand, is the casual joke-cracker. She's a people-magnet, diving right into the fray, and on the river she was having the time of her life.

I withdrew into myself, channelling my inner discomfort into my arms, water swirling and sucking at my paddle as I steered the big canoe down rapids and hauled on the rudder to keep it out of the eddies.

Māori legends tell the story of the warrior god Taranaki, who once joined my old friend Tauhara and the warriors Ruapehu, Ngāuruhoe and Tongariro in the centre of the North Island. All the mountain gods had fallen for the beautiful Mount Pīhanga, and a terrible battle broke out as they fought amongst themselves to win her heart.

After losing the battle to Tongariro, a disappointed and angry Taranaki travelled westwards, carving out deep trenches until he reached the sea. From here, he moved northwards to the Pouakai Range where he became Mount Taranaki, which at 2815 metres is the second highest peak in the North Island. When water arose from Tongariro and filled the scar left by Taranaki's departure, the Whanganui River was created.

I wonder how early European explorers felt about this wild

region, pushing their way through the dense, dark lowland jungle with its thick tangles of supplejack vines and broadleaf to emerge at the edge of this huge river. Were their hearts pounding as they negotiated sheer drop-offs and clambered slowly down steep muddy banks to launch their crafts into her dark waters? Did they stop to marvel at the graceful flight of the kererū and listen to the sweet song of the korimako and tūī? What about the thousands of men, women and children from local Māori iwi who once lived here, weaving legends around the whirlpools and rapids of the enchanted river as she carried them from deep in the mountains all the way out to sea?

As the Whanganui flows downstream, she widens and narrows, carving her way through mud and rock, deep and slow then shallow and swift, the fast-moving water channelling into a V-shape that I had to steer the canoe into, hanging onto the rudder and avoiding any obstacles that cropped up in the way.

Beyond the thrill of the rapids were swirling eddies that threatened to grab and twist the vessel sideways and make us fill up with water. Submerged rocks and tree trunks also lurked in the dark water for the chance to impale an oncoming canoe.

We'd all been warned of the infamous rapid after the haul-out site of Pipiriki, aptly named 50:50 because 50 per cent of canoeists tip out there and no one knows which side of the equation they'll land on.

Tom and Hils went first in a blur of paddles, skilfully steering their canoe through a tunnel of white-water that dug in close to a bank overhung with dead branches. I was teamed up with Stew and we hung back until the Dutch couple emerged out the other side. Then we lined up our canoe and accelerated into the rapid. Straight away it all felt wrong, the curve was so tight and we were heading straight into the bank. I hauled on the rudder to turn us around the sharp bend, but a counter-current sent big choppy waves slopping up over the canoe and into my lap. Turning with all the grace and vigour of a stricken submarine, the big canoe spun around slowly and filled with water.

My mother once told me that as a toddler, I'd laughed out loud to see the water burst through the destroyed hull of the 36-foot trimaran that was also our home. My parents were attempting to sail from New Zealand to Tonga via New Caledonia on their way to circumnavigate the world with my 18-month-old self and my three-year-old brother in tow, when a combination of bad weather and navigational errors saw us run aground on New Caledonia's notorious South Reef.

Thankfully, my rookie parents had invested in a Sabot sailing dinghy with a wooden hull, which my father had converted into a life raft to meet New Zealand safety standards, adding a hooped frame with a canvas canopy that could be zipped shut.

After it became clear that our yacht was well and truly wedged on the coral, with the relentless waves ripping through the open hull, my parents threw their two screaming kids into the bucking and kicking dinghy and abandoned the stricken yacht. They zipped the dinghy shut and huddled inside, then took turns to paddle and sail frantically to safety. We spent our first night anchored in calmer water inside the horseshoe-shaped reef, and our second night on a tiny tropical island teeming with giant land crabs, before eventually covering the 60 nautical miles to Nouméa Harbour, two and a half days later.

Triangulum, the uninsured Piver Lodestar trimaran that my parents had bought with the proceeds of our Waiheke home, broke apart on the reef and we lost everything, including my parents' dream to sail around the world.

Around 18 days after leaving New Zealand on our maiden voyage, we'd arrived in New Caledonia with only the clothes we were wearing and our flare gun and handheld satellite communication device, which, ironically, no one in New Caledonia had noticed.

I suppose I was too young to have any memory of these dramatic events, although from what I've read, the roots of trauma grow deep inside the body. In fact, trauma memories never make it through to the hippocampus, the part of your brain where normal, everyday memory is stored. Instead, traumatic memory can remain as fragmented, jumbled files in the amygdala, the part of your brain responsible for processing memory, emotions and your fight or flight reflex.

In everyday situations, the amygdala is the watchguard of the brain; its role is to help manage your body's response and keep you safe. If a dog barks, the amygdala responds — you turn your head to identify the sound. If it's a friendly neighbourhood dog then there is no threat and the amygdala will process this memory, to be stored away in the filing room of your hippocampus along with memories of Christmas holidays and other happy life events. But if you turn to see a wild-eyed, slack-jawed beast rushing towards you, then the amygdala will push the panic button to release a dose of adrenaline into your system so you can run like hell.

But what if you were caught and savagely mauled by the dog? Then the terror and panic of that traumatic event will remain mixed up with the memory of dogs, and perhaps even when you next see your neighbour's friendly dog, your amygdala will busily pump you full of adrenaline.

My therapist explained that this is because your amygdala, as well as being the brain's watchguard, is also the gatekeeper of traumatic memory, and it refuses to let these through to be processed and neatly filed like normal memories. Instead, these trauma memories fill up this part of your brain, becoming enmeshed and entangled, as if someone opened a folder and threw all the files on the floor.

One trauma memory can trigger another completely unrelated memory and, like a cluster of cancer cells, these grow and deform and grow again, allowing the smallest spark to prompt your amygdala to flood you with a series of terrifying and difficult emotions at any given moment.

While our tragic experience as shipwrecked sailors never stopped me loving the water, my mother baulked at the idea of getting on board a boat with my father again, and eight years later, when he went away to check out another boat, she left him.

I was thinking of my mother's terror of abandoning the rapidly deteriorating yacht for the yawning maw of the rough seas with two babes in her arms as I casually launched myself out into the swirling river to recover Stew's paddle, which, despite the stern lecture from the hire company, he'd somehow dropped.

One of you grab the kid and one stay with the boat — and hold onto your paddles! was the advice burned into my brain from our pre-river journey briefing. *Stay with Stew, Emilie,* I said, but her own instincts were stronger, and as I swam after the paddle she followed me with a cry of *Mummeeee!*

At least Stew had got the canoe, or rather it had got him, because after slowly filling up with brown water and submerging, it had spun around and was pinning him against the trunk of an overhanging tree.

Everything was happening very fast and soon I had Emilie, the paddle and an errant dry bag full of backpacks in my arms as I kicked for the bank. The sheer force of the water was pushing me downstream, while Tom was steering the single kayak to our rescue, paddling effortlessly against the current.

I've got Emilie, he said, and I focused on dragging myself out of the water and going to help Stew.

We pushed and pulled the canoe until Stew could wriggle free, then we dragged it towards the bank. The water wasn't particularly deep, and as we were out of the rapid, it wasn't even that swift, but the waterlogged Canadian canoe weighed a tonne and the plastic drums holding our gear turned out to be full of water too.

One of the drums slipped its rope and was off, bobbing down the river to freedom. Tom was in his element; he was winging the bright yellow kayak down the river with Emilie still perched up front.

I was busy helping Stew and Erin tip the worst of the deluge out of the canoe when Tom and Emilie slid up beside us, Emilie waving at me triumphantly, the blue plastic drum on Tom's lap. No tears or lasting trauma for her — she was loving every minute of it.

Once we'd all recovered from the excitement of the 50:50 rapid, we were buzzing with adrenaline and ready to tackle anything else the river had to offer.

Soon the river widened and slowed. We had to work harder and harder to cover the kilometres downstream. The sun eventually dried out our clothing, and we planned to wash and clean the rest of our gear, plus salvage our remaining food supplies, on arrival at the Flying Fox campground some 30 kilometres upriver from the 50:50 rapids.

When we arrived at the campground it was eerily deserted, so we drifted down river for a while before unanimously agreeing to haul out on a flat section of riverbank and freedom camp for the night.

It was a hard night and an even harder morning. I woke with the end of my sleeping bag stuck to the damp tent fly, and pebbles from the riverbank dug into my hips whenever I turned over on my thin inflatable mat.

My right hand and forearm were throbbing from hours of gripping a paddle, and I was dreading another day in the canoes. While the idea of the river journey had originally sounded like fun, I now found myself longing to get off my aching backside and back onto my feet. I couldn't keep up the group chatter, felt increasingly awkward and ostracised as Emilie vied for everyone's attention but mine, and found myself yearning to be alone in the bush again.

Moving quietly in case Emilie woke up and started chatting my ear off, I set about boiling water in our billy for breakfast. By now, my instant coffee was all gone so I drank my black tea silently and sullenly, desperately wishing for something stronger.

It was early, not yet 7am, and a low mist kissed the glassy brown surface of the water. A thin layer of sunshine warmed the high tops of the gorge. Soon the sun would climb higher and unleash its full force, burning our bare legs, arms, hands and the backs of our necks as we sat, helpless, paddling our way down the wide, muddy river.

I wanted to get moving, but I needed to wait for the group to pack up, so I turned my attention to sorting our damp gear and packing up the tent, shoving the dew-sodden fly into my barrel.

This far downstream, the river ebbs and flows with the coastal tides. If we managed to work the tides in our favour, then hopefully we'd make it to Whanganui the day after tomorrow and get back on our feet again.

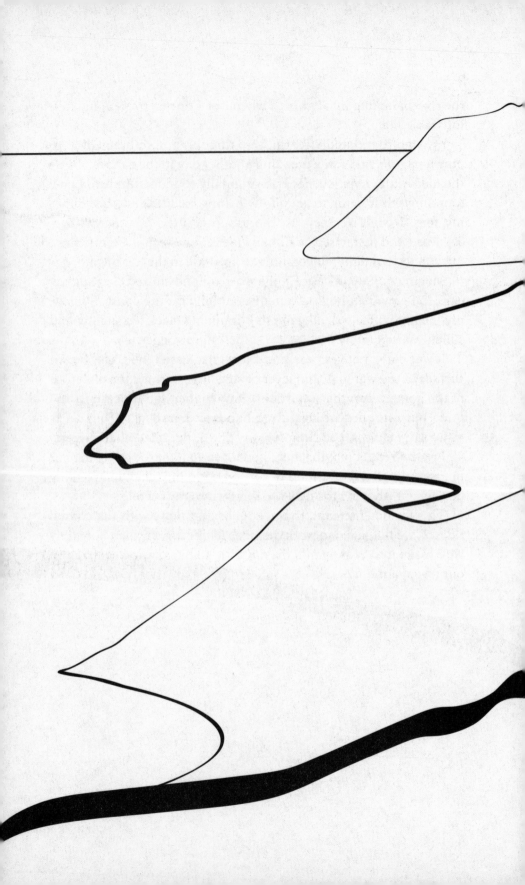

Chapter 4

Whangaehu Beach

Te Araroa
Day 22

THE DARK GREY SANDS OF Whangaehu Beach are filling my trail shoes as I wander along the tide line of this blasted beach, the sullen grey waves of the Tasman Sea on one side and a mixture of exotic forest and scrubby native bush on the other. Below the dunes the sand is soft and dry but here, dodging the lick and low of incoming waves, it is deceptively deep and boggy, making it impossible to set any kind of pace.

Emilie is also struggling. Although much lighter than mine, her bright blue backpack is stuffed with her sleeping bag, raincoat, water bottle and snacks.

There's sand in my shoes! she wails. The sand in mine is trickling down the outside of my socks with each sluggish step.

Over the past 10 days we'd covered 150 kilometres by river and a further 40 kilometres on foot. Once we'd recovered from our river dunking, the remaining days on the Whanganui were uneventful. After her long journey down through the foothills of the national park, the river eventually slowed to pass through farm country, becoming swollen and sluggish as she carried her load of detritus out to sea. I felt sad to see the river transition from clear, dark waters to an opaque brown, full of mud and silt.

Baking in the hot sun, we'd paddled doggedly on, no sign of a current to rush us along now. The smell of death was always in the air, and we pointed out rotting goat carcasses to each other with a mixture of disgust and laughter.

We'd arrived in Whanganui around 6pm, well and truly shattered. There, we farewelled Tom, Hils, Erin and Stew with warm hugs and best wishes for the rest of their trail journey. Tom and Hils were spending a couple of nights in a motel before heading on, while Erin and Stew and Emilie and I were staying with some local trail angels. A concept originating from the long-distance hiking trails in the United States, trail angels are people who offer kindness and generosity to hikers and trampers, often opening their doors to smelly, sodden Te Araroa walkers like us and providing shelter, food, a ride or just encouragement.

As we stood around awkwardly gawking at our sudden re-entrance to civilisation, a battered station wagon driven by a red-haired woman with a huge smile tore into the parking lot, with what appeared to be at least six little heads jostling in the back seat. It was Dani, a teacher at the local high school, whom I'd connected with through the local Kiwi Conservation Club Facebook page. Emilie and I were going to stay with Dani, her husband and their three kids for a couple of days while we cleaned our gear and sorted out our resupply packages.

After weeks of having only adult company, Emilie was over the moon to have friends her own age to hang with and, after suffering the length of the river with her backchatting me like a bolshy teenager, I was delighted to have a fellow mum in my corner.

I liked Dani immediately. An American who emigrated to New Zealand just over 10 years ago, she had a way of putting you instantly at ease with her easy-going manner and huge smile. Dani was chilled out yet passionate, hugely intelligent and empathetic. Even though we only spent a few days with her and her family, I felt the loneliness and sadness draining from my body. Dani helped me feel stronger, like a battle-scarred warrior woman, a wahine toa on a mission to find myself, instead of the mud-streaked self-hating ghost I'd found myself turning into on the river.

Dani introduced me to her friend Lydia, a fellow warrior woman, who lived in the little seaside town of Koitiata about 30 kilometres south of Whanganui. Emilie and I spent a night tucked up in Lydia's caravan, our bellies full of the homemade chocolate cake she had baked in our honour.

Lydia also knew what it was like to leave an abusive relationship, and the long and painful journey from being a woman broken to a woman reborn.

While Emilie was playing happily, Lydia encouraged me to be strong on my journey and gentle to myself. She also shared the wisdom of not taking on what isn't mine. This included other people's judgement, perceptions, harsh words and inexcusable actions.

I wondered what would be left of me if I stripped back all that wasn't mine. I wanted to shed all of it. Let me walk taller, step lighter, smile brighter. *I want to love and be loved,* I whispered to myself as I walked through the warm grey sand.

I wanted to laugh until my belly hurt. I wanted to decorate the outside of the black hole that had been following me around for half of my life with seashells and wildflowers and step away from it. *It's not mine.*

Lydia's words held me close, like the hug she had given me before we departed that morning to walk down the beach from Koitiata to Bulls.

Just outside of Koitiata there was a nesting colony of black-backed gulls, and we hugged the shoreline, our feet sinking into the wet sand, as we tried not to disturb the birds. The gulls are staunch but there's something to be said for group mentality, because when one huge bird spreads its wings and launches into the air, the others feel compelled to follow it. But one of these beautiful birds wasn't flying anymore, and we squatted down to feel the softness of its plumage under our fingers as it lay in the sand, eyes closed as if asleep.

It was soft and silky and the feathers were so tightly knitted together they resembled crushed velvet. I hoped it had simply died of old age and nothing more sinister. Emilie was quiet and concerned for the gull, and I showed her how to draw a love heart around its resting body with the tip of her hiking pole. She wanted to gather shells to decorate the heart, so we paused for a while, placing large white shells around the gull, holding hands to say a simple karakia for its passing.

It reminded me of the muttonbirds of my childhood, and how we'd find these beautiful, dark-coloured seabirds huddled amidst flotsam and jetsam on wild and windswept Australian beaches. Sometimes there were scores of them, just lying around, exhausted and slowly dying after their mammoth migratory journeys. We only knew them as muttonbirds, but their real name is short-tailed shearwater or slender-billed shearwater, and I now know that they spend the northern summer around Alaska before travelling a whopping 15,000 kilometres back to Australia.

We would tenderly gather the quiet birds in our arms to take them back to our campervan and attempt to rehabilitate them in a cardboard box stuffed with dried leaves, but almost always the exhausted muttonbirds would eventually die. How badly I wanted to save those birds, peeking quietly into the box every other minute, aching to see one recover and unfold its chocolate brown wings to fly again.

After Emilie and I left the black-backed gull and his carefully decorated grave, we swapped the sand walking for the firmness of a forestry road cutting through the adjacent pine plantation. Under the cover of the pine canopy it was much cooler. We were able to pick up the pace, out of the pine forest and down a narrow country back road until, many hours later, we stumbled into the town of Bulls and celebrated with ice cream at the local store.

Over the next week we covered a monotonous 40 kilometres of road walking from Bulls to Feilding and on to Palmerston North. The sprawling city is bordered by the Ruahine and Tararua ranges, a rugged 200-kilometre spine that runs parallel with the east coast of the North Island between East Cape and Wellington.

Rising inland of Hawke's Bay, the Ruahine Range is separated from the northern end of the Tararua Range by the mighty Manawatū Gorge, another spectacular geological feature perhaps best explained by Māori folklore.

Known by tangata whenua as Te Āpiti (meaning the narrow cleft or gorge), legend has it that the Manawatū Gorge was created by the mighty spirit Okatia as he fought his way through the impenetrable rocky fortress of these mountain ranges. A summary of Okatia's story goes like this: a long time ago, a giant tōtara tree stood on the Puketoi Range. The tōtara was home to a powerful spirit called Okatia. Despite living in the forest far from the ocean, the restless

Okatia became obsessed with reaching the Tasman Sea. To achieve his dream, he uprooted the mighty tōtara that was his home, then made his way towards the sea, destroying everything in his path as he went.

When the tōtara and its resident spirit reached a high, cloud-clad mountain range, it seemed Okatia had met his match. Driven by his need to reach the water, Okatia tried to smash his way through, but the mountain continued to hold him back. Eventually, an exhausted Okatia gathered the last of his strength and broke a path through the middle of the mountain range and powered on towards the sea. A river flowed through the gap he left and so Te Āpiti, the Manawatū Gorge, was created. What had once been a single mountain range became two — the Tararua and Ruahine ranges.

Of course, geologists ruin the magic of this story by explaining that the Manawatū Gorge existed long before the mountain ranges of the Ruahine and Tararua. According to them, as the land rose, the river continued to cut its way through the mountains, creating the gorge.

Our plan was to walk up into one of those cloud-clad mountain ranges to see if our endurance could match its strength.

In Palmerston North we headed straight for the bright orange suburban shelter of Whiowhio Hut, which stood in the backyard of trail angels, former trail walkers and keen conservationists Fi and Anthony Behrens.

From there, we'd planned to shower, sleep and resupply for the next section, but instead we joined a group of volunteers in a labour of love to restore Stanfield Hut in the nearby Ruahine Range.

For some time, I'd been hassling the Backcountry Trust's project manager Megan to let us in on a hut restoration project. This non-profit group works closely with DOC to take on the physical mahi of restoring and maintaining many of New Zealand's iconic backcountry huts and shelters. I was a fan of their work, and in Palmerston North the stars aligned.

Megan had a helicopter booked to take a load of building supplies and willing bodies into Stanfield Hut the day after we staggered into town, so we rushed around frantically to buy the extra food and spare old clothes we'd need to help fix and paint a hut. With a little help from Fi and Anthony, who also knew Megan, we scored a lift from a friendly DOC ranger out to the landing zone.

That's where Emilie made a new friend who she called 'Sally, the Queen of Flowers', a young lawyer and keen tramper from Wellington who was also helping fix up the hut along with her husband and their two friends.

As usual, Emilie was in her element with so many new faces to entertain. The helicopter pilot was pretty chuffed too and let her ride up front with him on the way to the hut and back again, while Sally and I hung on tight in the back.

It was my first time in a chopper and the deafening whump, whump of the rotors drowned out the instructions yelled by the co-pilot, although I understood the best thing to do was to duck down below those lethal blades and run for the safety of the cabin.

Once in the air, the exhilarating flight followed the scar of a valley deep into the hills where the chopper's downwash flattened the scrub beside a creek as my head rung with its almighty roar. We circled the orange roof of the hut twice looking for a landing spot, but the lush green canopy was so overgrown that the only suitable place was a few hundred metres downstream on the riverbank. After we'd landed and scrambled to safety, the co-pilot unloaded our gear and we formed a human chain to carry the heaviest of it up to the hut.

Megan was a human machine, wielding power tools and shouting instructions. It felt great to be part of such industry, although my skills were limited to scrubbing and prepping the inside of the hut, cutting back vegetation with a handsaw or passing tools to those on the roof.

Built in the 1960s by the New Zealand Forest Service to shelter deer cullers who often went bush for weeks on end, the sturdy little hut boasted two wide wooden sleeping platforms, a wood stove, a cooking bench and wooden seats. But decades of hard use by hunters and trampers had left Stanfield Hut in a sad state. Inside it was dank and stale, and outside, green mould was spreading over its bright orange tin flanks. Rats and mice had made their home inside the roof cavity. I helped rip down hunks of the old ceiling with a crowbar, cursing as a thick dust of powdered rat shit fell into my hair. Emilie helped out a bit, collecting old beer bottles and other detritus scattered in the scrub around the hut, but mostly she chatted, bouncing around everyone like an excitable puppy dog before returning to her favourite new person, Sally, the Queen of Flowers.

I am in awe of Emilie's social skills, how she is attracted to people like a bee to honey, tasting them all to find which one will yield the sweetest nectar. She has the ability to tailor her charm to warm even the gruffest or most introverted of people and soon has them eating out of her hand. Even the staunch Megan allowed Emilie to call her 'Meegie Weegie', although I didn't like Emilie's luck in pushing her teasing too far. I tried, unsuccessfully, to rein her in, but she ignored me, and I retreated with a bucket of river water mixed with sugar soap to scrub the mouldy green interior of the long-drop toilet.

Without much physical strength or technical skill, I started to feel a bit redundant on site. Megan was hopping around on the roof like the Energiser Bunny, installing the new flashing with help from one of the boys, while another couple were digging holes and pouring cement into the hard ground to lay foundations for the woodshed. But out at the musty old loo, I felt I could make a difference.

Under the cool shade of the giant ferns, bucket and scrubbing brush in hand, I used snippers and a hand saw to prune back overhanging vegetation to allow direct sunlight to shine through. Then I doused the walls with my sugar soap mixture and got to work. The green mould slid off under the friction of my sponge, revealing cream-coloured walls. With the door open, the loo didn't smell so bad. It had been a while since anyone had dropped a bomb in that dark, dank hole. I whispered an apology to the long-legged spiders that had made their home in its dark interior, then swept them, their webs and their collection of dead flies, moths and beetles out the door.

We'd already collected several rubbish bags of trash from the undergrowth around the hut — mostly tins, beer bottles and food packaging — and I retrieved a glass bottle to fill with river water and a couple of fern fronds. There. Now the loo looked a lot more inviting.

A brief movement caught my eye and I looked up to see a plump black-and-white miromiro or tomtit regarding me. He was after the insects I'd evicted from the loo. I sat quietly as he flitted around my worksite, snapping up bugs. The leaves rustled and there was another, a female, wearing her drab greyish-brown cloak. I watched mesmerised as the male passed her a morsel. Then Emilie's laughter broke the spell, and the birds disappeared silently into the canopy together.

Emilie was having a wonderful time with Sally and the others, bouncing around in a pair of bright red tights procured from a Palmerston North op-shop, enjoying the break from trail walking. She fed off the energy of the group, growing more and more excitable with each interaction. I am the opposite. Out beside the musty old loo, I was alone and in my element. These are the moments I live for, the privilege of sharing a private interaction with two of Papatūānuku's creatures.

Later that day, an old bloke called Bill turned up with one of his mates. A quiet, white-haired fellow in his seventies, I recognised him from the drop zone the day before. It turned out he was part of a group of volunteers who'd given Stanfield Hut a makeover in the 1990s, some 30 years earlier. Now retired, Bill, a keen hunter and tramper with a love for his local hills, had returned to help rip up the old deck and front porch he'd once built and replace it with new, treated timber. It was lovely to meet him and share some stories. I hope I'm still going strong in the hills when I'm his age.

In the quiet before sleep, I chatted to Megan, who was lying next to me on the platform bunks. Our talk turned to many things, including our own personal battles with the black dog of depression.

Despite the distance we'd covered in the past few weeks and the excitement of the hut restoration, I had felt my own black dog slinking along in the shadows, slowly creeping up on me. The signs were there: the low mood, the tears building up behind my eyes, the restless thoughts all leading back to that dark place inside myself, then one morning I'd woken to hear the slow thump of his tail upon the floorboards.

The dog and I are old companions. I don't like him, and he doesn't like me, but even though I've tried to shake him off many times he just keeps following me around, a familiar presence that I eventually, reluctantly, begin to accept as just being part of my life.

There were times when I'd had glimpses, moments of painful and poignant self-awareness in which I knew something was wrong with the way I was feeling — or the way I thought. It couldn't simply be justified by the situations around me. I could see other people managing life in such a totally different way, without the soul-destroying suffering that seemed to be ripping me apart.

The thing is, when you're so used to being mentally unwell, you forget what being well actually feels like. You don't realise your life has been hijacked by the dark cloud of mental illness and, instead, you start to believe that this is just how it is, that this is who you are.

I'm not sure when it all started for me. Maybe it was in my DNA, generations of trauma and suffering passed down to me by my stoic Scottish forebears. Maybe I was born with a predisposition for mental illness, which was compounded by my relationship with my troubled parents, their acrimonious divorce and my difficult teenage years of drugs and sexual abuse and not nearly enough rock and roll.

During my 18 months in foster care, I self-medicated with marijuana, a readily available drug of choice in New Zealand and Australia. From there, I dabbled in amphetamines, enjoying the buzz but hating the come downs, sampled magic mushrooms, LSD, MDMA and, once, cocaine. Then, at the tender age of 16, I stumbled onto heroin, a drug I'd vowed never to touch. At the time, I was between a rock and a hard place, so I sat back and let a 20-year-old Brisbane junkie shoot it into my arm.

Life quickly slipped away to a dark, desperate time where the only thing worth staying alive for was my next fix. Somehow, though, I'd pulled through, and 12 months later I was clean and empty as I enrolled myself in state-subsidised night classes.

Even after adding the accomplishments of my high school certificate, a diploma, a university degree, an unfinished attempt at an MBA and a string of well-paid positions to my CV, I still felt like a broken person masquerading at being whole. Some days I would put on my mask and go to work, and sometimes that was enough to silence the huge feelings of imposter syndrome, the ever-present low-grade rumble of panic and paranoia. If I looked my colleagues in the eyes for long enough, would they be able to see inside my head? Would they see there's something wrong with me? Why am I feeling this way, why can't I smile and laugh the way they do? All I want to do is cry. I'm so lonely, so lonely, so locked into the nightmare that's inside my head. And I'm so very tired.

What I didn't realise was that it takes tremendous energy to keep on functioning as though nothing is wrong when your body and brain carry the memory of terror, shame and vulnerability.

In the end, I put so much energy into keeping my shit together during the eight hours I sat in that open-plan office on the sixth floor of the Christchurch City Council building, that by the end of the day I'd weep quietly in the changing room before wheeling out my bike for the seven-kilometre commute home.

Even at home there was no time to myself to sit and think, space to unpack and repack whatever was eating me up inside. Because there was Emilie, beautiful and bright, my bubbly, bossy and magical girl, who I worried I was letting down because she deserved a happy, attentive loving family who adored her and not her broken ghost of a mother.

The thing about mental illness is that it can creep up on you so quietly, so softly and insidiously that you don't realise you're unwell until everything starts crumbling around you. Something is silently sucking the joy out of every breath you take, and you can feel yourself bleeding through the ragged hole in the depth of your soul. Even worse, it tints the lenses through which you view the world, subtly at first, until you realise you're approaching every human interaction with apprehension and fear.

Eventually, I didn't want to wake up, get out of bed, get dressed or drag myself back to the concrete prison cell my workplace had come to represent. I longed to throw in the towel, to admit defeat, to close my eyes and feel myself shatter into a million pieces and drift away. But I couldn't afford to lose everything, not now, not after the long battle I'd been through. There was no one to step up and take the load off my shoulders. The bills, the mortgage, food — who would pay for these if I wasn't working?

The words of French philosopher Jean-Jacques Rousseau would come to mind — memories from my third-year political science studies — *Man is born free, but everywhere he is in chains*. So true. I was chained, manacled. I had shackled myself to the capitalist regime, and I had gone willingly, no gun to my head (unless the metaphorical gun was a life sentence of poverty in low-paid employment, paying someone else's mortgage).

I had interviewed for the job that was now killing me, signed their employment contract and continued to uphold it by dragging myself, metaphorically screaming and kicking, back there every day in order to pay the mortgage on a house that I myself had made an offer on, negotiated the sale of and later hounded the government Earthquake Commission to pay out on after finding it riddled with cosmetic damage and shaky piles. I'd dealt with shady builders, then better builders, quotes and subcontractors, insulation grants, colours, benchtops and splashback tiles, not to mention the many hours of landscaping, fence staining and gardening.

So, no, I wasn't about to let all this hard work slip through my fingers. For myself and for Emilie, I had to keep going until I could find a way to gracefully bow out, a plan that would allow me the freedom to escape my all-consuming financial responsibilities without losing everything I had. I hoped Te Araroa would bring me the answers I was so desperately seeking.

Once we had left the Ruahine Range and returned to Palmerston North, I looked for a local doctor to prescribe me some antidepressants to help keep the dog at bay. Overcome with feelings of desperation and anxiety, this exercise in life administration took me back to another time when I'd tried to seek medical help, with a very different outcome.

I'm 16 years old and wandering through the steep streets of inner north-western Brisbane where the midday sun is melting the tar off the roads. The air is thick with the stench of it. I'm bent double, gagging, but nothing comes up except a thin stream of yellow bile that burns up my throat and brings water to my eyes. The top of the hill is barely 50 metres away, but that's at least 100 steps, maybe 200 at this agonisingly slow, bent-over shuffle. It feels like my bones have dissolved into a million pieces of glass, piercing and pulverising my tender flesh, and my brain has swollen inside my skull. A whimper escapes my dry mouth, but I'm too tired to cry, too numb to feel anything except the agony in every step and the blinding thump in my head.

Perched on a power line and waiting for me to die, a crow caws mockingly at me, its callous cry cutting through the thick, humid air. I'm weak and tired and it's been days since I've eaten or slept, but I'm not going to die, not today. I stagger on up the hill, past rows of pretty Queenslander-style houses with sweeping verandas and tin roofs baking in the heat. I keep going until I can see the white and grey outline of the medical centre that I hope will be my salvation. They run a methadone clinic and I need a hit.

But I live in a state of Australia where archaic legislation deems me too young for a doctor to legally prescribe a drug of dependence for a drug-dependent patient. In order to get a fix to replace the heroin addiction that's slowly killing me, I need to be at least 18, the nurse tells me sternly. Basically no, there's no help for me here. All that's left is to lie down and let the crows peck over my scrawny, wilted body.

This memory of my 16-year-old self came to mind as I walked the streets of Palmerston North. There, I learned that scoring a prescription for antidepressants is a challenge when you're an out-of-town trail walker, doing the rounds of local GP practices with your dirty-faced child with her big eyes and knotted brown hair.

But we're walking Te Araroa! I tried to explain to a poker-faced receptionist, who had no idea what I was talking about.

I don't have a local address because I don't live here, but this really is an emergency — I just need a prescription! She probably thought I was homeless or mentally ill — which I was — or a drug addict trying to scam her. Anger displaced the shame that burned the back of my throat. For fuck's sake, I wasn't asking for methadone, and it's not like I could get high on Prozac.

Stress and panic pushed their way up my throat, and I had to try really hard to swallow back the huge stone and remain calm. Emilie was sucking on an ice block even though it was only 10am — she'd jumped at the opportunity to corner me outside a dairy, and, with all my energy focused on not losing my shit, I caved easily to her request. I was so dysregulated, and my body was pumping huge amounts of cortisol and adrenaline around my bloodstream, so I was struggling to stay calm.

Have you tried calling your doctor in Christchurch? one kind-faced nurse asked me. *They should be able to fax the prescription to the pharmacy next door. Just give them a call and try.*

I don't know why I hadn't thought of that in the first place, instead of wandering the streets like a distressed junkie. I thanked her and we parked up at a local café while I made the call. Within 30 minutes, I'd collected my prescription, a box of what I hoped would be a magic potion in a brown paper bag.

I wonder if antidepressants would have done me any good as a teenager. I think my general distrust of authority figures, the social workers, psychiatrists, associated medical professionals and the police, probably put me off taking any prescribed medications.

After ending up a ward of the state in foster care at age 14, I remained incarcerated until I turned 16 and then immediately returned to Australia, a legal adult and a very angry one at that. I don't remember all the details, but in my case notes a social worker wrote about my desire to return to Australia, to live near my mother and attend a private art college.

I had stayed on in Brisbane when my mother moved 4000 kilometres across the country to Western Australia with my stepfather. When I returned from New Zealand, she organised a lease for me on a room in a boarding house and took me to the Department of Human Services office to set up my welfare payments. Due to my age, I could only qualify for a student allowance if I was enrolled in some kind of study. With no high school certificate and no money, I didn't qualify for the art college, so I ended up enrolling in some computing programme at the local polytechnic.

I only attended one class. It wasn't just truancy for the fun of it — I was broken, raging and roiling and in no state to participate in polite society. In the previous 18 months, I had been shuttled between more than 20 foster families and had spent several stints in various adolescent rehabilitation units, surrounded by unstable and dangerous people and predators. I ran away from almost every home the state placed me in.

In that time, I had been raped on two separate occasions and had narrowly escaped a third attempt. I had witnessed horrific domestic abuse. I had seen the brains of a neighbour blown onto the back of a foster family's car. I had been caught up in a gang haunt. I had watched a young man be beaten within an inch of his life. I had seen a young mother threatened with a syringe full of battery acid. The only way out of many of these dangerous situations was to placate my captors then escape.

Haunted by terrifying memories and overcome with anger and self-loathing, I sought only one thing — to get high and block out these overwhelming feelings. Marijuana was my drug of choice. It numbed me, chilled me, shut down my brain and wrapped me in soothing sensations as soft as the smoke I inhaled. I didn't need much — a $25 tinny would do me for a week if I smoked just a little bit each day, just enough to calm me down and keep my demons at bay.

Once back in Australia, though, I didn't have any contacts — hell, in those days barely anyone even had a mobile phone — so I asked the other inhabitants of that dodgy boarding house to help me out.

The house was a typical Queenslander, sitting high and proper with its pretty lemon-yellow weatherboards, white railings and sweeping deck. A purple bougainvillea wrapped around the front fence and, at first glance, it could have been any other grand family home in the inner suburbs of town.

Inside, however, it had been reconfigured into four large, lockable bedrooms separated by a wide corridor, with an open-plan shared kitchen and dining area and a back door that led to the laundry and bathrooms. The other occupants were two old guys and one younger one, and it was he who first offered me heroin.

With my brown paper bag of antidepressants safe in my backpack and my nervous system slowly returning to a manageable state, Emilie and I paused to enjoy the city life of Palmerston North.

We visited Bivouac to buy a better cooking pot, and in a thrift shop we found a beautiful children's book by renowned New Zealand author Joy Cowley. We visited a playground, then relaxed in the sunshine at an outdoor café, sharing a date scone as we waited for our hot chocolates with extra marshmallows.

Watching my little daughter smear jam and cream on her slice of scone, I thought about my 16-year-old self and all the things I'd say to her if I only could. Such as, please don't take heroin. It's not worth it. Perhaps I would drag her, kicking, screaming, swearing, into my car and take her far away from it all, to the beach, to the bush, to some backcountry hut several days' walk from the nearest road end. There, maybe I'd bundle her up in a sleeping bag and sit rocking her under the glowing stars at night. I'd show her why life was worth living and that she deserved to be part of it. I don't know if she would handle it, though. She was suffering so much, and those demons were so strong.

When 16-year-old me asked that young guy, Jed or Jarred or something, if he knew where I could get some weed to smoke, he said no, but he had something better. Heroin. Right there in his room, and he could give me a shot.

Of course, I said no because I wasn't fucking stupid. I had seen the movie *Trainspotting*, and when I was still in high school my older, cooler, drop-out friends had made me swear never to touch heroin. *It's like chasing the dragon, you'll never feel high enough again, but you'll keep trying until you're hooked*, my friends Leanne and Joel told me. They knew from experience.

When I was 13 and had just moved to Brisbane to live with my mother, brother and stepfather, I'd met Leanne and Joel on my way to school. They were five or six years older than me and they'd called out to me as they sat on the front porch of an old, battered house. At first, I was too shy to return their greeting. Eventually, one afternoon they convinced me to stop and chat, then welcomed me inside to listen to Pink Floyd and smoke a bong. It wasn't my first bong, and I was grateful to them for their friendship, their quiet acceptance in a world where I already felt like a social outcast.

I would stop in at their place most days after school, but sometimes they kept the door locked and wouldn't let me in. Those were their dark days, the days when they were coming down off heroin.

After Jed's offer, I thought about Leanne and Joel's warning for the next 24 hours until something set me off. Then, distraught and desperate, I knocked on Jed's door. He mixed us both a shot in a bent teaspoon, heating the metal with the flame of a cigarette lighter before sucking up equal portions into two hypodermic needles.

I watched, transfixed, as he wound a belt around my upper arm and expertly located a prominent blue vein in the crook of my elbow. The sting of the needle point piercing my skin was soon forgotten as he pulled back the syringe to make sure that he'd successfully hit a vein. The golden-brown liquid turned pink with blood, then his finger slowly depressed the syringe.

The warmth, bliss and euphoria of my first shot of heroin spread over me as I slipped off my seat and onto the floor. My brain exploded in ecstasy as it released an unnatural amount of dopamine, the neurotransmitter responsible for many positive emotions and feelings. It was as though I'd been dipped in warm melted honey, transcending my physical body and floating away to some ethereal plain. Finally, I had found peace, and holy fuck, did it feel good. *Trainspotting* was right. It was better than my biggest orgasm, more powerful than joy, stronger than anything I'd ever experienced. The chronic, nagging ache of loneliness, pain and sadness vanished in that moment as I sank into the warm, loving embrace of heroin.

Jed and I laughed, cried, hugged and I leapt down the slippery slope of heroin addiction, chasing that dragon as hard as I could.

But my old friends were right. It would all end in tears.

Six months later, I lay on a filthy couch in some even filthier share house and filled the room with my painful cries. Devoid of the powerfully addictive opiate drug that had taken over my life and too young to qualify for a methadone programme, I simply had to go cold turkey with my withdrawal. The symptoms were so strong that I thought I would die. In fact, I wished I could die just to make the pain go away. I could barely swallow; my gums were swollen and my hips jutted out beneath my skin. Everything hurt, as though my bones had dissolved into tiny pieces of broken glass and were working their way through every vein and artery.

A pock-faced, long-haired angel sat up with me on that filthy couch, feeding me spoonfuls of mashed-up Weet-Bix and sips of water. His name was Brad, and he saved my life. With his love and care, Brad helped me get off the heroin that was slowly killing me.

Only a year older than me, Brad had been on the streets for several years and was as wise as an old man. Jed and I had visited his place to score some weed to help ease the pain of our comedowns on the days we couldn't get a hit. Brad took one hard look at me and when Jed left the room said, *Mate, what the fuck are you doing with that loser? You're killing yourself. There's always a place here for you when you're ready to get off that shit.*

I was ready, more than ready, but heroin had me in its grip. I was terrified of the debilitating pain brought on by the withdrawal symptoms, but the next time Jed and I scored with a friend of his, the friend collapsed with the needle still in his arm. Jed ran for it, leaving me to stagger to the payphone and call an ambulance. The euphoria had turned into a nightmare, with terrible, jagged teeth.

Eventually, the withdrawals ebbed away, leaving me weak, tired and empty. For months, I seemed to exist in a vacuum. On the surface, I appeared to be a functioning human being, but inside I felt like a zombie. Brad and I began a relationship and most of the time he was loving and tender, although he was prone to the occasional fit of psychotic rage that matched my own. When I wasn't overcome by powerful feelings of anger, I simply felt emotionally dead.

We left the dodgy share house and moved into our own three-bedroom rental high above Red Hill, our bed a double mattress perched on stolen milk crates, bright blue plastic cubes that also served as side tables and bookshelves in our spartan home. Brad set himself up as the local tinny dealer to help pay our rent and fund our habit, and we had some flatmates move in.

I smoked with him but it made me dull and stupid, like those boys lounging on old sofas recovered from the local refuse station, spending their days smoking bucket bongs and playing *Gran Turismo* and *Street Fighter* on the PlayStation.

After a few mindless jobs in office administration, warehousing and waitressing — opportunities pushed on me by my case manager at the Department of Human Services — I found my way into an adult education programme that gave older adults and dropouts like me a second chance at gaining our high school certificate and, should we want it, entrance to university.

I grasped it with both hands and leapt, lying about my age for a start as you had to be at least 18 years old to qualify for this programme.

Over the next year and a half, I studied harder than I ever had in my life — all the core subjects, including English, biology, mathematics A and B, chemistry and physics. I broke up with Brad and moved out of that noisy share house full of bong-smoking boys and into my own little flat, where I could focus on my books.

Mathematics terrified me, physics made me cry, English was easy, chemistry was fascinating, but biology was by far my favourite. I walked away from my end-of-year exams with one of the highest grades in Queensland for year 12 biology, a credit in chemistry, and only just scraped through with a pass in maths and physics. I gained a distinction for English without really trying, much to the disgust of my teacher. What can I say? Reading and writing have always come easily to me. But even with my high school equivalent, my grade point average wasn't high enough to get me into zoology or marine biology, let alone vet school.

I applied for a few undergraduate courses, including medical engineering, and crazily enough I was accepted. Less than two months later, however, I withdrew from the programme. I never wanted to be an engineer, and the first-year papers drew heavily on my least favourite subjects — mathematics and physics. Alone, overwhelmed and distressed, I just couldn't seem to navigate the requirements of the course, let alone afford the textbooks. I sank into a deep depression and started using drugs again with a friend I'd made at adult classes — she was into amphetamines, a different, exhilarating high that never lasted long enough.

Eventually, I couldn't keep up with the rent and lost my flat. I guess after so many years of fighting, my resilience was low. I still wasn't convinced that I was going to make it in this world and I didn't have anyone in my corner to cheer me on.

I wish I could go back to my younger self and tell her everything would be okay. Maybe I'd help pay her rent, tell her to apply for another course mid-year, pay for her fees and textbooks, and make her go tramping with me in the mountains until her body was clean from those revolting drugs.

The private Blue Duck Bivvy in the depths of Tongariro Forest Conservation Area.

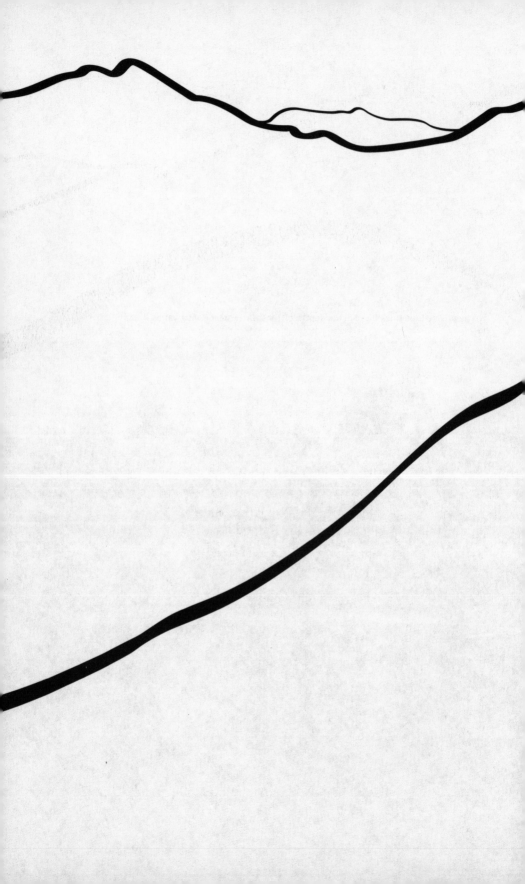

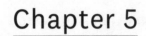

Chapter 5

Tararua Range

Te Araroa
Day 26

AFTER CROSSING THE SPRAWLING MANAWATŪ River on a foot/cycle bridge just outside of Palmerston North, the trail wanders away from the river and follows a series of walkways, country roads and green spaces into the foothills of the mighty Tararua Range.

I am happy to leave the weed-infested farms, fields and suburbs of the lower Manawatū-Whanganui region and head back into the bush, where I have an encounter with another of Papatūānuku's treasures. This time, it's a cave wētā.

Despite their name, cave wētā don't just live in caves — these shy, nocturnal creatures live under rocks, loose bark and damp places in forest and open country, emerging only at night to feed. Although the burning sun overhead signals that it is very much still daytime, one joins me for a skinny dip in a forest pool on the outskirts of the Arapuke Forest Park.

Despite their horrifying appearance, their small, humped bodies dwarfed by long, spiky legs and even longer antennae, cave wētā are completely harmless. I scoop it out of the water and place it on a rotten log so Emilie can take a closer look, then return to bathing.

All around me is thick native bush, five-finger, broadleaf and lancewood rubbing shoulders with tree ferns, and a thick carpet of moss blanketing the undergrowth.

A stream flows down some moss-covered rocks, creating a waterfall that fills a waist-deep pool. It is only big enough for one of us to bathe in at a time, and Emilie is hopping around in her underwear, watching the waterlogged cave wētā, while I breathe in deeply, then exhale and sink up to my neck in the cold, refreshing water. It burns and stings and then my body releases, enveloping me in an exhilarating tingle.

I know a little bit about cave wētā from my friend Danilo, an entomologist and veteran tramper. Upon hearing of my crazy plan to walk Te Araroa with Emilie, instead of trying to talk me out of it, he volunteered to be our emergency contact. Danilo told us cave wētā are part of a group of insects called Orthoptera, which includes their distant relatives, crickets, katydids and grasshoppers. Like the fairy tern and whio, these iconic New Zealand creepy-crawlies are also threatened or endangered, not only because they're a crunchy treat for hedgehogs, rats and mice, but also because the native bush that is their home continues to be rapidly transformed into farmland and property developments.

As I lie back in my watery sanctuary, it's hard to imagine that the sprawling city of Palmerston North is a couple of days' walk behind us, and that from here it is just two hours' drive south to reach the bustling capital of Wellington and the end of the North Island section of Te Araroa.

By my calculations, it should take us another three weeks to walk the remaining 200 kilometres between this spot in the Arapuke Forest Park and Wellington — that is if we can make it through the challenge of the Tararua Range.

These wild and notoriously rugged mountains run northeast-southwest for 80 kilometres from near Palmerston North to the upper reaches of the Hutt Valley, on the outskirts of Wellington.

Not particularly high by New Zealand mountain standards (the highest peak is around 1570 metres), the Tararua Range is infamous for its rapidly changing weather patterns. Even when there's clear sky elsewhere, a heavy bank of ice-tinged cloud often remains crouched over the jagged spine of the mountain range like a thick, grey fungus.

Now we were skirting along their foothills, travelling slowly south 40 kilometres through a mixture of council, private and conservation lands to the township of Makahika, where we would stock up on food before climbing 800 metres on a ridgeline to Waiopehu Hut, the first hut of the Tararua Range section.

The track had climbed and dropped and climbed again, winding its way around low spurs as the sun rose overhead. Although we'd packed up our tent and started walking before 8am, it was past 9am when we reached Arapuke Forest Park and almost 11.30 by the time we'd reached the waterfall pool, and our stomachs were rumbling.

I climb out of the water, suitably chilled, and carry my pack to a patch of sunlit grass beside the track. My sweat-soaked shorts and polyester T-shirt stick to my damp skin. I leave my merino sports bra to dry in the sunshine — it is simply too hot to wear it here.

Emilie is hovering like a dragonfly, ready to pounce on whatever morsel I offer her. Unravelling some slightly squished wraps, I shave off slices of cheese and salami with my pocketknife, roll it up for her and cut it in two pieces. She dances around with one in each hand, taking big bites out of one, then the other.

I make myself a wrap and lean back against my pack, close my eyes and chew, enjoying the creamy sensation of the cheese and the slight spice of the salami. It's hard to force myself to eat slowly and not devour the food with the hunger I always feel during these long days outdoors.

Emilie wants more, and this time I rummage around inside our food bag to find the little jar of peanut butter mixed with honey, a treat from our last resupply box. I fix her another wrap, then one for myself, and encourage her to have a big drink of water to help rehydrate and to bulk out the food in her tummy.

She picks me daisies from the grass growing in this patch of sun, exotic weeds no doubt blown up here from the farms and gardens outside the forest, and I pierce the stems and thread them to create a daisy chain.

It won't fit over her head, so she wears it as a crown. *Look Mummy, I'm the Queen of Flowers! Yes, you are, my princess.* You and Sally both.

Maybe it was the antidepressants, maybe I was just learning to live with myself, but somewhere between Palmerston North and here I realised the gaping black hole inside me had shrunk to a barely discernible crack. The racing thoughts that led to nothing and nowhere had slowed, and the physical feeling of floundering in mental quicksand had lifted. I felt light, despite the chronic weight of my backpack.

After leaving Palmerston North, we had continued wandering south, eventually leaving the sanctuary of the native bush to wander through dusty forestry roads until we reached the solid timber outline of Te Whare o Moturimu, a shelter established by the local council for Te Araroa hikers.

Although it was only 3pm, we were reluctant to press on, preferring to spend the rest of the afternoon between the refreshing embrace of the nearby creek and the warm grass outside the shelter. But as night fell, the eerie silence of the pine plantation hung over us and we went to bed early, snuggling up close together on the wide wooden platform.

We read stories from Emilie's *Snake and Lizard* book, chattered and giggled until we ran out of things to say and switched off our head torch. The blackness of night swallowed us up immediately. Spooning a sleepy Emilie, I returned to the silence of my thoughts, trying to ignore the strange sense of dread bubbling in the pit of my belly. To add to the sense of unease, the entrance to the wooden shelter had no door but instead was hung with thick curtains, which rattled gently in the night breeze. A particularly strong gust had me sitting bolt upright and scrabbling for my head torch, certain that some kind of intruder was coming to get us, but nothing was there.

The following day, we climbed the hill and out of the pine forest into a thick tunnel of native bush, following a track that dropped steeply down a wooded gully to the banks of the Moturimu River. The morning sun trickled through the dense canopy, creating dappled patterns on the forest floor. Brilliant green moss coated fallen branches and clumps of ferns sprang up everywhere. The music of little birds tinkled in the branches and my eye caught the movement of a korimako/bellbird dancing through the trees. The contrast to the silence of the dark green pine plantation less than a kilometre away was striking. Few creatures live in pine forests. Our native birds and insects can't feed on pine sap.

We navigated numerous stream crossings as we followed the course of the Tokomaru River, its clear waters gushing and gurgling around rocks and bends. Despite the apparent lushness of the undergrowth, we could see the tell-tale signs that something had been feasting upon the delicate vegetation. Chewed leaves, indentations in the damp track and the occasional cluster of liquorice-brown droppings all pointed to one culprit — goats — and where the track stopped at the edge of the river we came face to face with three of them, grazing busily on the opposite bank.

Despite their destructiveness, there's something very appealing about goats, with their intelligent eyes and expressive faces. As we paused quietly to observe them, the billy goat locked eyes with us and continued chewing, as if to say *Yeah, humans? So what?*

When I was small, we had a pet goat called Suzie, a tiny Angora my parents had persuaded the farmer next door to give us after her mother rejected her at birth. When she arrived, knock-kneed and trembling with her back end coated in foul brown muck, she was about three days old. My mother fed her milk from a baby's bottle and awful-smelling garlic-infused potion to help cure her scour.

After a week or so of feeding, washing and pampering, Suzie had gained weight and her curly hair was shiny white. She was heaps of fun, always entertaining us with her antics and games. She loved galloping between the lounge and kitchen, taking the corners so sharply that she'd skitter across the tiles, and would jump onto furniture, flicking her tail and leaping away just as we reached out for her. She also loved coming upstairs into our bedrooms to jump on our mattresses, but was discouraged from doing this after she paused in her play to pee on my brother's bed.

Suzie had free rein of our three-acre block on the outskirts of Huonville, deep in the Huon Valley in Tasmania. She would happily graze her way through the long grass towards the creek, where she would inevitably end up deep in the blackberry bushes. Once Suzie was well and truly stuck, she would cry out like a baby until my brother and I ran to help untangle her.

Unlike Suzie, however, these wild goats had no trust in humans and continued their brazen feasting for only a few more moments before the nanny called to her kid and the little group melted into the undergrowth.

I was still thinking of that block in Tasmania as we left the cool sanctuary of the river valley and cut uphill again, following a series of switchbacks until our path was blocked by a slip that seemed to rip open the landscape like an ugly wound, exposing raw, red flesh. Clambering up and over the slip, we marvelled at the sheer sides of the valley around us that rose almost vertically to a ridgeline.

Eventually our climb gave way to a flatter, firmer track, which grew into a four-wheel-drive track and led us to the corrugated iron structure of Tokomaru Shelter. Purpose-built in collaboration between Te Araroa Manawatū Trust and a local landowner, the shelter is for passing Te Araroa walkers and is basically a large tin shed with a concrete floor and a single wooden platform bunk. For two tired girls with only a lightweight tent as an alternative, it was a welcome home for the night.

I thought of my hardworking parents, their bodies worn out after another huge day of building their two-storey brick and batten house amidst the green wavy fields, and how the Tokomaru Shelter would have been a palace to our family back in those days.

When they first bought the Huonville block, we lived in a bus before moving into an on-site shed. My parents poured the concrete slab, then raised the framework of the walls.

Before they built the stairs connecting the top floor to the open-plan living–dining space below, we used a ladder to climb up to our bedrooms, often with one of the cats tucked under our arm. I helped my father lay the first brick on the lower storey as my consolation prize for losing in a maths test against my older brother. He won an ice block and I got to lay a shitty brick, one of many that we helped carry from their neatly stacked pallets to my father's worksite, their roughness grazing my soft hands.

At the age of seven I wasn't impressed, but now I am in awe of my parents' skill and dedication and how their team of two managed to transform that building site into a home.

A few years later, when my mother left, my father lost all interest in the block. The sheds, the paddocks, the dam we paddled our homemade canoes in, all of it could go to hell. He got rid of it all, even the dog. I don't know why I stayed behind with him. Maybe I'd had some childish fantasy that with my mother and brother out of the picture, I could finally be the centre of his attention and receive the love I always felt was withheld from me. Maybe I was just pissed off with my mother that day and was digging my heels in to see what would happen.

I never expected her to leave without me. I was mad at my brother for going with her, but he was always a mummy's boy, even though he was supposed to be my best friend. Hell, once when we were much younger, we'd told Mum that we were getting married when we grew up. She had laughed and told us we couldn't, so we were adamant that we'd live together instead. But now he was gone, and she was gone, and I hated them both for leaving me.

With my mother out of the way, my father plunged into a dark despair that both saddened and frightened me, so I tiptoed around him, wary of receiving the full force of his wrath.

By then, I was going to school, since continuing home education under my impatient father was not an option either of us wanted to consider. My mother's patient tutorage and my enquiring mind saw me sail through the end of primary school without much of a challenge.

I loved my teacher, had lots of friends and constantly received As and A+s on my report cards. I even have a report card somewhere with an A+++ for a particularly creative and inspired assignment about the ocean. Each member of our class was assigned a board in the hallway to present our assignment, with just enough space for four pieces of A4 paper. However, my friends and I filled our boards and the walls around them with handwritten text accompanied by brightly coloured hand-drawn illustrations.

My enthusiasm wasn't confined to the classroom — I took part in the school choir, the band, the athletics team, even the chess club, and revelled in our big end-of-year performances when we came together to sing and play music with other groups.

The haven of my final year at primary school was soon replaced with the uncertainty of my first year at high school. Somewhere in between, my father had sold the block and moved us to some ex-state house on the cheap side of town. Unlike many of my primary school friends who joined the ranks of various private schools, I went off to a raggedy public school where I knew no one.

At the tender age of 12, a budding pre-teen and the youngest in my class after being bumped up a grade due to my academic abilities, I was totally unprepared for the big, bad world of high school. But I was always an enthusiastic learner, and quickly realised that I could avoid teasing and scrutiny by hiding my academic ambitions and trying to be one of the cool kids.

I cut my beautiful, long, blonde hair short, pierced my ears multiple times with an ice cube and sewing needle, and wore whatever passed for op-shop fashion. I swapped afterschool band practice and choir for smoking bongs behind the boat sheds while waiting for the late bus home. Anything went, back in those dark days, just for the protection of being accepted into a ragtag social circle. At 14, I dropped out of school altogether.

Under the roof of the Tokomaru Shelter, I fell asleep with memories swirling through my head. After what felt like only a few moments of sleep, I found myself awake as the first light trickled into the sky. I was painfully aware that we were now only a day's walk from the official start of the track that would lead us deep into the Tararua Range.

Unzipping myself from the warmth of my sleeping bag, I crept outside to pee in the long grass, watching the tops of the trees switch and sway in the breeze.

Although it was only 6am, the wind was warm and the grass was dry and free of dew. I stirred milk powder into my instant coffee as a stream of mist moved up from the valley below.

By 8am, the wind, still warm, was blowing stronger. We could hear it whistling in gusts that rippled through the green and gold canopy, the leaves bending and flexing in unison under its force. In Canterbury, warm winds usually signal a nor'westerly weather front, which can swiftly change into cold wind and rain from the south. I was busy worrying about what this meant for us here when I realised that my mind was racing into unhelpful scenarios and I brought myself back to the trail.

I needed to focus on the task at hand, which was to feed Emilie and pack up our gear. But first, I switched on my InReach satellite phone and requested a three-day weather forecast. It didn't say much, just a 10 to 15 per cent chance of rain. But there was a message from Danilo, saying *Hello beautiful girls, I hope you're having fun out there!*

It was nice to know someone was thinking of us, let alone to be called beautiful with my sunburned lips and sweat-stained shirt. I drafted a reply, asking him to check the long-range weather forecast for me. Then I went inside to snuggle with Emilie, who was still wrapped in her bright yellow sleeping bag, and pack up our gear.

Come on baby, it's time to pack up! Mummy's got your porridge ready. I dived into the sleeping bag to catch her as she tried to hide from me, showering her with kisses. Oh how I wished we could stay there all day, rolling around together on the wide platform bunk while I breathed in her warm child's scent, but I knew she'd be bored soon, then hungry, and I only had a couple of days' supplies left in my pack.

After leaving the shelter, the four-wheel-drive track led to a narrow dirt road, which we followed for a couple of kilometres before plunging back into the bush. Tunnelling through the undergrowth, under the shelter of the thick green canopy, we were protected from the early-morning wind and soon distracted by the thick carpets of moss and ferns.

We had a 600-metre climb and an even longer descent before we could collect our next resupply box at Makahika, a hefty 18-kilometre walk away. It's an understatement to say that we were both looking forward to a hot shower and a big meal.

The cardboard box waiting for us at the Makahika Outdoor Pursuits Centre seemed so small — definitely not enough food to last nine days. Danilo had responded to my InReach message to say a front was passing over tomorrow afternoon, giving us just enough time to scuttle up Gable End Ridge to Waiopehu Hut. *Enjoy the Tararuas xxx* he ended his communication, a sweet end to a sensible message. I was certain he would have said otherwise if he felt we shouldn't be walking in there right now. I knew him well enough to be sure that he would have checked windy.com to watch the colours showing the precipitation and wind direction swirl across the screen and base his forecast on that.

The staff at Makahika weren't so sure. *Half of the trail walkers who come through here miss out on the Tararuas altogether because of bad weather*, the director told us. *Maybe you should just go catch the train to Wellington and play it safe. After all, you've got a little one with you.*

These words burned inside me as I repacked our gear. How bad could these mountains be? Despite my apprehensions, I really wanted to experience the magic of the Tararua Range. Surely Emilie and I could do it if we just took our time and walked from hut to hut. I didn't want to reduce myself to being a dumb mum who couldn't make her own decisions, but I also didn't want to make stupid mistakes.

With a rest day here and there, I figured we should make it through the next 90 kilometres in nine or 10 days. After the 15 to 20 kilometres per day we'd been averaging since leaving Whanganui, it seemed very luxurious to walk only 10 kilometres a day, but I knew that when every step was a careful negotiation of mud and roots and rocks, your hands reaching out to stabilise yourself on thin branches and slippery tussock, 10 kilometres could feel like an eternity.

With the weather forecast to close in late the following afternoon, I decided we'd head to Waiopehu Hut, taking the old Te Araroa trail up Gable End Ridge instead of the longer route that led directly to Te Matawai Hut. I reasoned that we could wait out the rain at Waiopehu then continue the six kilometres over to Te Matawai once the weather cleared. If the rain didn't clear after a few days, or the conditions got worse, we could turn back easily enough. For the plan to succeed, I needed to make sure we had plenty of extra food, enough to last us 12 days if we rationed carefully.

I turned to Geoff, a local trail angel from Levin some 10 kilometres away. He came to pick us up in his little red truck and took us to the supermarket to bolster our supplies, and wandered down the aisles to show me where they kept the sourdough bread.

You girls are trampers. I'm sure you'll be fine. Just take your time and make sure you keep that InReach charged.

The loaf of bread was too bulky to fit in my pack, so I asked Emilie to carry it. She shoved it into her bright blue backpack, eyeing up the jar of honey and slab of cream cheese I'd purchased to go with it. My pack was the heaviest it had been since Ninety Mile Beach, and I felt bad about Emilie carrying extra weight, but if she noticed, she didn't complain.

That night, I set my alarm to go off before the bellbirds because I wanted to make it to the hut before the rain set in. From our campsite at the Makahika Outdoor Pursuits Centre, there was six kilometres of road walking to cover in the warm, pre-dawn light before we even reached the forest park boundary, then a further nine and a half kilometres uphill to Waiopehu Hut. With a brutal 800-metre elevation gain and rough track ahead, I knew we needed all the daylight hours we could get if we were to make it up there before the weather unleashed its wrath upon us.

As soon as my brain registered the sound of the alarm, it released a squirt of adrenaline and almost immediately I felt a tingle of fear coursing through my body. I lay still and breathed, scanning my body to register how I felt. I noticed the burning knot in the pit of my stomach, flexed the aching muscles in my calves, curled my toes and pressed my shoulder blades into my sleeping mat. I told myself it was good to be scared before doing something brave, because attempting to walk 90 kilometres through some of the toughest mountain country in the North Island with my seven-year-old daughter at my side was a courageous, if not slightly crazy undertaking.

I reminded myself that we'd already walked and paddled over 300 kilometres, endured six days of being buffeted by the burning sun, wind and rain on a remote beach, got caught out in an alpine storm and survived a dunking in one of the North Island's longest rivers. Together, we'd visited over 60 huts in the Department of Conservation's 900+-strong hut network and, even before Te Araroa, our tramping adventures had seen us spend days alone in wild places.

It was just that I had no experience of tramping in this wild place — the dark and rugged valleys and ridgelines that make up the mighty Tararua Range. These mountains are one of a series of ranges forming the spine of the North Island, bounded on one side by the Wairarapa plains and on the other by the western coastal plain. We would be walking in from the western side, picking our way through the dense, tangled undergrowth, trying to cover as much ground as we could while the fine weather held out.

Wherever there are mountains, there is rain, and the Tararua Range is infamous for its heavy rainfall, high winds and thick, dense mist. One of my greatest worries was that I didn't know how to recognise the early warning signs of the fast-changing weather patterns that give these mountains their notorious reputation, or how quickly the rivers and catchments become impassable after rain. That type of knowledge is gained from spending time getting to know a place, visiting time and time again, in different seasons, under different skies, slowly learning how to read the sky and landscape and the living, breathing, changing forest all around you until you can intuit its every move.

Imagine knowing your local mountains as intimately as you know a lover, every curve and ridgeline, every bluff, every nook and gully leading you deeper inside. The lack of familiarity with the wild places we wandered through on Te Araroa had me permanently on guard, hypervigilant, subconsciously on the lookout for any danger. At the same time, I was removing myself from the stress of everyday life and I'd given my mind the space it needed to focus deeply on my immediate surroundings, including the rhythm of my own body.

When the restless, anxious energy of my dysregulated nervous system swept through me, I felt its presence as keenly as a chill southerly wind. With time, I learned how to channel this restlessness into action, energy in motion. With each exhale, I breathed this energy into my legs, feeling the strength in my thigh muscles propelling me forwards. Every other sense in my body would also become hyper-aroused, my eyes picking up movement and colour, my ears listening to all the little sounds of the forest. Without even thinking about it, my outstretched fingers stroked the tips of leaves, the tops of tussocks. As I moved through my environment, this energy moved through me, until it dissipated like tendrils of mist are absorbed into a sunny sky. In these moments, all that was left behind was a silent relief, a quiet joy.

In the morning, Emilie was reluctant to leave the warm cocoon of her sleeping bag and took a lot of coaxing, eventually emerging to the promise of a packet of strawberry and apple fruit sticks, a sweet treat to munch with her morning porridge.

Once she'd recovered from our early wake-up call, however, Emilie proved herself the superstar of the day. In fact, I was starting to wonder if she had magical powers, as her physical capabilities almost outmatched mine and her determination for good humour and camaraderie helped distract me from the weight of my pack.

Once we got across the farmland to the conservation park boundary, the beauty of the bush took over. Climbing up with a heavy pack feels like doing 1000 weighted lunges, and once you get your rhythm, there's something deeply satisfying in the sensation of a well-placed foot, with bones, joints and muscles all working together to propel you upwards and onwards.

The podocarp-broadleaf forest echoed a similar magic to the Tongariro Forest Park and giant tree trunks wrapped with thick vines disappeared into the canopy above our heads. While often muddy underfoot, the steep track was softened with leaves instead of being riddled with roots. I contented myself with observing how the leaf litter changed underfoot as we climbed higher, changing from dry, brown, spiked leaves to the delicate red and gold of mountain beech.

Several times, we wandered below towering rimu and giant tōtara, treading softly across powdered brown crunch, watched by flittering pīwakawaka and serenaded by the incredibly sweet melody of an invisible feathered songstress. The trees twisted and shrank as we climbed higher and higher, with mosses dripping from every living organism. A damp mist swirled around us, blanketing the valley below and softening the ominous drop on either side of the ridgeline.

Emilie had finished her pocketful of Fruit Bursts and run out of stories to tell and songs to sing by the time our heads popped out above the bush line and into the mist just as the rain hit.

Where is the hut? Are we nearly there? she asked. We paused to rummage for our raincoats, staring wildly through the dense fog for the angle of a roofline, the gleam of corrugated iron, a loo, anything to indicate that the end was near.

There is definitely a dangerous psychology in allowing yourself to crave for the track to end. I imagine it's like gearing yourself up for a final sprint at the end of a marathon — if you let go too soon, you'll burn out before you reach the finish line. We needed to push on, just a few hundred more metres through the mist and rain to the hut.

We found it damp, dark and spacious with a spattering of black mould growing up the wall of the open-plan living area, but it was a welcome shelter with the rain lashing outside. We unpacked our gear, made hot drinks to go with slices of sourdough bread, cream cheese and honey, then hunkered down for the night.

Later that evening, I wriggled out of my warm sleeping bag and ventured out for a pee. The dense cloud had lifted momentarily, and I paused on the western porch to admire the lights of Levin and Palmerston North glittering below.

The following day, we lounged around the hut, playing cards, reading the hut literature, Emilie drawing pictures in her hut diary, and trying to pace ourselves between mealtimes.

Let's have an afternoon nap, I encouraged Emilie, zipping my sleeping bag up around my neck and lying back on the grey plastic hut mattress on the wide wooden bunk.

No, Mummy! Let's play worms! Worm fight!

She wriggled over the top of me, a bright yellow worm with shining eyes and a gaping smile. My body ached from the previous day's punishment with that heavy pack, but soon I was wriggling around with her, pinning her down with the weight of my body as she erupted into glorious peals of laughter.

Then the hut door opened, and we froze, shushing each other with loud, dramatic noises, still high from our silly game. A dark form moved through to the other bunkroom and Emilie was off to investigate our new hut mate.

He was dripping forlornly, no doubt soaked through from the torrential rain that was buffeting the hut. I went to say hello and retrieved my little daughter in order to let the poor guy have a moment to settle in. I told her I was sure he'd feel like chatting a bit later.

Although our new hut mate was anything but chatty, we managed to squeeze out of him that his name was John, he was an English teacher, and he was also walking Te Araroa. From what I could see, he was also a big fan of Western novels, as he soon retreated to the sanctuary of his sleeping bag to read.

The following morning, despite the gusts of winds and smattering of rain, John was off again, stepping into his still-wet clothing and pushing on to the next hut. He said he'd wait for us there, and if we made it over later, then he'd walk with us up and over Main Ridge to Nichols Hut. This was all Emilie's doing, she'd managed to charm him with her magic spells. She'd got him to admit that he'd watched both *Frozen* movies with his niece, and Elsa was his favourite character. She'd shown him her Joy Cowley book, *Snake and Lizard*, which he agreed was a fine piece of writing, and I think I even heard him say he'd read it to her when we met up again.

I offered him a slice of sourdough bread and honey and quizzed him about his route intentions, but he mumbled through his two-minute noodles, his eyes reluctant to meet mine. Whatever. Maybe, like me, he didn't really know what he was doing there either, taking shelter from the storm in some damp, mouldy hut high on a ridgeline with the lights of the city twinkling in the distance far below. I hoped he'd be in a better mood later, or maybe he'd reconsider his offer of companionship and hightail it up the ridge before we got there.

Once John disappeared into the mist, Emilie was keen to go after him. I wasn't so sure. It still looked pretty wet out there. But after a few hours, we donned our wet-weather gear and ventured out into swirling mist to slip and slither along the narrow, overgrown track towards Te Matawai Hut.

The rain itself seemed to have called a ceasefire, but the mist quickly penetrated our shoes and slid down our necks as we pushed through giant tussocks and past spiky, stunted tree daisies, inadvertently shaking fat droplets off the vegetation and onto our bodies as we went.

Thick cloud wrapped around us, obscuring any views as we climbed up to the 1100-metre mark of Twin Peak, pausing solemnly to observe a simple memorial to a fallen tramper, who had died of hypothermia near that very point.

The lack of visibility was disconcerting as the track traversed a narrow ridgeline, where one wrong step would send us plummeting down through the mist in the valley below. Twice my feet slipped out from under me while negotiating a descent and both times I landed heavily on my arse, the weight of my pack pinning me to the ground. My shorts were wet, my merino knickers were wet and muddy water clung to my fuzzy blonde leg hairs like droplets on a spiderweb.

It was less than five kilometres from Waiopehu to Te Matawai Hut, but it felt much longer. Emilie put up with the damp and cold until the last kilometre, when we finally dropped down into a dark tunnel of bush that dripped water into wide puddles. We had no choice but to slosh through. Then she too unleashed some water, her little face screwing up as tears ran down her cheeks.

I felt so bad for her. The poor little thing had enjoyed skipping around in her pink pyjamas on our hut day and now here she was, soaked and muddy. I pulled out my phone to show her the map, reassuring her that it was just a little further to the hut where we'd be able to hang up all this wet gear and get dry again.

John kept his word and was waiting for us at Te Matawai after all, huddled in a down jacket and beanie, his breath forming clouds in the cold, damp air. I busied myself selecting the best of the semi-dry firewood from the porch. After I dropped a few hints, John took up the axe and we soon had a fire roaring in the wood stove, which took the chill off the air and dried our damp clothes.

The following morning, we stepped out of the dark, mouldy interior of the hut to marvel at the view of jagged ridgeline and beyond, blue skies. After spending days trapped in thick mist that had obscured everything, it was like waking up in another part of the world.

I felt slightly smug to see that John's pack was massive compared with my own, even though I was carrying food for Emilie and myself. Perhaps we all felt like rookie trail walkers at this early stage. Emilie quickly made it clear John was her conquest and therefore hers alone to chat to, so I wandered slightly ahead and enjoyed a few hours of solitude.

Hours later, once we'd dragged ourselves, using hands and feet, up to the heights of the Main Ridge, I gazed as far as I could in every direction and realised I could now appreciate the rugged beauty of the Tararua Range.

Before us was a sea of green, gold and burnt ochre and the occasional splash of red, an ocean of dark valleys and rugged ridgelines, rising and falling like waves as far as the eye could see.

A bank of fast-moving cloud descended on us, whipping our bare skin with icy fingers, and we fumbled in our packs for rain jackets and woollen hats that were still damp from the previous day.

There was no time to stand and stare at the scenery; instead, we scurried down the ridge towards the relative shelter of the stunted trees below.

Underneath their dark green canopy, the forest was a swirl of misty green. Long tendrils of moss reached down from the branches just as ferns reached up from the forest floor. We were in goblin forests of a lancewood tree daisy (*Olearia lacunosa*), its twisted limbs and flaking orange bark dripping in dull green moss.

The track was scant beneath our feet, the occasional plastic orange marker obscured by moss or lichen. The path undulated along the bumpy ridgeline, hidden by fallen branches, muddy holes and rotten logs already reclaimed by young growth.

Feeling thirsty, I realised I'd made a terrible rookie error by not filling my spare water bottle all the way back at Te Matawai Hut, five kilometres and a gruelling descent down slippery tussock ago. I'd just taken a deep draw on my soft plastic water bladder, sucking in the last of my water so all that was left was air. Even though it had been damp on the track, the big climb up to the ridgeline in the full sun had sapped my strength and I couldn't wait to get a refill from the tank at Dracophyllum Hut, still two very slow kilometres away.

All up, it took us six hours to reach the bright orange shelter of the hut, appropriately named for its setting amongst a grove of Dracophyllum trees. Our delight at reaching the bivvy was short-lived, because when I turned the tap below the rainwater tank, nothing came out. I could see the spouting from the gutter running into the tank, and it had been raining heavily for days, so it had to be full. I thumped the side of the tank to make sure, but it resonated hollowly beneath my fist.

Fuck. It was empty and I was dying of thirst. How could we possibly continue the next five kilometres to Nichols Hut with no water? There was nothing to drink up here on the ridgeline, and with these track conditions, we'd be lucky to cover a kilometre per hour.

I cursed myself for this massive, stupid oversight as I ditched my pack to climb up on the tank stand for a better look. From up there, I could see that the guttering was completely clogged with vegetation. When I unscrewed the lid of the tank, I saw that it was completely empty except for about five centimetres of water covering a film of muck at the very bottom, in which a couple of soggy earthworms were twisting about forlornly.

I sat on the front porch, as the few planks out the front of the hut might generously be called, considering my limited options. Emilie was already exploring the hut, which from her point of view was the perfect size for two grubby, sticky girls. We'd run out of daylight hours and energy to push on to Nichols Hut, so I unclipped my plastic cup and leaned deep into the tank, scooping out the remaining water and trying not to disturb the gunk at the bottom. Surely once I boiled it, it wouldn't taste too bad . . .

As the light faded from the sky, we shook out our sleeping bags and arranged ourselves on the narrow lower bunk — the top bunk was barely 30 centimetres below the ceiling and covered in mouse droppings.

John had decided to stay on too: clearly a full day with Emilie wasn't enough. I heard them singing 'Let It Go' together while I was searching for orange markers in the goblin forest, feeling slightly miffed that I wasn't invited to be part of the chorus.

I did my best to sweep the worst of the dust and dead leaves gathered in the corners of Dracophyllum Hut, but after a lifetime of offering emergency shelter from the harsh elements, its poorly ventilated interior was dank and dingy at best. It needed a good dose of sugar soap like that mouldy loo back at Stanfield Hut, but there was none to be seen up here, and anyway, I couldn't spare the water to go with it.

Despite my exhaustion, I was too wired to sleep and lay on one side of the grubby plastic mattress with my back pressed up hard against the wooden ladder that led to the top bunk. John was fast asleep on the floor and as Emilie wriggled against me, claiming more than her share of the bed, I contemplated climbing upstairs just to have some space, mouse poo or not. But before I could be bothered putting such plans into action, I drifted off.

The following morning, despite my eyes feeling bruised from

lack of sleep and one hip sore from being jammed against the wooden ladder, I found myself standing on an island surrounded by an ocean of cloud. Just a few metres below me was a thick white swirl of mist that completely obscured the deep gash of valley below. I felt like I could step out upon it, buoyed by its density and float slowly away.

My island was covered in dense clumps of golden tussock, olive green and yellow harakeke, reddish purple fingers of Dracophyllum. Across the ocean, ragged ridgelines protruded above the cloud like the backs of gigantic whales, the dark scrubby smear of bush on their flanks giving way to the lighter shades of the tops.

The sun was still hidden to the east, and the cool glow of daylight created an ethereal haze, as though I were sleepwalking through this magical landscape. The mist then flowed over the low lip of ridgeline and down into the neighbouring valley, a waterfall of opaque white silk. I sank down onto a plump tussock to wait for the sunrise, watching the background change from dark to light, thin whisps of white mingling into the blue sky.

Finally, the sun emerged in a glory of gold, and I closed my eyes and felt its heat upon my face. My fingers closed around the greenstone pendant I wear around my neck, the smooth stone strangely warm against my skin as though absorbing the light of the sun. Our pounamu was a gift from Timoti, a talented carver from the South Island. Mine is almost circular, more curvaceous than a crescent moon, and Emilie's piece fits perfectly inside it to make us whole. It's the most beautiful thing anyone has ever given me, made for me, a work of art created out of a piece of precious stone. It's more than a piece of jewellery though. It's a sacred connection with Papatūānuku herself, and wearing it makes me feel strong, grounded, safe. I hoped it would continue to protect us on our journey and that we would be permitted to pass through her wild lands unscathed. I felt that special gifts like this magical sunrise were a sign of her acceptance.

My early-morning meditation was interrupted as a rustle in the bushes behind me revealed a small child with golden brown curls escaping from two thick plaits. She was awake and had come to find me, sitting on my tussock throne in the morning sunshine. As she plonked down on my lap, I wrapped my arms around her and breathed in her sleepy, warm child's smell, still so sweet even though she hadn't had a wash for four days.

I'd left her all tucked up in her yellow sleeping bag, her little face slack with sleep, and crept out of the doll's-house-sized hut to enjoy a few quiet moments to myself before she woke up.

Main Ridge in Tararua Forest Park.

Chapter 6

Waitewaewae Hut

Te Araroa
Day 36

I'M SPRAWLED OUT ON MY very own hut mattress, the hood of my sleeping bag pulled tight around my head, watching my breath form white whisps in the cold air. It's dark and cold. Emilie breathes deeply nearby on the wide platform bunk.

There's no chance of catching the sunrise this morning as the wind is driving gusts of rain against the walls and roof of the hut, rattling like a fistful of wet nails.

In contrast to the tiny doll's house of Dracophyllum Hut, Waitewaewae Hut is a huge, open lodge-style shelter perched on the banks of the Ōtaki River, its high plywood walls stained dark with creeping mould, an inevitability for any dwelling that exists in the depth of this damp jungle.

I lie blinking in the semi-darkness, feeling the rush of adrenaline and cortisol from that awful nightmare coursing through my veins, like the junkie's rush from a bad batch of amphetamine.

I thought I would eventually escape the horror of these memories; that the natural aging process, combined with healthy living and a few hundred kilometres walking through the wild, would keep the nightmares at bay.

Yet during the night I found myself sucked into a dream world, running along a trail that's almost hidden by dark trees, long slender branches bent almost to the ground under the weight of their leaves. It's a tunnel, framed with vegetation and soft underfoot, but I can't run fast because there's a pack on my back and my cheap sandshoes are full of holes.

I'm moving at a kind of crab-like shuffle, but I need to hurry because once they realise that I'm gone they will be after me, and I don't want to go with them. The desire to escape is so strong that I fight my way through the tunnel that's suddenly opening up to a road, a highway, and waiting just up ahead on the shoulder is a white station wagon. I can hear its engine idling although the headlights are off, the grubby white paint reflecting almost silver in the moonlight. Suddenly, I'm knocked off my feet by a sense of pure, animal panic because I must get the fuck away from that car.

But the dream slows down until time sucks me in like quicksand and that leafy tunnel, now my only hiding space, is out of reach. All I can think is that it's too late, but too late for what? My arms and legs are leaden and heavy, I'm fighting so hard, but my body is paralysed under the weight of a bearded man as he lowers himself onto me, pinning me to the ground as he forces me open.

Shock gives way to pain then is replaced by an intense cold, and its only when the shades of black in front of me fade to a dirty grey mist that I realise I'm standing alone by the wet roadside with no sound or light to show where the car had been. My body is numb and uncaring and all I can hear is the intense roar of the trees screaming in rage as the storm rips through them.

Once I've fought my way out of my dreamworld and back into Waitewaewae Hut in the Tararua Range, I nestle deeper into my sleeping bag, pull my thermal liner up around my chin and snuggle against Emilie's sleeping back. I want to go back to sleep but the fear from my dream has come flooding back, riding a wave of memory.

I'm taken back to another night, more than 20 years ago, to a time when I was 14 years old, on the run and completely paralysed by fear. It was the middle of the night and we'd been driving for hours. At first, I'd been relieved and grateful to get a ride with this seemingly friendly guy in his old station wagon, especially when he lit up a joint and passed it across. The first few puffs spread a warm, soothing glow through my body and dulled my mind. I settled down into my seat, glad to be on the move, every kilometre putting more distance between me and my foster family.

The night rushed by, engulfing us soundlessly. This guy seemed okay. But as the night wore on and we left the lights of the town for the long dark tunnel of the highway, his questions started to creep me out. Did I have a boyfriend, why not when I was so pretty, had I ever had a boyfriend before, would I consider letting him be my boyfriend. I squirmed and shook my head, wishing he would shut up so I could get some sleep. He kept going, *What if I paid you, just this once, because when I get to Tauranga my mate is going to give me five hundred bucks for the weed that I'm carrying, and you can have it all, just for you.*

What a sicko, I thought, no way! Even in my drug-induced haze, the spiders of fear were already crawling deep inside my belly when he pulled the car off the highway and drove deep into the darkness of the forestry plantation.

My panic grew as he shut off the ignition and got out of the car to walk around to the passenger side, but for some reason I couldn't move, I didn't move, I just fucking sat there staring at him in disbelief.

The paralysing sickness of this fear pinned me to my seat, even when he opened the passenger door and leaned over me, reaching for the lever and roughly slamming the car seat back. I was trapped and I couldn't move or breathe with my knees pressing into my ribcage and his dead weight on top of me. He ripped at my clothing, his rotting breath hot in my ear as he warned me not to move or he would use his knife.

I don't remember where I went after that. It was like I was whisked away to a plateau, where everything sounded and felt as though it was coming from a great distance. The shock, pain and intense cold had frozen time and space, and it was only when the shades of black in front of me parted to a grey mist that I found myself huddled alone under a pine tree with no sound or light to show where the car had been. All I could hear was someone whimpering, and the sound scared me until I realised it was me.

You've got to understand how hard it is for me to go back to this place and release the memories that I've fought to keep hidden for so long. It's like opening a locked door in some forgotten part of my memory warehouse and walking into a room full of ghosts. They surround me and overwhelm me with their rotting stench and banshee wails. The panic is all-consuming and every nerve in my body is screaming, fight, run, do something!

Instead, I usually just freeze and fade away, but I can't keep doing that anymore, because I'm turning into a ghost as well. So, this time I close my eyes and step into the darkness. Once I'm inside, I visualise myself throwing open the curtains, sweeping out the dust, lighting a few candles and maybe helping those ghosts pass through to the other side.

It's a nice image, and yet going back there fills my body with a toxic cocktail of emotion so strong I seriously think I'm going to die. There's fear and rage, pain and shame, and even with my candle held high above my head, I just can't seem to see my way through them. *Why didn't you fight?* a ghost screeches in my face, a yawning black hole of rage and blame. It's a fair question, I guess.

Six years ago, I joined a Brazilian jiu-jitsu club with the aim of pulling myself out of my single mum shell, getting fit and meeting some people. I must say, I really enjoyed wrestling with those big guys and learning how to escape their grip and pin them to the floor, at least for a few moments before they overpowered me again. It wasn't really fair when I was only 55 kilograms and they were nearly 100 kilograms, but our instructor insisted it wasn't about size and taught us the grips and holds that would overpower even the biggest attacker.

One session, though, triggered some very difficult feelings. We were learning a new sequence and had to start off lying on our back, with our partner, the aggressor, leaning in between our legs. The idea was that with some swift leg and arm work, we could trap their neck between our strong thigh muscles and squeeze, putting pressure on the huge carotid artery and causing them to pass out. Right from the start, the burning lump of panic spread through my chest and I lay flat on the mat stifling back tears, causing the gentle giant on top of me to pull back in alarm. Once I'd regained my composure, I beat him up good, but the nagging question gnawed away at me for days — why didn't I try to fight that stupid fucker in the forestry plantation?

I guess it's not a fair question to ask a terrified, stoned teenager at two o'clock in the morning. But the rage I feel towards my rapist still surges through me and I wish I could go back in time and rip his face off, knife or not. I would welcome the bastard between my creamy white thighs then trap him in a headlock until his eyes popped out or kick his head against the windscreen to see which smashed first. But the rage is short-lived. Because it's not really rage that I'm feeling. Underneath there's only fear, terror, panic, compounded with a huge dose of sadness and grief.

For a childhood ripped away from me, for losing my family, my dreams, myself.

My therapist would remind me that the trauma of being raped was so deep, so devastating, that it had left lasting scars in my brain, severing my neural pathways in the same way that a prolonged storm will cause an entire hillside to give way and send tonnes of wet earth and rocks rumbling down to the valley floor, flattening trees and demolishing trails.

The therapist also explained that my shattered nervous system, in an attempt to 'keep me safe', had resorted to dosing me with the fight-or-flight hormone, adrenaline, and its toxic cousin, cortisol, which is why it's so easy for me to feel like I'm in a constant state of primal panic.

I can feel it building up beneath my solar plexus like the frantic fluttering of a thousand tiny butterflies, forcing their way up my throat and into my head until I'm overwhelmed by the urge to scream, to run, anything to escape this terrible, paralysing dread.

When I was younger and lacking the self-awareness to recognise myself slipping into this state, I would run, away from the countless uncaring foster homes, seeking solace in anything I could get my hands on: drugs, alcohol, comfort in the arms of a stranger. Because if I didn't find a way to calm this beast then it would continue to build and turn on me, compelling me to hurt myself just to make it stop.

Now, at my ripe old age of 36, I know that if I just lie still and ride it out, clinging on for dear life, eventually this intense discomfort will peak and subside. So, I lie here in the darkness of Waitewaewae Hut, breathing slowly, regularly, deeply, breathing deep into my belly and visualising the sickening sensation growing smaller and smaller, until eventually it fades and I am empty again. I think of my therapist in his pressed chinos and collared shirt, barely a year older than myself, yet possessing almost a decade of theoretical and clinical knowledge. Calm is safe. Calm is safe. In time, you will build new neural pathways. Your body will learn that to be calm is safe. I hope he's right on this one.

Above the wind and the rain I can hear the solid rumble of the Ōtaki River below the hut. We're not walking anywhere today in this weather, which is good because our rain jackets and walking clothes are hanging wet and forlorn from the line strung between the rafters.

Two days earlier, we had walked on along Main Ridge from Dracophyllum Hut, arriving at the solid little six-bunk shelter of Nichols Hut, complete with its full rain tank, in the early afternoon.

John, the English teacher, decided to push on to Waitewaewae Hut, so we said our farewells then spent the afternoon sitting around in the sunshine admiring the expansive views down the valley far below.

The tidy green and red shelter of Nichols Hut was the nicest we'd encountered so far on this trip through the Tararua Range. After the claustrophobic evening in Dracophyllum Hut drinking boiled worm water, it was wonderful to spread out on the wide platform bunks and relax for a few hours before evening fell.

Late in the afternoon, we were joined by Vicky, a solo French walker who had walked most of Te Araroa the previous season and had returned to the Tararua Range to make up a section she'd missed.

In the morning, thick mist swirled where the open valley had been, closing us off from the world and muting all sound with its cloying dampness. Vicky left the hut straight after an early breakfast, explaining that she hoped to walk all the way out to the road end on the other side of Ōtaki Forks that day, passing Waitewaewae Hut as she went.

After she disappeared into the mist, I dithered for a little while, taking my time to prepare hot water for our porridge oats and my morning dose of bitter instant coffee, and shooting furtive glances out of the hut window in the hope the sun would force its way back through the clouds. But just as the mist seemed to lift enough to view the track, another damp body of cloud would sweep in, releasing a spattering of raindrops that drummed on the roof of the hut.

This really wasn't a good place to get stuck. Although Nichols Hut was lovely, we were four full days' walk from the start of the track and at least another three, if not four, days from where we planned to exit the forest park at Waikanae. To get there, we still had to cross the highest point of this particular section — the long, exposed ridgeline that led up to Mount Crawford, perched at 1462 metres above sea level and a climb of over 300 metres from Nichols Hut — before we could drop down into the relative safety of the forest.

If the weather was closing in, I would rather it be when we were down the other side of the mountain where we would be sheltered from the worst of it in a valley, rather than stuck up here with kilometres of ridgeline in either direction.

With this logic, it made absolutely no sense to dally, but I couldn't help holding out hope for some kind of miraculous gap in the weather so we didn't have to go out into the wet, cold morning.

After five days of stumbling through the forest and along the ridgelines, our clothes were stiff with filth, and it took so much mental fortitude to peel damp cold socks onto warm feet, lace up our equally damp trail shoes and leave the sanctuary of the hut.

In fact, I calculated miserably, it had been 10 days since we'd had a proper shower and laundered our clothes, not since leaving Palmerston North.

Emilie didn't want to leave Nichols Hut. She rolled around giggling, a little yellow worm in her sleeping bag, but once she realised I meant business, her good humour disappeared, especially when it came time to squeeze her little warm foot into a soaking wet trail shoe. I couldn't blame her. I didn't want to go out in the rain either, but we had to push on towards Waitewaewae Hut.

I was beginning to see the trail not just as an act of physical capability, but one of mental fortitude. Endless days of physical discomfort have a way of breaking you down. There was the gnawing hunger of never quite having enough food to match the huge expanse of energy required to walk the distance, and the uncomfortable sensation of being constantly damp and dirty with no soft place to rest except inside your sleeping bag.

One could in fact question why I was doing this to myself, I mused, as I clambered up the narrow track, dripping wet tussock kissing my bare legs. Although the thick mist sometimes gave way to a light rain, it wasn't particularly windy and it certainly wasn't cold, as long as we kept moving.

The wind picked up as we neared the summit of Mount Crawford, looming head and shoulders into the clouds. It was hard to tell where the mist ended and the rain began, except by the time we'd dipped below the tree line, steady droplets had soaked our every pore. I wanted to take Emilie's photo beside a faded sign stating that we'd reached the summit, but her lower lip was wobbling as gusts of freezing wind blew wet curls across her face.

We've been wandering around in the mist for hours! I told her. *But the next hut is right down the bottom of this hill, and you can put your warm thermals back on and get into your sleeping bag.*

Yeah, she replied, a damp little poppet in a bright pink and blue rain jacket. *I hope you can read* Snake and Lizard *with me, Mummy.* We'd already read the book cover to cover, but the short stories, full of humorous dialogue between the ridiculous Lizard and his friend Snake always cheered us up.

Of course, I will. I'll make you a hot soup, read you a story and we can have a game of cards.

Anything, I thought, anything you want, my love. My heart swelled with gratitude at how this little child continued to walk with me through such tough terrain without complaining or questioning what on earth we were doing this for.

We unwrapped wet Fruit Bursts with numb fingers and sucked on the sweetness, hoping to gain some energy to help us down the mountainside.

Then began the long, slow descent some 1000 metres to the valley floor, following the steep and treacherously slippery track that wound its way down almost vertically in places. Our feet slid out from under us, landing us heavily on our behinds, or bruising our legs as we scrabbled over huge fallen trees, thick with slime.

A flicker of movement caught my eye, and then came an unusual sound, a mix between the cry of a baby and the mewl of a cat. It was a goat, a little baby goat. We paused and stared in delight as it bobbled about beneath the trees, balancing on a dark tree root, calling out with its shrill little voice.

A nanny goat responded with a deep, vocal bleat and walked up the path a few paces before registering our existence. Shaking her shaggy blonde mane, topped with a pair of somewhat regal horns, she eyeballed us with one rolling yellow eye, the elongated disc of her black pupil dilating in panic before she turned and crashed away through the undergrowth, her kid at her side.

Chattering excitedly about the goats, Emilie and I sprawled on a cushion of wet moss under a tangled tree to eat the last of the sourdough smeared with the last spoonful of cream cheese. It had been a bastard to carry this far, but I was so glad we had as sometimes it felt as though food was the only comfort I could give us on Te Araroa.

Yet eventually I seemed to transcend the physical discomfort, and I accepted that we were soaking wet and filthy, fingernails blackened by mud and earth , then my focus turned to the magic of the bush around us.

As we made our way downhill, I stared up at all the trees that were determinedly clinging to this sheer bank, silently reaching up towards the sky in a glorious jostle of long limbs and green leaves. A fallen tree had immediately been claimed by tiny fungi, slender saplings. The circle of life was right here before my eyes. It was humbling and empowering to witness the intense resilience and desire of these living things to thrive despite the difficulties they faced.

I was here because I wanted to test the very limits of my own resilience and reassure myself that, no matter what had happened to me, I was not ready to lie down and die.

After that slow and arduous descent from Mount Crawford, we were taking a rainy rest day at Waitewaewae Hut — where Vicky had left us the rest of her Skittles, much to Emilie's delight — when a group of four soaking-wet trail walkers turned up dripping all over the porch.

We spent the rest of the afternoon playing cards and swapping trail stories, and learned that the group had met each other during this section and planned to walk on to Pārāwai Lodge tomorrow, then over the hill to Waikanae the following day.

One member, a tall, lanky fellow called Sven, was a self-proclaimed veteran of the international thru-hiking circuit, which until then, I didn't know was a thing. He rolled out names such as the Pacific Crest and Appalachian trails, and engaged the others in lively debate about how many calories they were eating each day, what brand electrolytes they were taking and the merits of their lightweight gear. He didn't mention the ethereal beauty of the swirling mists above Mount Crawford or the bright whiteness of the mountain daisies against the muted palette of olive greens and russet reds. He had barely paused for a break at the sweet orange shelter of Dracophyllum Hut, let alone witnessed the serenity of the sunrise or encountered the goats.

Despite our obvious differences, it was amazing how quickly friendships form when you stick six sweaty strangers under one roof, eating, sleeping and drying their underwear together.

Emilie was particularly drawn to James, a slender Englishman from Wellington, who had joined his younger trail-walking friend for 'a bit of an adventure' through the Tararua Range.

They woke before dawn, lanky ghoulish figures, illuminated only by the red light of their head torches. My ears picked up a low, surreptitious rustling in the darkness as they packed and repacked meagre possessions into dry bags and backpacks, ferreted for food, and coaxed sleepy, warm feet into damp socks. I lay and watched in a kind of awe — this is the true breed of a determined trail walker.

That morning, our spirits buoyed with the energy of our new friends, we set off into the dark tunnel of trees that surrounded Waitewaewae Hut.

Even though it was only 10 kilometres between the huts, it took Emilie and me over eight solid hours of climbing, slipping and stumbling through the thick, damp bush, huge windfallen trees and washed-out track before we stumbled up to the red shelter of Pārāwai Lodge where the others were waiting.

The dried tears on a sopping wet Emilie's face transformed into a huge smile as the group applauded her, *Well done Emilie, that was bloody hard work wasn't it!*

James was right, it had been bloody hard right from the moment we stepped off the wooden deck of Waitewaewae Hut and into the deep puddles that had swallowed up the lightly marked and, in places, completely re-routed, track.

Down in the densely wooded river valley, the bush was thick and wet and the track was massively overgrown, eventually leaving the river to wind steeply up over a spur and across several side streams, still swollen with the recent rain.

The humidity smoked from the damp undergrowth, and huge old-growth trees reared up out of sight, their massive trunks green with moss and sprouting ferns and epiphytes. Over time, several of these behemoths had fallen, taking down smaller trees and completely obscuring the track. Tiny birds flitted through the forest, showy fantail and silent tomtit, emerging from the dense vegetation as if to show us the way.

We spent hours laboriously clambering up, over or around wind-fall, navigating masses of tangled branches and twisted trunks that the rain had transformed into treacherous and slippery obstacles. It was slow going.

I felt for Emilie. To her 120-centimetre-tall body, a fallen tree loomed like an impassable wall of slimy bark and broken limbs. But there were benefits to being little — in places where I had to climb over, she got down on her hands and knees and crawled under, emerging mud-streaked with dead leaves and strips of bark amongst her damp hair.

In most places, the tangle of broken trees was so dense and the hill so steep that we simply had to climb up and over. At one stage, Emilie got herself wedged, her body sliding down but her backpack jammed. I could feel my heart hammering in my ears as she shrieked, working frantically to unclip her pack and allow her body to wriggle free.

I hate this stupid forest! she screamed. The blood thundered in my head and her words struck a deep chord of shame and failure within my guts, because she didn't want to be out here in a muddy, wet forest with her stupid, rookie mother who didn't know what electrolytes were for.

My PTSD-activated threat detector swivelled around to locate

Emilie in its sights, a small, scowling, messy-haired child with a bright pink and blue raincoat sticking to her skin. *Threat!* screamed my body, still pulsing with fear and shock and shame. *Daughter*, said my mind, as I sucked in a lungful of warm, steamy air, pungent with rotting leaves and vegetation.

For fuck's sake, Emilie, stop screaming and get over that tree, I found myself wanting to say. Instead, I fought to swallow this down deep.

It's okay, Emilie, you got a fright. Mummy got a fright too. Let's have a Fruit Burst.

The shitty thing about trauma, about feelings in general, is that they often get activated by the people you love the most, simply because you are at your most vulnerable around them.

Sometimes parenting hurts so badly. No one tells you about the sting of shame you'll experience when you lose your shit at your kids, or how their whining and complaining stabs you deep down and stirs up feelings of complete inadequacy and rejection.

I could totally see why other walkers paired up together. It's such a relief to have the confidence and moral support of another adult human, someone to share the leadership role, to cheer each other up and egg each other on.

Once we recovered from the windfall and from each other, the track eventually flattened out and grew wider, following an old tram track that was a relic from early sawmilling operations. Suddenly, we could walk again, and relished the ability to stretch out our legs and simply walk instead of slipping, climbing and stumbling through the undergrowth.

Skirting a huge slip that had sent tonnes of rich, red clay tumbling down 100 metres of wooded hillside into the winding river below, we finally popped out of the bush into a field of long grass peppered with deep purple foxgloves, then we crossed the swing bridge and staggered the final distance to Pārāwai Lodge.

Despite any images of grandeur suggested by its name, the lodge is simply a lovely old 1970s-era tramping hut set back behind a grove of native trees some five minutes' walk from the confluence of the Ōtaki and Waiotauru rivers at Ōtaki Forks, which is at the main western entrance to Tararua Forest Park.

Heavy rain set in half an hour after we'd reached the sanctuary of the 18-bunk hut, but by then we had already managed a dip in the river to wash off the worst of the mud.

With no one else around, we stripped down naked on the shingle beach of the Waiotauru, delighting at the silky touch of the warm wind and cool water on our bare skin.

The Waiotauru was cold and swift. I amused myself by wandering upstream then letting the current wash me back down to our clothes. Emilie strode off naked, apart from her hut shoes, to play in a shallow pool. I observed her from my own watery sanctuary, a little brown nymph with golden pigtails, glowing in the afternoon sun. Even after a huge eight-hour day on the trail, she always had energy left to play.

Swollen, dark grey clouds obscured the sun as we wandered back up to the hut, and cicadas and crickets shrilled in our ears as the humidity peaked. We'd only just got inside when the sky opened and rain bucketed down upon the dark green corrugated roof, and the overflowing gutters erupted into rivulets that flooded off the porch.

We scurried around, rehanging damp clothing on the washing lines rigged up under the veranda, moving soggy trail shoes and socks away from the spray. It reminded me of those intense electrical storms back in Brisbane, where the tension in the air would build up all day, clouds ominously jostling each other with low rolls of thunder until suddenly releasing a wild downpour of lashing rain, intense winds and crackles of lighting.

The six of us gathered around the tables in various stages of meal preparation, talking to each other in loud voices over the roar of the rain on the roof, while Emilie skipped around trying to entice James into another game of cards.

As night drew in, the rain showed no sign of letting up. While the rest of the group made plans for an early start, a deep sensation of dread built once more in my stomach.

They were planning to tackle the remaining 24 kilometres of this section and follow the Pukeatua Track out to the village of Waikanae, before descending on the various motels and backpackers of the Kāpiti Coast to restore and resupply before walking south to

Wellington. Sven reckoned he'd be averaging 30-kilometre days, maybe more, and the others were making plans to walk with him if they could keep up the pace.

I slipped outside, away from the chatter, into the soothing sound of the pounding rain. No one could see me, so I squatted and angled my body so I could pee off the deck into the rain-soaked grass as there was no point getting wet just to run out to the loo.

I spotted a huge, yellow-and-black-striped Wellington tree wētā climbing up a post beside me, oblivious to the rain as he investigated a juicy patch of lichen. I went back inside to tell Emilie, but she was busy playing yet another game of cards with James, so I grabbed my phone and InReach, one to take a photo of the tree wētā and the other to send Danilo a message about it. At least he'd share the excitement of my discovery and maybe he'd have an opinion about the rain.

With the sky obscured, the satellite phone took a long time to pick up a signal, but as soon as it did a message popped through.

Hello beautiful girls! Hope you've got a good place to sit tight during this rain!

I laboriously typed my response on the heavy keys. *Sitting tight at Pārāwai Lodge and walking out to Waikanae tomorrow. Huge Wellington tree wētā here with me!*

I sat and watched the wētā as raindrops drummed fast and furious into the drenched ground. I imagined I could hear the roar of the river over the rain, thinking about the huge, red gash of the slip we'd walked over earlier that day and feeling relieved that the hut was up on a terrace well away from the river flats.

No one with any sense should go walking in this weather, my tramper's intuition told me. But it was so tempting to keep going. Just another big day's walk and we would be somewhere warm and dry with hot showers and real food. Hell, it wasn't as though we were walking into the Tararua Range in this weather; we were at the boundary of the forest park now and after another 24 kilometres of forest walking, we'd be out.

Then my InReach beeped. *Good news about the wētā! I wouldn't walk anywhere in this rain! Maybe just hunker down for a few days xx* came Danilo's reply.

I suggested to the others that they should consider sitting out the heavy rain and walk out the following day, but their alarms were set and their gear was ready. I went to bed telling myself that if the rain stopped overnight then we would consider walking out as well. If not, well, we were in for another rest day.

The following morning, the rain continued to fall as my companions went about the grim job of cooking breakfast, packing gear and pulling on a range of damp, smelly clothing.

Emilie slept through most of it while I lay and watched them, caught up in my own inner turmoil.

This was an insane amount of rain and surely no one should be out walking in this weather.

Are you sure you guys don't want to sit it out? I asked, self-conscious of the pleading tone in my voice. *It's not safe walking in this kind of downpour. The rivers are up, there could be a slip or fallen trees on the trail.*

But my words landed on deaf ears and I fell quiet, wrapped up in my own internal struggle. If they were really doing it, surely Emilie and I could too?

I traced and retraced the route on my NZ Topo50 map: after taking the walking bridge across the Waiotauru River, follow Ōtaki Gorge Road a couple of kilometres, then take a track up into the bush, climb steeply some 300 metres to a long spur, then keep climbing steadily another few hours to the summit of Pukeatua (812 metres) before descending back down towards the Waikanae River, which was bridged.

There didn't appear to be any obvious rivers or creeks crossing the track, just a very long slog in less-than-ideal weather.

Still . . . my tramper's intuition told me to stay put — no one should be out walking in this downpour . . . but if four other trail walkers could do it, surely we could too . . . ?

Silence settled over the big wooden hut as soggy footsteps disappeared into the rain. It was only 6am, and Emilie snuggled into her sleeping bag while I dragged myself up to boil water for hot drinks. We were down to a whisper of milk powder and just a few grains of hot chocolate powder and granulated coffee, but it was better than nothing.

That night, we'd finish the mashed potato flakes with one of the spicy chickpea freeze-dried meals. Emilie would complain but it was too bad, she would just have to eat it or go hungry as I didn't have anything else.

I tried not to think of the other walkers tucking into burgers and chips over a cold beer or ordering triple-shot flat whites to sip while they effortlessly strolled down the Kāpiti Coast towards Wellington, smug with their long legs, ultralight gear, high-calorie meals, self-confidence and absence of small children. Then my coffee perked me up and I decided, fuck it: if they were walking out, we were too.

By 8am, we'd stepped out into the rain, determined to make it over the Pukeatua Track to Mangaone South Road, then on to Waikanae. But my resolve was crumbling as we crossed the mighty Waiotauru River, now a churning brown mess, a far cry from the swimming hole of yesterday.

Emilie was prepped and primed. She'd agreed to tough it out in the rain in return for the gift of a new doll, post-Te Araroa. What's more, I'd promised to let her look up the Toyworld website on my phone to browse the dolls and their clothes once we were happily ensconced in our motel room.

As we stepped out into the driving rain in all our wet-weather gear, I could see I had my day cut out for me.

Quiet and sleepy, Emilie wandered slowly behind me with her wet pigtails swinging in the rain. She was already daydreaming as she poked her hiking poles at the weeds and flowers. We walked up the gravel road to the start of the Pukeatua Track, and I noted the raging side creeks diverted under the road. I was preparing myself mentally to turn back and sit this one out if we got to a creek too wild to cross.

We climbed steadily through the mixed forest and grassy clearings, our bodies heating up as we gained elevation. The low cloud filtered through the dense scrub and tree ferns, and water oozed out from beneath our feet. In some places, the track was a river of water, as rain slid down the trees and cascaded down the steep spur. It wasn't cold, but our damp clothing and shoes quickly absorbed any excess heat created by our tired bodies.

At maybe 700 metres up the spur, we hit the scrubby tops on the eastern side of Pukeatua Summit. Now gusts of wind were driving the rain in vertically, as though we were walking inside an angry cloud. As we reached the 800-metre mark, we cheered then began our long descent, following the track down the south side of a westerly ridge to a saddle and beyond.

Now it was all downhill, down to the river, onto the road and out to civilisation, food and hot showers. Even Emilie had finally made it out of second gear and we were making speedy progress down the hill when a pile of windfall stopped us in our tracks. We were startled by the black shape of a giant wild boar moving just behind the tangled logs, head to the ground, rooting his way through the sodden leaf litter. *Hey!* I shouted as it turned towards us. *Hey! Get out of here!* The boar looked up, side-stepped, then turned and bolted into the undergrowth. My heart pounding, I turned back to the challenge blocking the track in front of me.

I started climbing over it and was straddling a thick trunk to help Emilie up when a long-legged ghost emerged out of the mist and staggered towards us.

Still pulsating with adrenaline from seeing the boar, my brain took several moments to register that it was a tramper, because I didn't understand why anyone in their right mind would be walking in here in this weather, and whoever he was, he must simply be going the wrong way.

To my surprise it was Sven, the fast walker from the group that had departed at 5am that morning. He was staggering back up the track with wet-weather gear plastered to his long white face.

There's a creek in flood and no way we're getting past it, he told us.

What creek? Where are the others? I asked.

They're coming. We're all going back to the hut. This way is impossible. The creek came out of nowhere.

We were digesting this information when James popped around the corner, followed by David, who confirmed what Sven had said was unfortunately true; the creek was surging down a gully, a dirty brown torrent of detritus deeper than a hiking pole. No one had picked up this stream crossing on the maps or trail notes.

Our hearts sank to the cold depth of our muddy trail shoes at the thought of trudging back up onto that ridge to begin the long descent back to the hut.

I cursed myself for following them out into this weather after having cautioned them not to go. I thought about setting up the tent there and then and waiting for the rain to stop and the floodwaters to ease, but there was nowhere flat on the narrow, bushy ridgeline and everything was sopping wet. And how many days would we be huddling there in our wet gear, waiting for the water to go down? I felt so bad for Emilie. The poor thing was drenched, wet and cold and bitterly disappointed, having made big plans with Mummy to find a cheap motel with a hot shower and a TV with cartoons for our rest day.

She perked up a little to see the others and did her best to hustle back up the hill, but as the cold wind blew through the forest, I could see her lip wobbling and her chat turned to tears. Bless James, for I think he felt as bad as I did for her.

David and Sven had burned on ahead to the hut to prepare plan B, while James walked with Emilie and me. We fitted her gloves, gave her some chocolate and took turns carrying her backpack for a little bit, which saw her speed up exponentially as she tore down the hill with us in hot pursuit. I had a few slips and trips on the way as the track had disappeared under torrents of rainwater, and in several places we were walking through calf-deep mud.

Finally, we got back to the hut where the other guys had lit the fire. There, we went through the process of stripping off wet gear and warming ourselves up. I tried hard not to think about the relaxing, warm hut day Emilie and I might have had if I'd heeded my own advice and stayed put instead of covering 20 pointless kilometres in the rain.

Imagine if we'd stayed here all day, Mummy! Emilie chirrups, mirroring my thoughts. *These guys would have come back all wet and we could have said, did you have a nice walk?* Her ability to bounce from sadness and misery into boisterous good humour never failed to impress me.

Pooling our remaining food, we had a fairly decent group dinner of assorted pasta and Mexican chilli beans as we made plans for the next day — this time walking out via Ōtaki Forks to the highway.

Several years ago, a huge slip cut the Ōtaki Forks campground off from Ōtaki Gorge Road after a similar heavy-rain event caused part of the road to slump towards the Ōtaki River, raging several hundred metres below. No vehicles could get in or out and, as a result, this once-popular camping spot at the main western entrance to Tararua Forest Park lay in a strange state of disrepair as nature swiftly reclaimed all human infrastructure. Without regular maintenance, weeds, flowers and seedlings sprouted from the gravel road, between cracks in concrete, and empty parking lots transformed into grassy, flowering paddocks.

The plan now was to walk down Ōtaki Gorge Road, then take a five-kilometre emergency track that leads walkers up and over a spur to avoid the slip. There was just one ford we'd have to cross.

By this stage, I had lost a lot of faith in the group's wisdom, but this seemed like a fool-proof enough plan, plus James had managed to contact his wife who would drive in to meet us on the other side so we didn't have to walk the long way to Waikanae in the rain.

But the next day when we walked up to the swollen ford and got ready to link our bodies in the mutual support method, Sven turned to David and asked, *Mutual support? What's that?* I couldn't believe that they didn't know the basic river-crossing techniques essential to safely navigate New Zealand's backcountry. At this point I realised that from now on, I would always rely on my intuition.

Although powerfully swift, the ford was knee deep, and the combined force of our six determined bodies saw us cross it with ease.

After 10 days in the grip of the Tararua Range, our time in the mysterious cloud forests that almost thwarted the warrior Okatia was coming to an end.

After our dramatic exit from the Tararua Range, we spent a couple of days in the luxury of the capital city, Wellington, with James and his wife, before catching a bus and resuming Te Araroa just south of Waikanae. I'm not sure what happened to the other walkers, but having escaped the mountains, I am sure they legged it down the coast without any further trouble.

I learned an important lesson at the outskirts of Tararua Forest Park — to trust my own judgement and make my own decisions. Even though my chronic insecurities and fear often drain my self-confidence, I realised that I need to trust my own decision-making process and not follow others, especially into heinous weather. My tramper's intuition tried to warn me, as did Danilo, and I was lucky the consequences weren't worse for Emilie and me. I felt sick to learn that another part of that road out of Ōtaki Forks had been completely wiped out by a second huge slip, right over the top of where we'd been standing just a few days earlier.

Beside the Waikanae River, evidence of that huge storm could be seen in the tangled branches and receding floodwaters. The river drains the western flanks of the Tararua Range then curls through the township before entering the Tasman Sea at Waikanae Beach on the Kāpiti Coast. From there, Te Araroa walkers cut along the heavily populated beachfront for nearly 25 kilometres, gazing out at Kāpiti Island before heading inland alongside the main trunk line to Plimmerton.

Plimmerton is where Anne and Russell live in their home overlooking Te Awarua-o-Porirua Harbour. Now retired, Anne is a keen tramper and no stranger to the wildness of the Tararua Range. She'd taken us in for the night, opening her doors, and arms, to a pair of weary walkers who were still feeling shell-shocked about their abrupt re-entry to society.

I've run you a bath, now why don't you take this and go have a nice relax, said Anne, placing a tall glass of gin and tonic into my hand. I thought I'd died and gone to heaven, if heaven was a three-bedroom brick home that felt as warm and welcoming as my grandparents' house used to when I was a little girl getting spoiled with cartoons and hokey pokey ice cream.

Anne had even popped a pink fizzy bath bomb into the tub, and

I lowered myself down into an ecstasy of warm water like a prawn into a glass of pink champagne.

Even the bathroom reminded me of my grandparents' home with its Formica fittings, decorations and plush, carpeted floor. I've always thought there was a special kind of trust bestowed upon handing over the use of one's bathroom to a stranger, an intimacy in sharing the space where one bared one's body and restored one's soul. Especially if they were likely, as I was, to help themselves to your shampoo and bath gel.

I could hear the humming of the television set — Emilie was snuggled up on a rug in front of it — and the noise of the kitchen as Anne prepared our meal. We'd been taken in by another trail angel, and in Anne's case, I felt she was the real deal.

The hot bath combined with the generous dose of gin in my aperitif sent a warm glow through my body as I sank lower into the water. I raised my feet and saw my toes, all 10 of them, and my strong, well-muscled calves, brown and hairy from months in shorts. My stomach was flat, and my breasts were small but firm, with pink nipples spreading across the creamy softness.

Maybe now it had carried me so far, I was finally beginning to like my body and feel comfortable with its bumps and edges. It was a good body, strong, small and compact, a body that had carried and given birth, with a little assistance, to my beautiful daughter.

It was just that I had no feeling in my body, I mean, as a woman. No desire to be touched, nor even the urge to masturbate. Any need to orgasm had been dampened by chronic stress and sadness, exacerbated by shame and stigma. Perhaps being forced into sexual maturity so young in my life meant I was now some kind of female eunuch. I used to enjoy sex, but perhaps I'd been single too long and had forgotten what desire felt like. All I knew was that, for me, male intimacy was accompanied by such an overwhelming sense of shame and worthlessness that it sent me into a dark spiral of self-loathing, often for weeks after the event.

My stream of consciousness and sexual self-analysis was inter-rupted by Anne calling me to dinner.

After a huge and deeply satisfying meal, eaten on trays in front of the TV and accompanied by another glass of dizzying gin and tonic, I excused myself to collapse for a while on my single bed. It was beautiful to feel so loved and cared for, so completely welcomed into this simple, warm home.

Having been on my own since I was 16, moments of feeling safe and looked after are few and far between, but Anne reminded me of another mother who once took me in and tried to care for me, someone who managed to plant the seeds of hope into my young mind and teach me that I was worthy of being loved. Her name was Mary. She was the mother of my friend — well, not really a friend, but one of the gang that had hung out at the house I'd visited after school as a lonely teenager in Brisbane before getting booted to foster care.

We'd bumped into each other again when I was about 18, between homes and a little broken, although by that stage I'd kicked the heroin habit and had earned myself the adult education equivalent of my high school certificate with a high distinction in English and biology.

My friend took me home to his parents' house and suggested I take up residence in his old room, since he was moving out to live with his girlfriend. He drove off with a wave, and I waited around nervously for his mother to get home. Eventually I met a warm-faced lady, who poured us both a generous glass of wine and asked me if I'd had dinner.

I stayed with Mary for almost a year, feeding greedily off her love and attention, relishing in simple tasks like doing the grocery shopping together and watching TV in the evenings. I guess what I really craved was not the drugs or the shady boyfriends but the solid, dependable, non-judgemental love of a parent.

Mary ran a nursing home for old ladies, and eventually I took a job in the laundry there, sorting buckets of fouled underclothing and managing the huge industrial dryer. Later, I was promoted to the role of kitchen assistant, but what I loved best was chatting to the women and feeling helpful and useful. The consistent routine and sense of purpose helped pull me back from the brink of despair I so often found myself teetering on, as did Mary's love and friendship.

I'd never thought of becoming a nurse, but I realised that I liked taking care of people, especially the elderly, and I already had the biology and maths requirements to get into nursing school.

Eventually, I enrolled in a 12-month Diploma of Enrolled Nursing at a private college in central Brisbane, and worked night and weekend shifts as an aged-care assistant to help fund my way through.

After graduating, I survived six months in a full-time position at a private hospital before signing up with a temp agency that paid lucrative casual wages to eager nurses willing to fill in shifts at the various private and public hospitals across Brisbane.

I worked as an endorsed enrolled nurse (EEN), the additional E referring to the medication endorsement, meaning I was qualified to dispense an array of medications to the patients in my care. Despite my previous career as a junkie, I wasn't qualified to deliver any intravenous medications, or Schedule 8 medications, those strong analgesics and distant relations to heroin commonly known as controlled drugs, but anything else was fair game.

I worked as a nurse on and off for almost five years, even after returning to university to tackle a three-year undergraduate degree in journalism. I told myself journalism was a continuation of nursing, a means to give a voice to the many voiceless people trapped within a social system that continued to fail them.

Working as a nurse gave me a deep insight into the socio-political system of our time, and I didn't like it. Vulnerable people — especially the alone, the mentally unwell and the elderly — fell through the cracks, their lives at the mercy of the endless flow of over-tired, under-resourced health professionals. Despite their different health conditions, many sick people shared one thing in common — they were sad, lonely, and hurting deeply at a level the medical world didn't understand and couldn't fix.

I understood that kind of emotional pain all too well. I just didn't know how to make it stop, for myself or the patients I cared for. When I was in my nurse's uniform, I was warm, outgoing, attentive, caring. But as soon as my shift was over, I was alone, so alone, and I didn't know how to turn that love and care upon myself.

Waiohine Valley, with the plush Nichols Hut below.

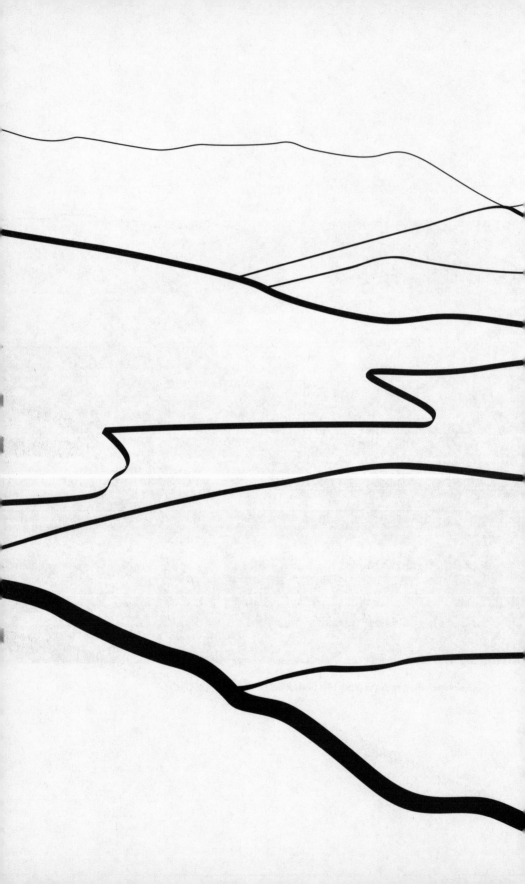

Chapter 7

Queen Charlotte Sound

Te Araroa
Day 46

I'M SITTING ON A BANK waiting for Emilie. The forest is ringing with the buzz and clicks of cicadas, and bright patches of turquoise water are visible through the trees.

It's another day in paradise in the Queen Charlotte Sound at the top of New Zealand's South Island. My map says we're halfway between Schoolhouse Bay and Camp Cove. It's 2pm, the sun is out and it's scorching.

Emilie has slowed down to a snail's pace, preferring to amble along by herself on the gently graded track instead of keeping pace with me. When she catches up, we'll have a snack to keep up the momentum.

Twenty-four hours earlier, we'd stepped off the looming bulk of the Interislander ferry in sunny Picton and made our way across the terminal to find the Cougar Line water taxi that would take us to Ship Cove at the northern end of the Queen Charlotte Track.

For southbound trail walkers like us, Ship Cove is the official starting point of the South Island Te Araroa trail. From here, we will wander some 75 kilometres along the Queen Charlotte Track to Anakiwa, then a further 41.5 kilometres to Pelorus Bridge. There, we plan to resupply before tackling the Pelorus River and Richmond alpine tracks through the notoriously steep, long and rugged Richmond Range.

The warm, almost tropical island scenery of Queen Charlotte Sound is another world compared with the hustle and bustle we'd endured over the past week. After leaving Anne and Russell in Plimmerton, we wandered through the outer Wellington suburb

TOP Victoria (aged seven) with her pet goat Suzie in Huonville, Tasmania. **ABOVE** First cuddles with baby Emilie. **LEFT** A young Victoria at Pony Club in Tasmania.

TOP Victoria and Emilie (aged four and a half) on Emilie's first overnight tramp to Woolshed Creek Hut. **MIDDLE** Packing up our lives for six months. **LEFT** Emilie and Baby Kiwi on the long flat stretch of Te Oneroa-a-Tōhē/Ninety Mile Beach. **OPPOSITE TOP** Victoria and Emilie beginning their Te Araroa journey, from Te Rerenga Wairua/Cape Reinga at the northernmost tip of the North Island. **OPPOSITE BOTTOM LEFT** Team 'Best Team' on the dawn of our epic Whanganui River journey. **OPPOSITE BOTTOM RIGHT** Emilie working hard on the Stanfield Hut restoration.

TOP Big smiles at reaching the turn-off to the solid wooden shelter of Nichols Hut after several hard hours of tramping, climbing, slipping and sliding along the Main Ridge route. **RIGHT** The iconic orange shelter of Dracophyllum Hut, where we scooped five centimetres of muddy rainwater from the bottom of the water tank. **OPPOSITE TOP** Emilie navigating the rain-soaked slippery tussock near Mount Crawford in Tararua Range. At times, the dense sub-alpine scrub was taller than Emilie. **OPPOSITE LEFT** Enjoying breakfast in our trusty tent, the 'little yellow motel'. **OPPOSITE MIDDLE** Ten Man Hut, Tongariro Forest Conservation Area. We needed to give the dilapidated old hunters' hut a good clean, and Mum was delighted to find a full can of bourbon left behind by a hunting party. **OPPOSITE BOTTOM RIGHT** Emilie writing in her hut diary at the end of another long day.

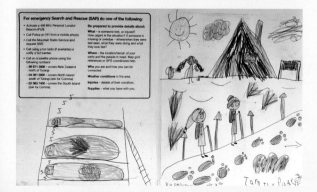

TOP LEFT Card games like Spot It! were a great way to keep entertained during down time at the end of the day. **MIDDLE LEFT** Emilie kept a diary for each day of Te Araroa, where she wrote stories and drew pictures of our adventures. **BOTTOM LEFT** With drawing paper scarce, Emilie also took every opportunity to leave an illustration in the DOC hut books. **OPPOSITE TOP** Trying to avoid wet feet on yet another river crossing along the Pelorus Track on our way into Richmond Range. DANILO HEGG **OPPOSITE BOTTOM LEFT** We spent Christmas Eve playing in the Pelorus River before camping on the grassy flats behind Middy Creek Hut. DANILO HEGG **OPPOSITE BOTTOM RIGHT** Fighting the mud monsters on our escape from Tararua Range.

TOP A quick photo opportunity on Mount Rintoul with Mount Richmond Forest Park in the distance. DANILO HEGG **MIDDLE** DOC workers Chris and Mel dropped in for a visit after spotting us from above. **LEFT** Top Wairoa Hut. The sturdy ex-New Zealand Forest Service hut, painted in Dulux DOC Rescue Orange. These remote huts and shelters are often maintained by the Backcountry Trust. DANILO HEGG **OPPOSITE TOP** Shaky legs while navigating the steep descent between the two peaks of Mount Rintoul in Mount Richmond Forest Park. Emilie took to the slopes like a mountain goat with her little red trail shoes gripping the rocks. DANILO HEGG **OPPOSITE BOTTOM LEFT** A brave wahine toa with a swollen face from wasp stings, and scrapes and bruises from her big fall. **OPPOSITE BOTTOM RIGHT** Top Wairoa Hut. Danilo and Emilie recuperating after a long, hard, death-defying day navigating the narrow Wairoa Gorge, where Emilie took a terrifying tumble.

TOP Descending to the emerald
waters of Hinapouri Tarn in the
cradle of Maniniaro/Angelus Peak
in Nelson Lakes National Park.
MIDDLE Celebrating the end of
another section with Melissa and
Nadia. RIGHT The prima ballerina in
her beautiful hut dress. OPPOSITE
TOP Wild camping in the post-
glacial basin of Rotopōhueroa/
Lake Constance. OPPOSITE
BOTTOM LEFT Victoria and Melissa.
OPPOSITE BOTTOM RIGHT Giving
the hut a good sweep before
heading off on the trail.

TOP The iconic Camp Stream Hut. **MIDDLE** Enjoying the spacious interior of Royal Hut in Two Thumb Range. **BOTTOM** Victoria's dreamy watercolour of Highland Creek Hut on the Motatapu Track. **OPPOSITE TOP** Celebrating our one hundredth day on Te Araroa at Camp Stream Hut. DANILO HEGG **OPPOSITE BOTTOM** Following the Motatapu Track from Lake Wānaka to Arrowtown.

TOP Picking our way through the wet tussock forest in Takitimu Conservation Area. **LEFT** Goblin Forest in Takitimu Conservation Area. **OPPOSITE TOP** The historical Martins Hut in Longwood Forest Conservation Area — the final hut for southbound walkers. **OPPOSITE MIDDLE** Crossing the Aparima River. One of several hundred swing bridges on Te Araroa. **OPPOSITE BOTTOM** Taking a break three kilometres into the Greenstone Track, still recovering from concussion.

RIGHT An excited Emilie near the end of the trail. **BOTTOM** The adventures continue post-Te Araroa through the Mataketake Tops Route in South Westland. DANILO HEGG

of Porirua and over the hills of Colonial Knob and Mount Kaukau, finally arriving at Island Bay on the south coast of Wellington several days later. With our thru-hike of the North Island section officially finished, the shower of confetti that I was hoping for came in the form of lashing rain, much to the disapproval of the driver of the number 1 bus.

We scuttled aboard the big red double-decker bus, Emilie excitedly choosing a seat up the top, and watched the city zoom by as water dripped off our wet trail shoes and onto the floor. The afternoon commuters either stared blankly at our dishevelled appearance or didn't notice us at all, their downcast eyes glued to glowing screens.

The dreadlocked clerk behind the desk at the Waterloo Hotel and Backpackers gave us both fist pumps, a handful of extra towels and a small heater as we retreated to our room to celebrate with hot showers, cheesecake and fresh blueberries.

The rain-swept concrete jungle of downtown Wellington was ugly, noisy and confusing after our 10-day wilderness immersion in the Tararua Range. However, there were benefits to being in a big city.

We did what girls apparently do best, taking a day off from trail walking to wander the streets of the capital, making a beeline for the outdoor stores after an indulgent breakfast at the local French patisserie.

My first pair of Altra Lone Peak trail shoes had lasted me some 800 kilometres and now it was time to buy a new pair. I felt a tinge of sadness to part with my ragged and torn footwear, for they had become an extension of myself over the last month as we'd travelled over 100 kilometres of hard-packed sand and coastal scrub down Ninety Mile Beach, circuited around the volcanic landscape of Tongariro National Park and navigated the rain-soaked ridgelines of the Tararua Range. Their seams had split and their rubber lugs had worn smooth, each step was grinding my poor little feet into squashed sausages.

Although it boasts a rich collection of cafés, boutiques and galleries, I quickly realised Wellington wasn't an epicentre of outdoor wear. Frustrated by the lack of choice in Macpac, Bivouac and Dwights,

I called Further Faster in Christchurch, who had supplied my first pair of shoes, only to learn that Covid-19 had disrupted shipments and they couldn't help replace my kicks.

The dedicated staff talked me through some options in different brands to look for locally, and we found ourselves at Shoe Clinic, where a very lovely shop assistant helped me try on trail shoes while playing a game with Emilie on the side.

After several unsatisfactory choices, I laced up a pair of Hokas and their wide toe-box immediately felt like a hug in a shoe.

Urghhh . . . I'm so bored . . . can we go now? asked my clearly non-shopaholic daughter as she lay spread-eagled on the floor, attempting to tie the shop-assistant's shoelaces together.

You're a cheeky monkey! I think I've got a little present for you behind the counter. Come and help your mum pick a new pair of socks, the assistant said.

I could have hugged her. The noise and chaos of the city and the stress of finding a pair of shoes before our ferry departed in the morning was burning up inside of me, and I wanted to growl at Emilie for not understanding or giving me the space I needed to sort stuff out.

Once I had my new shoes and a pair of bright red Salomon trail shoes for Emilie, I felt much lighter. It was fun to be tourists in New Zealand's capital city, slipping through the crowds of lunchtime inner-city employees, knowing I didn't have to go to work and Emilie didn't have to go to school. We had escaped the monotony of the daily grind and were on an adventure all of our own.

I took Emilie to the Museum of New Zealand Te Papa Tongarewa to ogle at the exhibits and purchase a new children's nature book, bought her sausage rolls at a café, procured more fresh fruit from a nearby farmers' market and caught the cable car up to Zealandia, Wellington's inner-city wildlife sanctuary, for a guided tour.

Emilie's eyes popped to see kākā playing noisily in the trees, chunky tuatara lying in the sun and striped Wellington tree wētā, with their shiny cigar-shaped bodies and spiny legs, making themselves at home in wētā motels — purpose-built holes in dead tree stumps with Perspex windows for people like us to peek inside.

She chatted non-stop to our guide while I stood back and

observed the scenery and my beautiful, excited, happy, little daughter, absorbing fun facts and details like a sponge with two messy pigtails.

Any guilt I had about her missing a term of school was assuaged by experiences like this. The lovely people at Zealandia had picked up on our Te Araroa journey and reached out through Instagram to offer us complimentary passes to the sanctuary, and back in Palmerston North, we'd also enjoyed a private tour from the staff at Wildbase Recovery, a facility where native birds can recover from illness or injury before being released back into the wild.

I could tell these experiences made a big impression on Emilie as they enriched the detail of the stories she told me each day, shaping the characters she created and the adventures they went on together.

Storytelling has always been a big part of our tramping adventures. It's a way to pass the time, to keep Emilie's busy mind occupied so she doesn't linger on physical discomfort or boredom, and also a way to connect deeply with each other on a creative level. Back when I was trying to encourage a five-year-old Emilie to walk longer tramps with me, we invented a character called the Bush Baby, a kaitiaki or guardian in the form of a little girl who is sent by Papatūānuku to take care of her many wild creatures.

The Bush Baby doesn't possess magical powers, although she's a wise, caring and deeply charismatic persona who can create simple healing potions out of native plants. Together with her various forest friends including a weka and an orphaned kiwi chick, she goes on adventures, faces challenges, rescues native creatures and wanders, with us, across the varying terrains of Te Araroa.

The Bush Baby enjoyed the inspiration of Ship Cove, where she teamed up with her friend Willy the Weka to sail to an offshore island and search for a special seaweed that held certain magical powers, with the help of the local half-crab population.

After the water taxi dropped us off on the jetty, we stood and soaked in the scenery of the Marlborough Sounds, its densely forested hills rising steeply from the sea. There, at the tip of the Queen Charlotte Track, the brilliant blue water revealed crystal-clear shallows as wavelets from the departing jet boat lapped the sandy shell-encrusted shore. Beyond the jetty was a track that disappeared into lush vegetation peppered with towering tree ferns.

Mummy, I'll tell you a story, Emilie announced as we set off, side by side, along the gently graded path. And she did, with plenty of detail adding colour to the images and characters, including the newly built cable car woven from dried flax that ran on a string from ground level up into the branches of the tree where the Bush Baby made her home.

We wandered another four kilometres before deciding to call it a day and spent the afternoon searching for half crabs amongst the rocks at Schoolhouse Bay. It was warm. Peaceful. Calm. I was so happy because we were here. We'd made it back home to the South Island.

After a relaxing evening making friends with the local weka population, we packed up the next morning and started walking. The morning sun intensified, reminding us that the 75-kilometre Queen Charlotte Track from Ship Cove to Anakiwa wasn't a simple walk in the park. The well-cushioned bounciness of my new Hokas helped offset the weight of my heavy pack and the stunning coastal views and lush forest distracted me for a while, but I'd woken up with a nagging sensation of unease, that something was eating me from the inside out.

Something had triggered my PTSD. I told myself this nervous, raggedy feeling was my body responding to a big dose of adrenaline. But there was something else lurking underneath — a sense of deep sadness and grief that felt so out of place in this beautiful setting.

My therapist would tell me to focus on the feeling, to describe its size, shape and location inside of my body and breathe deeply into it. But for most of our sessions, I arrived too flustered from the compounded stress of my workday to be able to isolate the unpleasant sensations that had engulfed my mind and hijacked my body. I couldn't distinguish which was trauma and which was simply the pure adrenaline that was keeping me alive. The inappropriate fight-or-flight reflex of my dysregulated nervous system was preventing my body from returning to its proper functioning, to a place where this persistent emergency response could come to an end, and I just knew that I felt like I was dying.

Yet out here, 46 days into our long walk across New Zealand, I could feel the stress and busyness of my former life falling away, leaving me lighter, emptier. After all, everything had become so much simpler, and while each day consisted of intense, hard, physical work, my cognitive tasks were few. My routine was to wake up, prepare breakfast, pack up our gear, walk, eat, find somewhere to camp, unpack our gear, prepare dinner, relax then sleep. As the kilometres passed under my feet and my cardiovascular, respiratory, energy and muscular systems united to propel me forwards, my body felt more like my own again.

It was as though the singular focus of walking Te Araroa was helping strip away the thick exoskeleton of self-defensiveness, and my body was slowly revealing deeply buried and long-forgotten sensations and memories.

I knew this was part of the healing process; that to fully understand my trauma I needed to explore these uncomfortable internal sensations to help me locate the imprints of past trauma on my body.

It was just that I felt like a cave diver who has leapt into the gloomy depths without a head torch, map or reel, that crucial piece of kit that provides divers a lifeline back to the entrance of the cave. My visibility was low and my oxygen tanks were almost empty. I was stuck in there without any way out, and I was scared that if I leaned any deeper into this overwhelming sadness, I would lose my will to live.

Lost in thought, I realised I'd got a few hundred metres ahead of Emilie. I leaned back against the bank and waited, closing my eyes as the shade from the lush, green canopy fell across my face.

I breathed deeply and tried to let my mind wander to see where it ended up, floating on a subconscious current of thoughts and memory. It was interesting to observe where it lingered like a scratched record and other places where it recoiled as though burned.

I'd learned from painful experience that it was better to sit back and observe, rather than to jump in and try to wrestle it to submission.

That day, it was sifting and searching through my subconscious, on a mission to find something or somewhere — a chink in my armour. It arrived at a door. I don't remember the colour or detail, just my 14-year-old self stepping through it with my heart hammering in my ears as I was shown down the hallway to a room in a family home of people who weren't mine.

I don't remember much (I don't want to remember much), but there was a Pākehā woman and her Māori husband, a blended family with two noisy little boys and a seven-year-old girl who was smiley and shy. I wasn't used to hanging out with younger siblings and didn't know what to do with any of them, although the little ones liked me watching cartoons with them snuggled on the sofa, and the girl, I think her name was Belinda, liked art.

I don't remember the house. It was nothing special, a dank three-bedroom place in the back streets of Waihi. There was an outdoor area where I'd sometimes lurk after dark. They were my first foster family . . .

Foster care. How did I end up a ward of the state in the country I was born in but left when I was just two years old? I didn't grow up in New Zealand, I didn't know this place.

Twenty-two years ago, I began my foster-care journey in the little town of Waihi, just north of Tauranga, on the east coast of the North Island.

I'd been staying with my favourite set of grandparents in a house my brother and I had visited as kids, which was filled with happy memories of holidays, Christmas presents, Sunday morning cartoons. Away from our parents and their drama. I was there because I couldn't live with my father in Tasmania anymore and I'd quickly worn out my welcome with my mother and her new partner in Brisbane. After moving to be with my mother at age 13, I'd begun year nine at Corinda High School, feeling hopelessly out of place in my class of bubbly, soccer-mad, sporty female peers with their Adidas- and Nike-branded backpacks.

I missed my neighbourhood gang in the lower socio-economic suburbs of Tasmania, the easy access to cigarettes, stolen beer and the leaves and tips of their parents' dope. Sharing a house with my absent father suddenly felt like a much better deal than the structure of my over-bearing mother, stepfather and annoying older brother. Then I'd met Leanne and Joel and been indoctrinated into their gang, much to the horror and disgust of my mother.

After the freedom of Tasmania, the rules and expectations were too much for my angry teenage self and I rebelled. I hated seeing my mother with her new partner, hated her because I felt she had left me behind with my father only to take up with Roger and forget all about how important I used to be to her. My adult self knows it wasn't that simple, but as a teenager, that was how I felt. When I tried to tell her this, she would shut me down and turn away, back to him, who would tell me off for upsetting my mother. My brother would pull faces at me and go to be close to my mother. Feeling shunned, cast out, unwanted, my teenage pain and grief burned as fierce as my anger. I spent more and more time at Leanne and Joel's, sometimes wagging school completely to smoke bongs and watch music videos. Getting high and dropping out of life, avoiding bitchy high school classmates and family dynamics. But only on weed, never anything stronger. Pot was all I needed, it relaxed my body and gave the sensation that all my senses were numbed out, wrapped in a smoky layer of cotton wool. But my mum wasn't impressed. Eventually she and my stepfather gave me an ultimatum — go back to my father or go into foster care. I was running out of options in Australia. And then my grandparents in New Zealand stepped in.

Perhaps they had memories of a happier me in my white-blonde pigtails in mind, but what they got was a sullen, angry 14-year-old, who had no interest in going shopping with Nanny or helping Poppa in his garden. I found the hunting grounds of Waihi full of interesting distraction and shady characters, leading my poor grandmother to call the police to help locate me after a few late-night adventures.

What can I say . . . it wasn't like I was having fun. I just wanted to find some pot to smoke and escape for a little while, either by myself or with other strange souls who didn't judge me or expect anything of me except to share a joint, a laugh and some company for a while. I'd slink off to the local skate park and hang around with its other occupants, bumming smokes and hoping for something stronger.

Everything went pear-shaped after my grandfather had his stroke. The police came to find me at the skate park and so did social services. My grandmother was at the hospital with Poppa, which left an underage minor on the loose. It was quickly established that my mother in Australia did not want me back, my father was unfit, and none of my other relatives wished to step up to the challenge.

So the state stepped in and declared me its ward. This meant I was now under the legal protection of the Governor-General of New Zealand, managed by the government agency then known as the Department of Child Youth and Family Services, or CYFS (pronounced Siffs). I would be placed with a foster family.

It's just for a while, the social worker said, *until we can figure out what we're going to do.*

Enraged by the faceless entity that was now in control of my life, deeply hurt by my mother's refusal to allow me to return to her in Australia and distrustful of the various social workers and medical professionals, I was angry and uncooperative. I refused to attend high school, ran away from many foster placements and spent periods of time roaming the streets, seeking to get high while hiding from the police.

I was well out of my depth. While my neighbourhood gang in Australia had enjoyed joints and bongs with the occasional beer, I had generally been surrounded by older friends who looked out for my wellbeing. In New Zealand, I knew nobody and the dark waters of the underworld were full of sharks. Older boys and men would seem friendly, help me score weed and get high before proffering harder drugs, then would put the hard word on me to pay up with the only collateral I had. Every neighbourhood seemed to have a certain tinny house that unstable and frightening people frequented to buy weed and other drugs, causing chaos and preying upon the needs of others.

My first set of foster parents in Waihi lived a few doors down from such a house. My foster mother was good friends with the 'tinny lady' who lived there along with her skinny 18-year-old son, Michael. He wasn't a bad guy, introverted and quiet, and he'd often invite me to hang out in his room to listen to music or watch movies and smoke his personal supply of weed.

The house would often pack out when the local biker gang was in town, and that was when I first met the Spider. Small, dark and lithe with tattooed forearms, a thick black beard and shaved head, his beady black eyes would follow me soundlessly as I wandered through the house and out to Michael's room.

I'd like a go when you're done with her, I once heard him whisper loudly to Michael, and a sensation of disgust and shame burned deep between my legs. Michael and I weren't lovers, although I cared for him deeply because he seemed vulnerable and nerdy, holed up in the dark safety of his bedroom. We were just friends. He shared his dope with me without ever asking for anything more than my company in return, for which I was deeply grateful, because it wasn't as though CYFS provided us foster children with pocket money.

I felt uncomfortable around the Spider and made a point never to return his penetrating gaze. Soon, though, a rollercoaster chain of events unfolded when I went to the tinny lady's house on the wrong day, at the wrong time. She wasn't there, and Michael wasn't home. But the Spider was.

Despite the intensity of these unstable, frightening situations, I don't remember much. My therapist has asked, gently, encouraging me to acknowledge what happened so I can start to recognise the invisible demons that I'm struggling with and begin to integrate the trauma memories. But I can't. My mind simply won't give anything up. It's all a blur of faces and places, a burning hot blur accompanied by a roaring in my ears and an asphyxiating sensation in my guts, chest, throat and jaw. It takes all the energy I have to fight back the tears of rage and pain and shame, to hold myself together, to keep on living the only way I know how.

My case notes state that I ran away from that blended family in Waihi, probably after certain events that I didn't trust the social worker enough to share with her, only to be located and placed elsewhere. I moved from Waihi to Thames, out to the Coromandel Peninsula, across to Hamilton, up to Auckland and down to Tauranga, where I was placed in a youth residential home called Arndt House, the staff of which were apparently instrumental in helping get me off drugs, at least for a while, and made plans for me to return to Australia.

Once I got out of foster care, I went straight back to Australia and worked hard to erase all memory of these traumatic times from my memory warehouse. An enthusiastic and experimental drug habit helped a lot, until even that didn't work anymore. Memory has a way of resurfacing, like water from deep underground, carving its way through the hardest of stone until it reaches the surface.

As I waited for Emilie, I wondered why my mind was going back to this time. It was a beautiful sunny day, an easy track, stunning scenery . . . and yet I was stepping over the threshold of darkness into the memory of my first foster home.

I was deep in this rabbit hole of memory when Emilie wandered up behind me.

Mummy, can I sing you a song? she asked.

She launched into her favourite song from *Frozen*, as I nodded numbly. Oh Emilie, I love your joy. Emilie is my cave-diving reel, my grounding force, my lifeline. It was time to pull myself back together, to take a page out of Anna's book and 'Let It Go'. But it was so hard to come back from that place, and so easy to get lost in the darkness that had followed me around for so long.

I woke to the dawn chorus and stayed awake to listen to the beautiful melody of hundreds of little birds as they celebrated a new day — a day with clear skies and strong winds that came through in gusts every few minutes, sounding almost like the roar of heavy rain. But my tent fly was dry and, with the exception of Emilie's hiking poles that had been dragged about the clearing, nothing seemed to have been pilfered by weka during the night.

Emilie continued to sleep as I opened up the tent and lay watching the tops of the young trees move with the wind. I loved the shapes of their leaves and the collage they made — some long, some fat, some shiny, all tilted skywards in clusters like a green bouquet.

A weka with a swollen cheek, which we'd met the previous night, came by to peek in the door of the tent, but I gave him a stern look.

Apart from our dinner dishes stacked neatly together and my trusty trail shoes, there was nothing worth stealing.

I hoped today would be a shorter day with beautiful camping and swimming, as I wanted very much to soak up some sunshine and stare at the scenery, and I was sure Emilie would love some downtime on the beach, setting crabs to sea in little boats made of upturned shells.

As it turned out, we decided to stay and play at Camp Bay, packing our rest day full of seven-year-old entertainment activities.

After breakfast, we secured the tent against invasion by inquisitive weka and headed down to the bay, skinny dipping with delight in the cold, clear water.

I lay on my back in the water with my eyes closed and the warm sun on my exposed skin, listening to the gentle lap of water on the shore. It was as constant as a heartbeat, as comforting as being held in the womb. I treasure those small moments of being completely at peace with myself and my surroundings.

The sandy seabed was covered in large stingrays that, just like us, seemed to be hanging out enjoying the morning sun.

A tūī fluttered among the harakeke, sipping from the tubular orange flowers. Emilie played . . . and talked . . . and played, while I tried desperately to be a good sport and keep up. We combed the high-tide line for treasures, finding fragile green and purple dried kina, tiny shells, glittering rocks, fern fronds and fragments of Neptune's necklace for her to arrange into a garden for the seashore pixies.

We built a sandcastle in the silt-laden sand and dug a moat around it, complete with a couple of bewildered tiny crabs crouching in the shallow water. Emilie brought a book she'd got at Te Papa, *At the Beach*, part of the wonderful *Explore & Discover* series by New Zealand author Gillian Candler, down to the shore to identify seashells. She held tightly to my hand as we waded out into the shallows to observe the stingrays, which tolerated our presence momentarily before gliding away across the seabed to deeper waters.

The sun rose higher, and the sounds of other humans walking into camp had me reluctantly reaching for my clothes, while

Emilie remained capering around, a little golden fairy surrounded by graceful green punga.

I fetched my watercolours and sat and painted the scenery in a happy trance.

We retreated to the shelter of our tent only to find it boiling in the midday sun, so we moved it a few metres into the leafy shade. The weka returned with a friend and together they stalked the campground, eyeing up sandals and hats with their beady red gazes.

Emilie played in the grass with a pair of tiny soft toys I'd permitted her to carry on Te Araroa, scratching at sandflies while twisting long blades of grass together to form a tipi tent to house her baby kiwi and tūī.

Intrigued, the weka drew closer. Emilie waved her toy kiwi at it, then we both gaped in horror as the weka lunged forwards, grabbed the toy out of her hands then legged it into the nearby scrub.

It all happened so fast.

Mummy! My toy! Emilie wailed, stumbling a few feet towards the bush before sinking down to cry. I batted away feelings of frustration — why did she have to tease the bloody weka in the first place? — then I got into weka-hunting mode.

At first glance, the dense scrub appeared impenetrable. Aside from Emilie's sniffs, everything was deathly silent. The weka was clearly holding its breath to see what we would do next, but I'd dealt with these cheeky thieves before.

Bending over double, I scanned the scrub and found several weka-sized tunnels leading away into the bush. After a few false starts, I found a small brown toy kiwi abandoned and looking a little sorry for himself.

With baby kiwi tucked up for a nap inside the tent, Emilie and I ate sweaty cheese on crackers for lunch then returned to the cool of the bay. It was low tide and the sun baked down on the exposed sea grass and shells. Emilie was becoming hot and irritable as I followed her around with a tube of sticky sunblock.

After successfully slathering her with it, I took her to the jetty and showed her how to climb down the ladder and swim around the wooden pillars from one side to the other. To my surprise, she followed me, enthusiastically doggy paddling and giggling through the turquoise water.

All those years of swimming lessons and still doggy paddling, but nothing a week on the beach and some more confidence couldn't improve. In fact, she had no trouble in the confidence department. After a couple of goes at swimming from the end of the jetty to the rocky beach and back again, she set her sights a bit further afield.

Pointing to a distant orange buoy she declared *Come on Mummy! Let's swim out to there!*

I redirected her back up the ladder to sunbathe.

By 3pm, I was dying for a nap. You might not realise how exhausting it can be when your only companion is an energetic seven-year-old with an almost insatiable appetite for attention. Emilie's only companion was her sleepy old mum, who she loved to boss around as much as possible. I guess I was making up for all those long days at the office when she was at after-school care.

The Queen Charlotte Track passed quickly. After a few days of easy trail walking, we wandered from the last of the low, forested ridges and into Davies Bay on a glorious, golden day. We were only three kilometres from the small township of Anakiwa and the official end of the Queen Charlotte Track, but neither of us felt like leaving this beautiful place just yet. From Anakiwa it was another nine kilometres to the larger town of Havelock on a purpose-built walking and cycling trail called the Link Pathway. Havelock offered a supermarket, backpackers and other accommodation, but we had enough food for another couple of days and were clean enough from our daily swims.

So even though we'd only covered 10 slow kilometres that day, we decided to set up the tent in a quiet corner of Davies Bay and get back in the water, pretending to be marine biologists on a mission to explore.

The magic of low tide was all around us, a symphony of tiny movement within the soft, muddy sands. If we were still and watched closely, we could see the shallow water teeming with crabs, so many shapes and sizes — hermit crabs rocketing across the seabed in borrowed shells, mud crabs sizing each other up for a fight, and a drift of reddish-brown seaweed that turned out to be a camouflage crab with humorously long limbs and beanstalk eyes.

I held Emilie's hand as we wandered further out, cold water passing the tops of our thighs, the sunlight reflecting off the ripples and casting shadows on the seabed. Translucent schools of skittish mullet darted and twisted around us.

If you stand really still, I whispered to Emilie, *they'll forget we're here.*

So we stood, holding our breath as the fish flickered closer and closer, almost close enough to feel the movement of water against our thighs. Their silverish scales almost completely camouflaged them in the clear water and only their yellow eyes gave them away.

We moved slowly forwards, sliding our bare feet through the muddy silt of the bay, feeling out large clams with their deep tap-root buried into the mud. As we reached the far side of the bay, wet rocks hid slithering gangs of half crabs with huge pincers disproportionate to the rest of their little bodies. More hermit crabs rocketed around in the shallows, the most charismatic of all the crabs with their funny gait and little pop eyes. Some sort of sea snail was also cruising around at a surprising speed and, as I sat on a rock with my toes dangling in the water, a small sea star made its way up onto my foot.

I love the magic of low tide. It summons up all kinds of warm memories of exploring rock pools for tiny marine treasures with my brother long ago when the world was small and full of magic.

I hope I can pass these feelings of joy and wonder on to my little daughter.

The following day, we shouldered our packs and walked for eight hours in the sweltering summer heat, all the way from Davies Bay to Havelock. There was scant shade from the relentless sun that scalded the backs of our bare legs as we walked out of Anakiwa.

We found a sheltered spot to take a phone call from Kathryn Ryan at Radio New Zealand. Emilie burbled about the baby weka chicks we'd spotted a few days earlier while I attempted to keep cool and give succinct answers to Kathryn's questions. *What were a mother and daughter doing walking the length of New Zealand?*

I tried to share some of the messages I'd prepared for our Givealittle page, which had already received several thousand dollars from donors, explaining how I hoped that taking time out in nature would help reset my shattered nervous system and release me from some of the debilitating symptoms of post-traumatic stress disorder.

I didn't tell Kathryn about how my deeply buried memories of being mauled by predators during foster care were pushing their way to the surface as I walked one of the jewels in the crown of the Marlborough Sounds. Still, I imagined she would be keen to listen and maybe even offer some insights of her own if I ever bumped into her in person one day.

There is a certain irony in hiding the secret shame of being an unwanted foster child — and a sexually abused one at that — for most of my life, then coming out on national radio. It brought to mind the time when, as communications advisor for an industry training organisation, I'd sat in the auditorium at Te Papa and listened to a speech by the chief executive of the glossy new Ministry for Vulnerable Children, who told us how their research showed that care-experienced children fail to achieve much in life. He spoke about *high rates of educational disengagement and under-achievement.* Instead of noting down his quotes for the press release I was preparing, I wanted to stand up and shout at him, *I'm not just one of your statistics, you fucker!* That would have made for a good headline.

It seemed that a single mother with mental health issues taking on New Zealand's backcountry with her young child also made for a good headline and, while the publicity we received for our Te Araroa adventure triggered a waterfall of intense, unpleasant emotions, I was buoyed by the many private messages and comments received from supporters through our Facebook and Instagram pages. Apparently, there was a whole army of people out there who were also sick of pretending that everything was okay, when it wasn't.

After the interview with Kathryn Ryan, I wondered if I should try to get back into journalism once we'd finished walking Te Araroa, instead of the soul-destroying world of corporate communications. Or maybe I should bite the bullet and study psychology — after all, I had great personal experience. But deep in my heart remained the dreams of my childhood self to be a marine biologist, zoologist or ecologist, immersing myself in our natural world.

I was deep in thought as we stumbled into Linkwater and stopped for a breather outside its only store. The store attendant took one look at Emilie and her backpack, a little red-faced girl with golden wisps of hair escaping her knotty braids, and asked us where we were headed. We explained about walking Te Araroa and our fundraising mission, and the good bloke said Emilie's ice cream was on the house.

As the day drew on, the temperature rose and Emilie slowed down, signs of distress showing on her little face. From Linkwater, it was still another 14 kilometres to Havelock, following the gravel pathway along Queen Charlotte Drive before climbing into the bush above the road. Up there, at least we had some shade.

We stopped for another break, soaking our washcloth in a tiny stream and holding it to the backs of our necks, sweaty faces, arms, chests — anything to try to cool ourselves down and get respite from that heat.

I took Emilie's sleeping bag from her pack and stuffed it into mine. I only had a few items of food left now and I wanted to take the load off her, to help keep her moving through the hot, still air.

We eventually staggered into Havelock, a small town located at the confluence of the Pelorus and Kaituna rivers at the head of Pelorus Sound, 35 minutes northwest of Blenheim. Once a gold-mining town, today Havelock's old-world colonial buildings house boutiques, galleries and fancy restaurants that entice passers-by to sample the town's famous green-lipped mussels.

I wasn't in the mood for mussels or to face the hordes of holidaymakers getting ready for Christmas. It was 23 December and the campground was heaving, so I decided to splurge on our own private room in a lodge that overlooked the main road.

After washing the past five days of swimming in Queen Charlotte Sound out of our hair, I dived into our dirty gear. In just two days' time, we would be meeting up with Danilo at the Pelorus Bridge campsite to walk the 44.5-kilometre Pelorus River Track and 95.7-kilometre Richmond Alpine Track together as one huge, back-to-back section. I was quietly freaking out as I wondered how the hell I'd ever fit enough food for it in my 50-litre backpack.

I took a break from sorting out gear to meet up with Mark, a friendly local outdoor enthusiast, who had been following our journey on Instagram. It felt a little strange to be meeting face to face with someone I'd only met online, but this wasn't Tinder, I reminded myself, just an invitation to eat fish and chips from a takeaway down the street.

With all her walking clothes in the washing machine, Emilie demanded to be allowed to wear my red Icebreaker singlet with the little pink plastic shoes she usually only wore inside huts. It fitted her like a mini-dress, and I could tell she thought she looked cool as she eyed up the other children waiting around for a feed in their summer clothes.

It turned out (the completely harmless) Mark was up from Blenheim to visit his parents and enjoy a spot of fishing. His dad had heard our interview with Kathryn Ryan and thought the whole idea of our long-distance adventure was great. His mum had been a keen tramper in her day, so after our greasy meal, we wandered a few doors down to their house and invited ourselves in for ice cream.

It's hokey pokey, do you want one scoop or two? Mark's dad asked an effervescent Emilie, who'd transformed into a Christmas fairy with her bright red dress. Then, learning of my Scottish heritage, he offered me a dram of whisky to go along with my ice-cream cone. I could have hugged him.

Back at the lodge later that night, I resumed my packing while Emilie dozed on top of the blankets in our stuffy upstairs room, quietly sweltering while the cool night air passed by outside.

Leaving her asleep, I padded downstairs in search of a pair of scissors to help wrap some lightweight Christmas presents: lollies, chocolate, and a promise of a more substantial gift at the end of the trail.

Danilo messaged to say he was excited to be seeing us very soon, and that he would be leaving Dunedin tomorrow to make the

700-kilometre drive up to Nelson Lakes, where he'd leave his car and get a shuttle to Pelorus Bridge.

The feelings of anxiousness and overwhelm that had plagued me as we walked into Havelock had dissipated under a haze of Scotch whisky, and everything I'd worked so hard to organise seemed to be coming together.

A while back, I'd connected with a good soul called Karen and given her some photos to use on a new website she was creating. She'd launched an on-demand personal shuttle service for trampers and other travellers, and had offered to bring Danilo to us all the way from Nelson Lakes on Christmas Eve.

While I'd had internet reception, I had also been emailing the Nelson-based freeze-dried food company, Real Meals, to see if they'd be keen to work with us, and they'd agreed to supply food for our Richmond Range section. A big box of assorted meals would be waiting for us at the Pelorus Bridge campground, along with a modest resupply box containing my usual oats and muesli bars. I hoped like hell that it would all fit in my pack.

The trail notes recommend that anyone attempting the Pelorus River Track and Richmond Alpine Track together as a single section should prepare for at least a nine-day tramp, but I knew we'd be slower, so I'd planned supplies for 12 days with a couple of additional emergency meals in case things didn't quite work out. The long-range weather forecast didn't extend that far into the future, and I knew from experience that the weather in the mountains can deteriorate rapidly.

The following morning, Emilie and I arrived at the campground on the banks of Pelorus River/Te Hoiere, and set up our little yellow tent amongst a towering stand of kahikatea, beech and rimu trees.

I could barely carry my resupply boxes the short distance from the camp office to our site and was cursing my decision to radically change up our food routine, swapping our tried and tested porridge oats and pasta for bulky, brightly coloured packages.

I clipped our tent to the outside of my pack to make more space for food — a huge bag of porridge oats, milk powder, instant coffee, dried fruit, nuts, OSM bars and a dense mass of dehydrated meals and snacks. As small as Emilie was, she ate just as much as I did, and so my 158-centimetre frame was quite literally carrying for two. It was the heaviest my pack had ever been and I couldn't believe it when I managed to clip it shut with everything crammed inside.

When a beaming Karen pulled up with Danilo riding shotgun in the front of her new sign-written minibus, I was relieved to see his pack was ridiculously huge as well, although I soon learned he was also carrying five kilograms of camera gear and specimen containers so he could hunt for wētā and cave wētā within the depth of the ranges.

This rugged backcountry section involved a 115-kilometre stint through remote terrain and high mountain passes, following the icy blue waters of the Pelorus River up into the foothills of Mount Richmond Forest Park and beyond. Spanning the boundary between Marlborough and Nelson, the track wanders through a sequence of environments from river valley and beech forest to sub-alpine wonderlands. It summits two scree-covered peaks, the highest at 1731 metres, before winding its way through an impressive landscape of unusual geological significance, a mineral-rich boulder-strewn area famous for the intensity of its red colour. Closely resembling the outback of Australia, these red hills are home to some strange and unique vegetation amidst the tussock-land low shrubs, as well as a rich diversity of insect life.

From our previous trips together, I knew Danilo was a talented photographer and aspiring entomologist, however I hoped he wasn't just joining us for the fieldwork opportunity to find and photograph the many invertebrates of the Richmond Range.

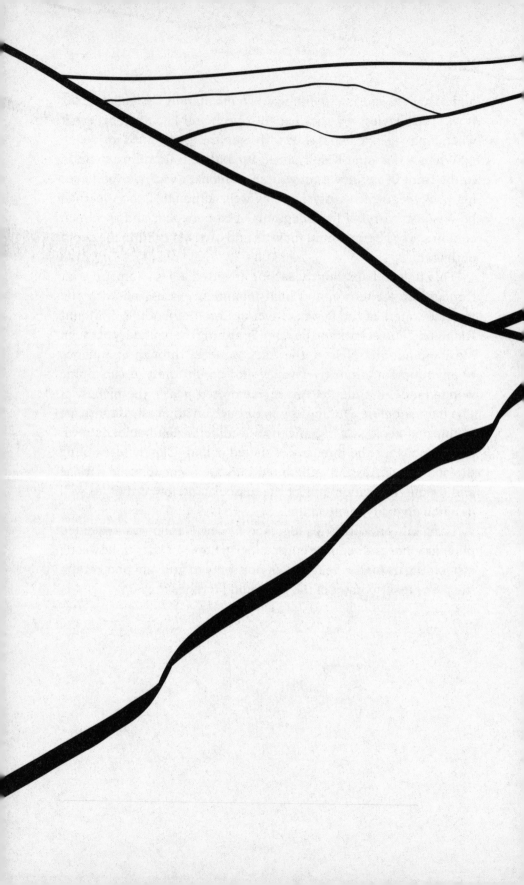

Chapter 8

Mount Richmond Forest Park

Te Araroa
Day 53

THE EARLY-MORNING THROBBING OF CICADAS and three sweat-encrusted socks modestly bulging with lightweight treats greeted us on Christmas morning. My companions' reactions to their gifts ranged from delighted to less-than-impressed, once they'd ripped off the brown-paper wrapping that I'd carefully decorated with hand-drawn and coloured pictures.

Aww! I didn't just want a stupid chocolate bar! exclaimed one of them.

Yum! I'll eat it for you then! said the other.

Despite her initial show of ingratitude, Emilie stuffed some chocolate into her mouth and clambered outside to pee, before returning a moment later to inform us delightedly that Santa really had been because Rudolf had left a big reindeer poo right outside our tent!

I wonder why he didn't dig a hole or pack it out like a good tramper, she mused.

The deer must have wandered right past our tent nibbling the dew-soaked grass, pausing to gift us their droppings before disappearing back into the forest.

I tried to tell myself my pack was all the lighter having dispensed my surprise gifts, but it wasn't, and my legs trembled as I heaved it onto my back. Back when we talked about the logistics of him joining us, part of me had hoped Danilo would gallantly offer to help carry some of my heavy load through the next huge section. In fact, I had thought that was partly why he'd offered to chaperone us across the Richmond Range . . . but that wasn't the case. In the end, I swallowed my pride and asked if he could carry Emilie's snacks and a couple of extra Real Meals packets, in addition to the half of my little yellow tent that we were all planning to squeeze into at night. His help made all the difference between a pack I could barely clip shut and a load I could barely lift.

Even though my pack was big, filled as it was with the other half of the tent and food supplies to last 14 days for both Emilie and me, Danilo's pack was bigger as it was jammed full of heavyweight tramping gear and a gigantic professional camera and macro lens. At each stop, he would strew his gear all over the grass, then take forever to pack up. Then, once we were off, he walked at a slow, steady pace, like a giant bull, whereas I'd dash off ahead then stop and wait for him to catch up.

With three of us on the trail, the dynamic changed, and my little glue went to glue herself to someone else, chattering non-stop as she stomped along in front of him. Left to my own devices, I wandered ahead, trying to focus on lugging my huge pack uphill without stumbling and falling flat on my face.

After a few days wandering alongside the mighty Pelorus River, we climbed back into the beech forest, walking on a soft carpet of red, yellow and brown leaves. I could hear a robin calling in the distance and the soft whisper of wind in the trees, high above my head.

It was just past 9am and we'd already been walking for a couple of hours, trying to cover some distance before the heat of the day melted all motivation. The track climbed through the forest, winding though huge silver beech, and there looked to be clear blue sky above the canopy.

I knew my little mate and my big mate were coming up the hill as I could hear Emilie chattering away and Danilo responding.

Danilo, what is the biggest wētā you've ever seen?

Hmm, let me think, do you mean the largest body or the longest legs? Because some species of cave wētā can be thirty centimetres long from the tips of their toes to the tip of their antennae, whereas the largest species of giant wētā, the wētāpunga, can grow to the size of a sparrow.

Wow! My mummy and I saw a really big wētā on the Round the Mountain track and I know it was a girl because it had a spike on its bum.

You're right! Your mummy sent me a photo of that one and it was a beautiful lady Wellington tree wētā.

You said wētā are nocturnal — but we saw this one at nine o'clock in the morning! Mummy said maybe she was coming home late from the nightclub!

Or maybe she was day clubbing!

It was so lovely to have the companionship of another adult, not that I was getting much company since Emilie had made it pretty clear that she was going to monopolise the conversation. But even that was nice. I loved seeing her happy, chattering like a little bird, telling stories and learning fun facts about insects and nature from our resident entomologist.

Danilo's large, calm presence had a soothing effect on my ragged nerves and this morning I was enjoying my solitude as leader of the group, wandering through the forest a few minutes ahead of them, stopping every now and then for them to catch up. This time, I'd boosted up the track high above them, almost enjoying the sensation in my strong thigh muscles as I leaned forward to help my ascent.

Then I came around a bend in the track and she was there, staring at me through narrowed slits — my teenage self. I had felt her stalking me for days, lurking sullenly just out of reach, but now she was so close I could touch her face, and I would have, if only she hadn't looked like she'd bite me if I tried.

It was hard to be around her, to feel so much emotion simmering barely below the surface, to see palpable rage and pain and fear contorting the smooth features of her face.

She fell into step beside me without a word and, together, we continued the long, slow grunt through the beech forest, following the crest of the broad ridge as we gradually climbed to the highest point, some 1030 metres, before flopping down in the shade to wait for Danilo and Emilie to catch up.

I watched her out of the corner of my eye, still afraid to meet her gaze, which was turned to the ground. Her cheap sandshoes were ripped, no good for trail walking out here, and she was wearing a pair of cut-off shorts and a tie-died camisole, which might have once belonged to our grandmother. Tiny nubs of breasts poked out from a grubby crop-top and her arms were bare, although I could see angry red lines snaking up her pale wrists. She had multiple studs rammed in her ears and her hair was matted with homemade dreadlocks.

I wondered when she'd last had a wash, or something decent to eat. There was an adultness, an aloofness in the way she held herself, watchful, on guard. I wanted to hold her in my arms and feel her slump against me the way Emilie does when she's peaceful or tired. I wondered when was the last time that anybody had held her.

I was still musing when she turned to meet my gaze, and a sticky, electric shock jolted me out of my reverie. A huge sob broke the silence, then another, then I was bent double with my head between my knees, keening, tears leaking out of my eyes, saliva dripping from my open mouth as I lay amongst the crown ferns and cried.

I made a grab for her, but she was gone, her words echoing in my head. *Why didn't you look after me?* repeated over and over again, the accusation in her voice draining all my strength away.

I'm . . . so sorry! I gasped, *so sorry, so sorry my darling. I'm so sorry you had to go through all of this, all on your own. To feel so abandoned by your own family, so unloved and unworthy, it hurt you so much, too much, and then you hurt yourself and the toxic cycle of grief and shame and rage and pain spiralled out of control.*

Why hadn't I looked after her? Because I couldn't look after myself, so I raged and roiled, on a rampage of self-destruction, running from one foster care family to another, telling authority to go fuck itself — the litany of useless and uncaring social workers, the police officers who came to pick me up and return me, the medical professionals who tried to prod and poke at my brain with their inept tools.

I knew all this because, a couple of years earlier, in an attempt to empower myself and come to terms with this gap in my history, I'd submitted an Official Information Act request to Oranga Tamariki, the agency formerly known as the Department of Child Youth and Family Services. I had the right to know about my past, I reasoned, and my journalism training meant I was experienced in asking difficult questions to get the information I needed. Only this time, I wanted to uncover what was lurking behind the void in my memory and to see if re-familiarising myself with this lost chunk of my childhood would give me the closure I needed to heal.

Upon reflection, it was a reckless and dangerous move that,

combined with my limited toolkit of self-awareness and soothing strategies, would serve to retraumatise instead of restoring me.

When the paperwork finally arrived, well beyond the statutory 20 working days the agency was required to abide by, I ripped open the plastic courier bag with a sense of dread. What was I doing and why was I doing it? What benefit could there possibly be in opening the lid to this Pandora's box of mine and rehashing the painful memories I'd kept buried deep down inside for so long? I faltered, fearful, picking up the single A4 cover letter on top of the thick manila folder with shaking hands.

There, typed under the agency's letterhead and addressed to me, read a dispassionate message to thank me for my request for all the information about myself as a child. *Here*, they explained, *within this folder, was the information covered by my request. However,* the letter continued, *please note one of your paper files has been unable to be located so the information in that file has not been included in the release. I regret any inconvenience that may cause you.*

I re-read that last sentence a couple of times in a haze of almost comical disbelief. What the fuck sort of sorry excuse was that to give someone? If the agency that was supposed to care for me couldn't even keep track of my file, what did this mean for my mission to uncover the truth about certain traumatic events that had derailed my life so badly?

I flipped casually through the folder with a growing sense of floating far above myself. Photocopies of handwritten social workers' reports, copies of emails and other correspondence, doctors' referrals, psychiatric assessments — but what stuck out the most was a piece of paper titled 'Transit Sheet', scrawled with dates and signatures. I had been like an unwanted parcel with no sender to be returned to. A parcel covered in hastily stuck-on labels, all of them meaning one thing — damaged, open at own risk. Labels like oppositional defiant disorder, borderline personality disorder and suggestions I was impulsive, drug-seeking, manipulative, self-harming, attention-seeking, all scribbled in my case files by bemused physicians, none of whom stopped to ask what terrible, painful and traumatic childhood experiences were fuelling my angry and destructive behaviours.

My young voice was completely absent from these files, as though my wants and needs hadn't even existed. Instead, those needs were misinterpreted and paraphrased within badly written entries by burnt-out social workers, whose prose ranged from unsympathetic to scathing. Indeed, it seemed I had given the whole lot of them the run around, quite literally.

Vicky has run away. She is in Waihi somewhere. Stopped the car to get her and the kid slammed the door shut and took off again. I advised (a black redaction line hid the name) *to report her to the police.*

Yes, you bet I slammed that door, you stupid bitch, my younger self snarled from behind me. She was standing there in the leaf litter with the sun glinting off her hair, fists balled.

No one can tell me what do, it's my life, they don't have a fucking clue about me anyway, she continued, the fire burning brightly behind her eyes. *They don't understand and they don't care, nobody cares.*

The fire was fading, and she looked less self-assured, because it's scary to realise you're just a kid all alone in the world.

I care, I told her, *I love you and I'm so proud of you for being so strong, and if you could just hang in there, I promise it's all going to be okay.*

The look on her face told me she didn't believe me, although I knew she so badly wanted to. She fingered those dark scars on her wrist, and I could see the emotion sweeping over her like a tidal wave about to drown her, so I reached out and pulled her onto my lap, legs wrapped around me, head against my chest, holding her so tight while she choked out huge, angry, painful sobs. I rocked her a little and stroked her hair, like I do with Emilie.

It's not your fault, sweetheart. Everything is going to be all right; everything will be all right. You'll see, my love.

I snapped out of my daydreams to find myself sitting on a fallen log, leaning my heavy pack against the tree and watching hundreds, no thousands, of tiny-winged insects shimmering in the sunlight.

They were so tiny and so numerous that they appeared to be simply hovering in one place, but if I tried to focus my eye on one, they quickly dipped and disappeared.

Still, it was beautiful to sit and watch this manifestation of forest magic in the swarms of these tiny shimmering creatures.

In my mind, I took my 14-year-old self's hand, taking care to avoid the sullen, red scars on her wrist, and we climbed quietly through the beech forest until eventually we popped out above the tree line and into the twisting collage of reddish-orange sub-alpine scrub near Starveall Hut, perched on a ridgeline at 1200 metres with impressive views of Mount Starveall.

The thick carpet of moss and creeping coprosma outside the hut gave way to lichen-stained scree and clumps of white and yellow mountain daisies. The following morning, I left my younger self sitting there, bundled up in a sleeping bag with a cup of soup in her hands, watching the bright orange sun rise up from behind the solid bulk of rock. I thought she'd be happy up there for a while. I shouldered my pack and kept walking, for both of us.

Four days later, we tackled the Rintouls. There were two parts to that long day — a steep climb up to the ridgeline above Old Man Hut, then an even steeper climb over the highest points of the Richmond Range; Little Mount Rintoul (1643 metres) and his towering brother, Mount Rintoul (1739 metres), then a gruelling descent to Mount Rintoul Hut and on to the peak of Purple Top (1532 metres), where we would set up camp for the night.

At Old Man Hut, heavy cloud and intermittent rain had dampened our plans to make the lengthy trip over the Rintouls, so we had called it a day and joined several other groups of trampers to wait for the weather to clear.

Emilie, the social butterfly, was in her element and quickly corralled the men and boys into a game of catch the wild goats, zoning in on a handsome French guy, whose accented voice rose in good humour as he played with her. They tried to sneak up on a few grazing goats, and after the feral beasts ran off, the group spent a joyful hour sharpening sticks into spears and practising their throws, all under the direction of a chatty seven-year-old. When she eventually wandered back to me, I asked her how it went.

We made a hunting group. I was the boss and we all had to practise with our spears, but we waited for ages and the goats didn't come back, so I got bored. What's for dinner, Mummy?

Early the following morning, after clearing the damp bush line, we scrabbled up the loose rocky flanks of Little Rintoul. The thick clouds of the previous day fell away below us to reveal rank upon rank of mountains to the southeast, and north to Motueka, the steely blue expanse of Tasman Bay and the north-western tip of the South Island.

Higher still, thick-stemmed mountain daisies sprang out of cracks between rocks, bright yellow buttons fringed with papery white petals, the common *Celmisia spectabilis* and its silvery-leafed cousin, *Celmisia incana*. More delicate and beautiful still were the tiny blossoms of *Raoulia grandiflora*, the large-flowered mat daisy, a spreading plant that forms cushions or mats resembling an inconspicuous grey rock until it erupts in a spread of miniature yellow and white flowers.

The thick, claggy cloud that had kept us confined between our tent and the crowded shelter of Old Man Hut the previous afternoon had clearly been appreciated by these fragile alpine plants, growing precariously nearly one and a half kilometres above sea level.

As we descended to the saddle between Little Rintoul and Mount Rintoul, I slipped on still-wet shingle, the morning sun yet to absorb water from the wet rock, and plunged down heavily on one knee. Although it wasn't a dramatic fall, the sharp edges of scree dug into my kneecap and scraped off a layer of skin. Blood quickly seeped into the space my exposed flesh now filled. But I couldn't stop there, on that narrow scar of track with an almost-vertical drop below me.

By the time I'd reached a flat spot, the blood had coagulated with the red dust on my leg. I gave it a wipe with the back of my hand and transferred my blood to a passing vegetable sheep. Otherwise known as *Haastia pulvinaris*, these iconic alpine plants are so named because when you spot their extremely compact, rounded masses of grey, fuzzy growth from a distance, they look just like the woolly backs of errant sheep.

She'll be right, I told myself, *it's just a scratch*. In fact, after the shock of the initial impact, it barely even stung — worse yet was the impossible weight of my pack still filled with another seven days' worth of breakfast, lunch, dinner and snacks for two ravenous females.

I'd been concerned about Emilie falling off the side of a mountain, but soon saw that I had no need to worry — that kid was a mountain goat with her little red Salomon trail shoes gripping the rocks. I only had to remind her to stop chattering and watch where she was going!

Even though we'd woken early to get a head start on the huge day ahead of us, a few groups overtook us as soon as we'd cleared the damp tree line and Emilie was busy socialising.

She wanted to make sure the French-Italian party she'd befriended at Old Man Hut kept their eyes open for feral goats. It was a fair request, and they answered solemnly that they would do their best to catch one, plus leave some goat chops for her dinner if they got lucky.

We didn't spot any goats on the climb to the summit of Mount Rintoul, and once we'd dragged ourselves up the raggedy scree and boulder-strewn tops, we flopped down on the burning shingle to admire expansive views over the Tasman and refuel our tired bodies with dried fruits, nuts and stale crackers.

Then, since in this environment what goes up must come down, we set out on a knee-burning slide down the scree slope towards the bush-clad ridgeline, eyes fixed on the tiny brown dot of Mount Rintoul Hut far below. My feet struggled to find a hold in the soft, fine pebbles and sand, but once we changed to the larger rocks and boulders, I felt more stable, although my thigh muscles trembled with the strain of our steep descent and my grazed knee was starting to throb.

We paused at Mount Rintoul Hut to refill our water bottles and demolish muesli bars, and were delighted to discover a handwritten message of encouragement and some snacks, including an extra freeze-dried dinner, left behind for us from a group we'd shared a rainy afternoon with at Slaty Hut two days earlier.

There, I'd got talking to Rose, a friendly Aucklander who was doing the Richmond Alpine Track with her two friends, and confided my concerns that, despite having packed supplies for 12 days, we might not have enough food to cover the long haul out to Nelson Lakes, given that wet-weather days had already eaten into our plans.

It was impossible to go any faster over these rough alpine tracks without tempting fate, especially when one of our group was only seven years old. But in your mid-twenties, as Rose's group was, superhuman activities come easier, and their group had chosen to push on over the clagged-in tops of the Rintouls, while we old and cautious folk stoked the fire in the hut. Their shorter route would lead them out of the Rintouls the following day, so they'd left behind their spare food as a gift for us hungry trail walkers.

It was a welcome discovery, and the act of kindness buoyed our spirits as we continued a further two kilometres along the ridgeline to scramble up the mauve-coloured head of Purple Top, so named because of the tinted rock around its crown.

There, amongst the wide-open silence of the mountainside, we set up our little camp after wandering off track a few hundred metres to find a perfectly flat spot surrounded by clumps of mountain daisies and tussock at around 1400 metres.

It had been a huge day, as we'd covered eight kilometres in almost as many hours, but we'd made it and were basking in a golden warmth of sunset and gratitude — for the gift of food, the perfect weather conditions and for having the hardest part of the Richmond track firmly behind us. If we'd had anything to celebrate with, we would have — an extra muesli bar had to suffice until I remembered the chocolate bar that had been left for us at Mount Rintoul Hut, which we split three ways between us. Maybe it was the joy of acing a challenging day, or the pleasure of being here in this beautiful place with my two companions, or just my bottomless hunger that made the chocolate taste so sweet.

Fabio, the cheerful Brazilian guy who called me his 'landlady' as he rented the self-contained sleepout at the rear of my property, knew I loved frogs. That's why he'd ordered me a bumper sticker for my car with a picture of a bright green Australian treefrog and the words, 'MILF, Man I Love Frogs.'

He'd surprised me with the sticker one afternoon after a

particularly demoralising day at work when I was still agonising over how to officially check out of life and walk Te Araroa. I had been feeling pretty down on myself, but Fabio was supportive of my plans and had told me, *Most people are just ordinary, but you, Victoria, are extraordinary! I'm sure you would be amazing at doing something like that.*

We'd dreamed and schemed over a couple of beers while our kids played in the back garden of my Christchurch house, where my little blue truck with its bumper sticker was now parked up over 1000 kilometres away.

And I was here, squatting beside a shallow tarn that was teeming with thousands of big brown tadpoles, watching a tiny baby froglet emerge into the sunshine.

Ever since I can remember, I've been obsessed with frogs. There's a strange magic that surrounds these amazing amphibians with their ability to transform from water-dwelling wiggly things to climbing, hopping and swimming animals, not to mention their large-eyed cuteness and wide range of colours, sizes, sounds and habitat. Australia, where I grew up, has thousands of them.

In the deep south of Tasmania, the frogs are generally smaller and darker than the bright green hues of their larger, tropic-dwelling companions, or at least the frogs my brother and I found in our local creek were.

We discovered a way to lure the frogs out of the creek by placing slabs of thick bark on the lower banks for the little creatures to crawl under. Then we would return the next day to turn the bark over and uncover the dazed frogs.

My brother didn't mind helping with the bark, but he never wanted to hold the frogs, whereas by the age of seven, I was an agile and experienced frog-handler. I even had a book about frogs that explained how they can absorb salts, oils and chemicals from your hands, due to their semi-permeable skin, which allows them to absorb oxygen from water. I knew that, to protect their skin, I had to wet my hands before gently picking up a frog, although this also gave the more energetic specimens a better chance of slipping through my fingers and hopping away.

I took some of the frogs home to live in an aquarium my folks had picked up at a weekend market, back in the days when people came together to sell their wares rather than through the socially disconnected world of online trading sites.

My aquarium sat on a bench beside our giant, galvanised rainwater tank, out of full sunlight, and I filled the bottom with river gravel and fresh water. I placed a big rock with a flattish top in the middle for the swimming frogs to haul out onto, and a nicely rounded piece of bark to huddle under. I'd carefully collected a handful of weed from the creek, roots and all, to transplant into my tank for the frogs to enjoy. It was a miniature wetland hotel, I decided, just for the frogs to enjoy.

Through painful trial and error, I'd learned that frogs don't like too much water, and if there was not enough space for them to haul out, they'd eventually get tired of swimming and drown. Almost as bad, on one particularly cold morning I'd gone to check on my frogs and found them all crowded under the bark except for one poor fellow who couldn't quite fit, and whose leg was frozen solid in the water as a result. The diligent biologist in my seven-year-old self was devastated at the harm my ignorance had inadvertently caused my amphibian friends, and a trip to the library was called for to borrow more books.

Out on the Richmond Range, I didn't have a bucket and I wasn't going to startle the froglet by picking him up, because I was just thrilled to be watching him navigate his natural environment. His world had just become infinitely bigger as he crawled, slowly but surely with the help of sticky, amphibian feet, out of the clear brown waters of the tarn and onto a sun-flecked rock. I wondered if it was his first real time above the surface, as he'd still got the remnants of his almost-translucent tadpole tail hanging down behind.

Tall greenish-grey arms of mānuka and kānuka stretched out into the empty space above the tarn, reaching up to the sun that was blazing overhead. We'd arrived at the aptly named Tarn Hut about 20 minutes earlier with lunch on our minds but instantly became distracted by the discovery of the tadpoles. Emilie was wading through the shallows with her plastic cup, trying to catch one, while Danilo and I sprawled together on the bank and observed the determined progress of the tiny froglet.

After lunch, we pressed on, reluctant to leave the cute little hut and its delightful tarn, but aware that we needed to keep moving to the next hut if we were ever to make it out of the Richmond Range and to our next resupply point.

I pointed out that I'd be quite happy to stay behind and make Tarn Hut my home, and maybe tame some goats to travel to St Arnaud with me once a month to collect supplies of rice and beans and flour. But the nature of trail walking unfortunately meant that we had to keep moving, or we'd simply run out of food.

No one wanted to stay and play huts with me, so I shouldered my pack and followed my two companions back into the dry beech forest. The track that had been slowly winding along the low ridgeline now plunged off the side in a steep, thigh-trembling, knee-throbbing descent, all the way into the depths of the Wairoa River valley far below.

Someone with a good sense of humour had written funny little messages on the wasp bait stations along the way. My favourite was a handful of pebbles placed inside an empty station and the words: 'U Rock'.

We arrived at the busy grounds of Mid Wairoa Hut around 5pm, the sun still strong but not strong enough to heat the swift, icy blue waters of the river nearby.

Built on a flat benched section some 20 metres above the Wairoa River, the six-bunk hut makes up for its limited bunks by offering several choice camping spots, but by the time we arrived, legs aching from the steep and punishing descent, they were nearly all taken.

It was disconcerting to see so many other humans after a full day of feeling completely alone in the mountains. After finding a tent space tucked away in the bush, Emilie and I disappeared to swim in the sapphire waters of the swimming hole, two little frogs in our own watery realm.

Top Wairoa Hut sits up on a hill between the meeting point of two rivers, at the foot of the geological wonderland of Red Hill, which is aptly named after the ultramafic geology and mineral composition that give the rocks their brilliant colours. After the crowdedness of Mid Wairoa Hut, we were relieved to find this small, bright orange hut completely empty, and as dusk fell we spread ourselves out over the bunks, grateful to still be alive.

From Mid Wairoa Hut the track had followed the Wairoa River some eight kilometres upstream, gaining 400 metres elevation as it carved its way through the steep-sided bush-covered valley and sidling multiple times across precipitous slopes.

The narrow track was often slippery and scrambly, with only rocks or tree roots between us and a steep drop to the deep limestone gorge and river rushing below. The trail notes state: 'Some trampers will find this section challenging', but we almost found it deadly.

It was the section where I nearly lost my daughter. She was in front of me on the narrow scar of a track when we came to the trunk of a black-tinged beech tree thrusting horizontally out of the slope. I climbed over it while Emilie went under it, hanging on to the rough bark until her fingers slipped and she fell backwards in terrifying slow motion, rolling head over heels down the steep bank towards the gorge below.

Mummeeee! she cried, her voice shrill and panicky until her cries were muffled by her fall.

Emilie! I screamed back at her, our eyes locking as she came up from another dizzying, sickening somersault. *Emilie, stop!*

It seemed that for an eternal, paralysing moment I simply stood and watched her, waiting for her to respond to my command. My brain flapped frantically like a caged bird, screaming a thousand jumbled messages at me as I tried to register the urgency of the situation.

Mummeeee! Emilie cried again as her head came up again on the climax of another horrible turn, her little body limp as a ragdoll.

My stomach dropped as my body secreted an enormous dose of stress hormones, and a blood-curdling sensation of panic and doom flooded through.

My baby. My baby was in danger. I was losing her. Emilie. My everything.

My brain finally caught up with my body. I threw my pack to

the ground and leapt down the slope after her, thinking of nothing other than catching her and cradling her in my arms before the slope disappeared into the sheer rocky sides of the gorge. If we fell into the river together then perhaps I could cushion her fall and pull her to safety from the swirling torrent. Rocks and vegetation scraped bare skin off my thigh as I slid down the slope after Emilie, arms outstretched to catch her.

But a tree caught her first — a slender sapling, growing some 10 metres down the almost-vertical embankment, the last stop before the gorge. It was a tōtara tree, *Podocarpus totara*, known in Māori legend as one of the favoured children of the forest god Tāne-mahuta, the Soul of the Forest.

No more than six centimetres in diameter, it stood tall and firm with Emilie wrapped around it, her big brown eyes swollen in terror.

Am I safe now, Mummy? she whispered as I reached for her and pulled her into my arms.

My heart was hammering in my throat, but instead of my usual panic, I felt strangely calm. *Yes, love. You're okay. Come on, let's climb back up to the track.*

Slowly, carefully, still sitting on my bum with my feet wedged against the little tōtara with Emilie safe in my arms, I unclipped her backpack and placed it on the bank beside us. Then I stood, shakily, and lifted Emilie back onto her feet, trying not to look down the sheer 10-metre drop into the river below.

Danilo was standing on the bank about 10 metres above our heads. It felt like a million years had passed in a matter of moments, and he'd stood there waiting, turning to stone like those Māori mountain gods. I wondered if his guts had dropped with a big dose of adrenaline and whether, instead of being propelled to fight or flee, he'd simply frozen stiff in horror at the situation unfolding before him.

Once Emilie and I had clambered back up to the track, fingers digging for grip amidst the rotting leaves and tree roots, Danilo held her tight and stroked her hair, picking some of the moss and leaves out of her curls.

Miraculously, Emilie was stunned and a bit scratched up but unhurt. Still pulsing with adrenaline, my big leg muscles started to shake uncontrollably as I fumbled for lollies in my pack, while encouraging her to sip some water and suck on something sweet.

I wanted to sit down, or better still, to lie down, holding Emilie close against my body as I breathed into the panic and waited for the terror to pass. But it wasn't safe to stay here, balancing precariously on a section of track some 30 centimetres wide, with a steep bank above us and a dizzying drop below.

We had been walking for hours already and were some four kilometres from Mid Wairoa Hut with some hairy steep sections behind us and another four kilometres ahead of us to Top Wairoa Hut.

It was our eighth day of moving slowly through the wild, rough and sprawling landscape of the Richmond Range. It was New Year's Day, the day one of us had nearly died, and yet we were all still alive, stumbling slowly in convoy, one foot in front of the other, stepping, climbing, scrabbling, all the way up the left branch of the Wairoa River until it reduced to a clear, harmless trickle, barely ankle deep.

I repacked Emilie's bag to a minimal weight, taking her sleeping bag and thermal liner into my own pack. I wanted to make it as easy as possible for her to just keep walking, even though I knew it was the last thing she felt like doing.

Somehow, she had lost an earring, a tiny golden kiwi, and her little face screwed up to cry again when she realised it was gone. I tucked her pounamu pendant inside her shirt and gave her a kiss.

Maybe the earring is your gift to the tōtara tree in return for saving you — he held you in his arms safe from the river and you gave him your beautiful golden kiwi, I said.

Emilie's eyes widened at the thought, and I tried to breathe a little more magic into a tragic situation. *Maybe tonight your kiwi will come to life and run around in the forest, happy and free. I think your pounamu kept you safe, so make sure you wear it close to your skin and it will help you feel strong and calm.*

With that, she followed me closely along the narrow track, talking about her fall, the golden kiwi and the magic tōtara tree.

After an eternity of slow, relentless climbing, the dry and stunted beech forest gave way and we stepped out into a wide creek bed, evidence of the Wairoa in recent flood was scattered around us in the form of twisted, shattered trunks and branches.

I couldn't help but shudder involuntarily. The notes warned that the river could rise rapidly and the section from Mid Wairoa Hut to Top Wairoa Hut would be impassable in bad weather. The image of Emilie's limp little body being sucked away in raging floodwaters flashed into my mind, and I knew my body wouldn't have given my brain enough time to think rationally before compelling me to leap in after her.

We hung about in the stream, gulping cups of icy water, observing how the power of previous floodwaters had carved a deep chute through layers of gravel and grit. Then it was time to gather the last of our energy for one more push, clawing our way some 20 metres up the steep bank with its treacherously loose handholds to emerge at the top, smothered in sunshine and surrounded by a tunnel of gently swaying mānuka. Their sharp-tipped leaves, laden with delicate white and pink-flushed flowers, reached out to stroke us in quiet congratulations as we stumbled the final few metres to the bright orange sanctuary of Top Wairoa Hut. It was empty. It was ours — our salvation, our refuge, our bunk for the night.

The world was red. The rocks were red. The heat of the sun reflected off the red ground. We were slowly melting as we trudged through the alien landscape, feeling like we'd lost the trail and had instead wandered deep into the Australian outback. I turned my head, searching for huge cactuses and termite mounds, but instead I saw mānuka and Dracophyllum, speargrass and tussock. The air was thick with the frenzied hum of a million invisible cicadas. Giant dragonflies zoomed past, occasionally pausing on a rock until we were close enough to marvel at their brilliant yellow and black markings, before taking to the skies again. We were still in New Zealand, moving slowly through the geological wonderland of Red Hills on the outskirts of Mount Richmond Forest Park. In a couple of days' time, we'd make it out of the desert and into the cool beech forests surrounding Nelson Lakes National Park. From this vantage point, however, there was only red rock as far as the eye could see.

The brilliant red colour was due to a high concentration of minerals in the ground, and from such unique soils grew even more exceptional plants. Although these magnesium-rich soils were too toxic for tree growth, other strange and wonderful vegetation was thriving amongst the low bushes and shrubs.

A splash of bluish-purple caught my eye and I discovered a patch of native harebells, their tiny flowers a delicate contrast to the thick and fleshy leaves. Apparently, the composition of the soil brought out their blue colour. Suddenly my head was ringing with sound — a cicada had mistaken my backpack for a bush and was clinging to a strap, vibrating his wings loudly in the hope of attracting a lovely lady cicada to mate with.

As we climbed higher, the plants became shorter, sprawling across the ground in clumps and patches, often displaying tiny flowers or brightly coloured berries. A ground beetle scurried along a cool path cast by their shade, minding his business as he scavenged for tasty things to eat.

Emilie was walking beside me, pointing to this flower and that. Beneath the brim of her sunhat, her cheek was slightly swollen and grazed from the previous day's near-death fall, but otherwise she seemed to have escaped unscathed.

I knew she would have loved to ditch her pack and drop down amongst the plants and the beetles — it was the perfect place to make a fairy garden.

I loved seeing the wonder of the world through her child's eyes, where everything was tinged with magic. I paused to pull her close in a warm embrace, marvelling at her composure, my beautiful, brave girl.

I wondered how I would have coped at her age. I was glad she felt safe enough to cry in my arms, to feel the feelings and let them go. If there was one thing my daughter was teaching me, it was the ability to bounce back from adversity without losing your joy for life.

Once we reached the saddle, the red world opened in front of us. We dropped our packs and rummaged for muesli bars and crackers, always hungry yet not daring to go beyond our carefully allocated rations. There was still a long way to go until I would be able to fill up my food bag. My pack had been full to almost bursting 10 days ago, but I was now able to twist the roll-top down several turns before clipping it shut.

Emilie played in the dust where she was sitting, reaching for pretty rocks with their swirls of ochre, orange, black and gold.

It felt like we'd been out there for so long that we were becoming one with this expansive landscape. I stretched my legs out, I couldn't believe they'd carried me this far. They barely even hurt, except for a slight stiffness in my calves first thing in the morning, which melted away after stretching. But my back ached. After the previous day's slide down the riverbank to rescue Emilie, I felt as though my spine had been beaten gently with a lump of wood.

Somewhere in the distance, I could see the greyish-blue flanks of real mountains, their base hidden in a sea of olive-green. From where we were, my map showed that it was less than 40 kilometres to the road end from where we'd walk the final few kilometres to our destination of St Arnaud in Nelson Lakes National Park.

At our pace, in this burning hot weather and on these painfully rugged tracks, it would probably take us three or four days to get there. The worst of the Richmond Range was now behind us and all that remained was to survive the long, slow trudge through the desert, hoping our food rations would last the distance.

We'd spent the night on the wide wooden platform of Hunters Hut after a long, hot day clambering up to the 1374-metre saddle above Top Wairoa Hut, then following a high, exposed ridgeline dotted with beautiful flowering alpine plants. The ridge ran westward below Mount Ellis before winding its way down to the left branch of the Motueka River.

With the shade of the beech forest behind us, we realised the desert landscape of the Red Hills reached unbearable temperatures at the height of the day. That morning, we'd set an alarm for 5am to try to cover some distance before the sun reached its zenith. My eyes throbbed in their sockets and I ached to lie down and rest some more, but slowly, mechanically, I started stuffing my red and grey sleeping bag into its compression sack and reprimanded Emilie for messing about with hers.

But I can't do it! It won't go in, see!

A tired Emilie was bolshy and uncooperative, and threw her half-packed sleeping bag towards me. She was sliding towards the typical stubbornness of her Taurus star sign, but my parenting bucket was empty, and I wasn't in the mood for a battle of wills right now.

Look, just go outside and calm yourself down, I snapped at her, crying on the inside for another cup of coffee, a hug, someone else to come in and do some calm, collected parenting because I was just too tired to deal with it right now. She'd managed to pack her sleeping bag just fine over the past 60+ days. Why now, why this morning when my morale was at an all-time low?

Danilo either ignored or didn't register our mother-daughter mini drama and focused intently on fitting his expensive camera gear into his large white pack.

Emilie stomped off, slamming the hut door behind her, bloody little shit with no consideration for the other hut occupants, a young couple who were moving around quietly in their own world, oblivious to the battle raging on the far side of the hut.

For whatever reason, this brief confrontation had triggered something deep inside of me and an explosion of stress hormones was now coursing through my body, like a barrage of tiny, red-hot arrows that left deep furrows of cold, numbing shame and loneliness in their wake. I hated myself whenever I lost my temper at Emilie. Of course she's not a shit, just a frustrated kid expressing her big emotions. I wondered what she was doing now.

I finished sipping my lukewarm coffee, staring out the window and reminding myself to breathe as my heart hammered in my chest. Yes, I was stressed out and tired, but it was a beautiful time of day to be alive as the dawn bathed the red desert landscape in cool shades of blue and the sweet piercing chimes of bellbirds rang through the olive-grey scrub.

Peace had resumed inside the small hut when a series of bloodcurdling screams pierced our ears. I ran outside to see Emilie staggering towards me from the scrub, writhing and clawing at herself.

Wasps! she shrieked. *There's a wasp biting meeee!*

Shit. My brain shot off a series of unhelpful expletives as I tried to hold her still and pull off her fleece jumper to examine the stings. But she kept screaming, horrible, agonising sounds, and I realised there was a wasp crawling in her hair, hunching its body to pierce her skin again and again with its sharp stinger. I squashed it and held her tight, feeling incredibly useless, as she stiffened and moaned with the intense pain that was shooting through her little body.

Jacqui and Shuma, the young couple we had shared the hut with, looked a bit pale as Danilo held a writhing, shrieking Emilie in his arms while I wet my buff and applied it to her burning red skin. We all felt so bad for her.

Shuma produced a tube of topical antihistamine, which I applied to Emilie's stings. Then I lay down with her on the bunk and cuddled, our packing aborted, while Danilo attempted to distract her with a story from her beloved *Snake and Lizard* book, his lilting accent rising and falling above her little sobs.

So much for our early start. I wondered what else could go wrong!

After an hour, the involuntary spasms had calmed and, after some coaxing, we got Emilie ready to leave.

Our small group staggered morosely up the hill behind Hunters Hut, aiming for Porters Creek Hut some four to five hours away.

Poor little Emilie. She'd been stung on the temple, the back of her neck, in her hair and on her elbow. One eye was swelling up and, combined with the red scab from her tumble down the bank, she really looked like she'd been in the wars.

But the kid was pretty staunch about it all. She asked me to photograph her face so she could see what it all looked like, and I repeatedly told her how strong and brave she was. A real wahine toa, a warrior woman. We talked about wasps and how they sting when people go near their nests, as well as about other insects that bite.

Danilo shared some great stories about his own misadventures with wasps, including disturbing a nest in a rotting log while climbing down a riverbank and having to dive into the water with angry black and yellow insects swarming on his back.

I told her about Australia and the agony of bull-ant stings —

everything seemed to want to sting or bite you over there! Big red ants, jumping ants, green ants and those chunky black ants that nip you from the grass.

In the lush, wet depth of the Tasmanian forests lurked blood-sucking leeches, waiting patiently for little juicy legs to brush by. I still remember the horror of discovering a massively swollen specimen buried into the soft flesh behind my knee, and my squeamish attempts to pull it off.

Emilie's eyes boggled. *Let's never go tramping in Tasmania!*

It was 1pm when we climbed over a little bluff and saw the bright orange roof of Porters Creek Hut in the distance, a tiny speck in a sea of green.

Even from that distance, though, it was clear to see some of the green belonged to invaders — wilding pines! Soon we could see them everywhere amongst the darker tones of the native shrubs. As their seeds blow across fences from forestry plantations, these fast-growing exotic trees are popping up all over New Zealand's high country, crowding out native plants and sucking much-needed water and nutrients out of the soil. Millions of dollars are spent every year in efforts to control their invasive spread and limit the damage they do to our country's fragile biodiversity.

Emilie gasped. *We need to call Fiona*, she cried, *so we can get a group together to pull them out!*

I melted with love for her earnest and practical solution. She was of course referring to the wonderful couple, Fi and Anthony Behrens from Whiowhio Hut in Palmerston North, who had shown us a YouTube video of Fiona orchestrating a wilding pine-clearing expedition.

The couple had left a lingering impression on Emilie, and she often declared she wanted to learn to set traps to save the native animals. When we saw a particularly nice river or stream, she'd ask me, *Do you think whio would like to live here?*

We arrived at the empty hut, sweaty and sore, and decided to have a rest before determining whether we wanted to continue another six kilometres to the river. It would make tomorrow's walk out to St Arnaud a bit shorter, but we were all worn out and lacking motivation.

I took out my tiny watercolour kit and wandered off quietly to paint a scene of the hut and surrounding landscape, the bright green contrast of the flowering hebes soft and round against the reddish blue of the rugged ranges.

Half an hour later, a small group of northbound trail walkers, known colloquially as NOBOs, turned up. Emilie and I got chatting to them, then a lovely older southbound couple arrived. Emilie was in her social-bunny element with all the new faces, showing off her swollen eye and wasp stings and receiving gasps of horror and admiration in return.

I could only socialise for a short time before I got tired out and craved the magical solitude of the bush. Even after 12 days in the Richmond Range, I was in no hurry to leave.

No one could be bothered pressing on to the river, so we set alarms for 4.30am and planned to make tomorrow one big day, walking all the way out past Red Hills Hut to St Arnaud and civilisation.

Richmond Range. DANILO HEGG

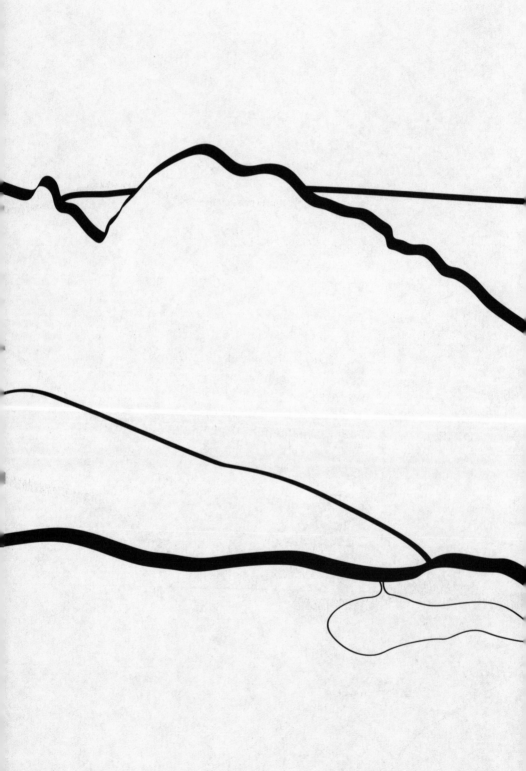

Chapter 9

Hinapouri Tarn

Te Araroa
Day 67

SOMEWHERE HIGH IN THE MOUNTAINS, alpine springs and snowmelt trickle into a glassy blue tarn where two little girls are playing.

I lie sprawled out on a bed of moss and tiny alpine plants with one cheek pressed against a cushion-grass pillow, the warmth of the sun on my bare legs.

The water must be freezing but the girls don't seem to notice. They're high on life and the joy of being together.

I watch them splash and laugh, shorts hiked up high as they stir the mud at the bottom of the tarn with their feet. Next, they'll haul out to bask in the sun before chasing each other through the tussocks.

We're camping beside Hinapouri Tarn in a huge rocky basin below Mount Angelus on the Travers Range, one of four main ranges within Nelson Lakes National Park that extend like splayed fingers at the northernmost limit of the Southern Alps. The alps stretch some 500 kilometres along much of the length of New Zealand's South Island, with Aoraki/Mount Cook its highest peak. The path of Te Araroa winds along its lower limits and foothills.

The pretty, elongated mirror of Hinapouri Tarn is broken in two by a narrow stream, and we're camped on a flat spot right between both waterholes in what feels like pristine wilderness, even though it's only a short walk from the larger, more popular Lake Angelus and the gigantic structure of Angelus Hut.

I'd rather be over here in the relative peace and quiet beside the tarn than crammed in the 26-bunk hut with all the other humans. After 12 days wandering through the Richmond Range with only

Danilo and Emilie for company, I'm in no rush to be surrounded by the noise and energy of other trampers. Besides, we're here with our dear friends Melissa and Felix and their daughter Allegra.

After farewelling Danilo in St Arnaud, Emilie and I are spending a few days with Melissa and her family, exploring this special part of Nelson Lakes National Park. Melissa is a botanist and I'm thrilled to be having a private ecology lesson in this beautiful part of the world.

The previous day, we'd tackled the short, steep scramble up the Cascade Track, named for its many tumbling waterfalls that distract the tired tramper from the punishing climb up the almost sheer mountainside.

The clear waters of Lake Angelus and Hinapouri Tarn feed into Hukere Stream, which falls almost 1000 metres to the valley floor before joining the Travers River. This, in turn, flows into Lake Rotoiti, one of the main lakes of the national park.

Today, I'm reclining at 1600 metres. Tomorrow, Emilie and I plan to go even higher as we're taking a detour from Te Araroa to climb over Mount Cedric before dropping into the Sabine Valley, which runs up the western side of the Travers Range. We will join Te Araroa at the head of the Sabine River in a couple of days' time.

Why the detour? Simply because I wanted to follow Melissa up to this botanical wonderland and hang out for a few days in the company of friends, allowing Emilie and me the time to recharge our social batteries before heading back out on the trail. I also wanted to explore the parallel river valley of the Sabine instead of continuing up the Travers.

Right now, though, the thought of moving any further exhausts me. I just want to lie here on the ground and sleep. The constant movement, the need to cover multiple kilometres every day is becoming too much for my shattered body. The strain of carrying my freshly refilled food bag, crammed with 10 days' worth of food for two, and the general discomfort of life in the wild has caught up on me and I'm craving the sanctuary of soft mattresses, clean sheets, a full refrigerator and fresh, nourishing food.

My mind is swirling with thoughts of chickpeas and baby spinach salad drizzled with fresh lemon juice and topped with juicy strips of spiced lamb, although I'm trying to make do with a cup of peppermint tea while I stir hot water into a bowl of couscous and soy protein.

Maybe we could just go home with Melissa and Felix, wash the dreadlocks out of our hair, burn the feral tramping clothes we've been wearing for the past 65 days, then collapse into a warm bed.

But although our friends would welcome us with open arms, I know I can't go with them. My legs might be willing, but my heart would break. There's only one way forward: to keep slowly wandering south.

We left our friends at their beautiful campsite by the tarns under Mount Angelus and climbed up and out of the basin, sidling along the ragged ridgeline of Mount Cedric and plunging down through the beech forest into the Sabine Valley some 1000 metres below.

Avoiding the big and busy DOC huts that were not covered by our annual Backcountry Hut Pass during the peak summer season, we opted to tent on the banks of the Sabine River for a couple of nights.

As I sat outside our little yellow tent surrounded by a grove of slender young beech trees, I noticed a female robin in one of the trees staring back at me. Soon she was on the ground, inspecting my trail shoes, tugging the striped laces with her beak. Those worms didn't taste very good, so she bounced over to the tent to check out the guy ropes instead. She was a mokorā, a South Island robin (*Petroica australis*). I could tell she was a female because of the small pale area on her belly; males have a larger, distinctively creamy patch amidst their dark slate-grey feathers.

Many of New Zealand's native bird species have evolved to take on the attributes of the mammals absent from the unique and isolated ecosystem. With her long thin legs, round body and large dark eyes, and her preference to hop around in a series of little jumps, the mokorā could be the bird version of a little mouse.

She bounced through the undergrowth as I moved about our

campsite, securing the tent pegs, setting up our cooking gear and sending Emilie down to the river to collect water.

Which way should I go? she asked. It was a fair question, as we were camped on an island in the middle of the confluence of the Sabine and West Sabine rivers. It was a strip of land maybe 50 metres across at its widest point and just a couple of metres higher than the water itself.

There was water all around us, perfect for filling up cooking pots, as long as Emilie didn't accidentally float one downstream while pretending it was a boat.

Once I'd finishing organising our gear, I wandered down to the riverbank to join her. She'd found a calm patch with sandy shallows and was busy digging out a little pool to sit in. The strewn rocks and bleached branches told me that this island got inundated when the river was in flood, although the tiny grove of beech trees I'd chosen to camp under seemed sturdy enough, and my InReach weather forecast told me there was no sign of rain.

We'd been wandering up the river track when I'd spotted the island, surrounded by a shallow channel of knee-deep water on one side and the grey-white force of the Sabine rushing through a narrow chute on the other. At that point, we'd been going for almost 13 kilometres, a respectable enough distance along the rooty, bumpy and undulating valley track that would soon fork off along the western arm of the Sabine River.

We were tired and already scoping out flat spots to camp on when the island appeared, calling to us above the noise of the river, through the darkness of the trees.

What a delight to have our very own island to call home, to sleep surrounded by the soothing sounds of flowing water. Although far from tropical, hopefully the thin canopy of stunted beech trees would shelter us from the early morning dew.

Although most of the heat was already gone from the afternoon sun, we couldn't resist stripping off and wading into a deep blue pool below a huge dead tree, our breaths coming in sharp gasps as our bodies adjusted to the cold.

Even though the burn of the icy water hurt when I first immersed myself, I loved the hot tingle that spread across my skin following such a brave feat. Emilie preferred to splash and giggle, dunking her bare bottom in the shallows.

Something caught my eye and I saw that I'd been joined, yet again, by a long-legged invertebrate of sorts — our splashings had disturbed a wētā, which had leapt into the pool.

He was so light and tiny that his six spiky legs didn't even pierce the surface of the water, but he couldn't swim to safety and so would either make a tasty morsel for a swooping bird or drown.

I scooped him up in one palm to show Emilie. His rescue was a good excuse to leave the frigid pool and return to the warmth of our camp. We placed the wētā on the grass and watched him, admiring his long antennae and the swirled pattern of brown and gold on his back.

Danilo had showed me how to tell the difference between wētā and cave wētā, although at first glance these long-legged creatures all look the same. I thought about how delighted he would have been at our discovery, and wondered what he was doing now. He was probably deep in the wilderness of Kahurangi National Park, his next destination after St Arnaud.

Part of me wished Danilo could have accompanied us through this next section, or at least over the challenge of the Waiau Pass, simply because I felt good when he was with us. It was a strange discovery to realise I felt safe when he was around, as though a warm calm had descended on me, safe and comfortable even in the silence of our own thoughts.

Someone once asked what triggers me and I didn't really know what to say. But now that I think about it, it's often related to interactions with people: my desire to join and be accepted by them is in stark conflict with my instinct to withdraw and hide from these often volatile, unsafe creatures.

As humans, we seem hardwired with the desire to be accepted and affirmed. Then, when we perceive that we are not, we suffer the burn of rejection and the deep shame that comes with being a social outcast.

For my trauma-affected brain, this knee-jerk reaction brings about a violent change in my biochemistry. It's almost palpable. Have you ever sat quietly and watched a snail or a hermit crab timidly come out of its shell — seeking, searching — only to recoil and telescope itself back inside? During those moments of primal panic, no amount of coaxing will bring it back out in a hurry.

It's taken me a long time to understand that I've become hard-wired to perceive rejection and judgement from my fellow humans, and to pre-emptively hide my inner self from them. This place of relative safety has become a terribly lonely sanctuary.

Out there in the wilderness, though, there was nothing to judge me. Nature was far too preoccupied with its own dealings to notice my presence, let alone bother to affirm me. Maybe Danilo, deeply absorbed in the ponderings of his own scientific mind, hadn't noticed me either.

Usually, it's difficult for me to let my guard down around people until I know them well, and many men don't want to wait that long. While being tough is easy, being soft, open and loving screams of a vulnerability that my hypervigilant brain finds very unsafe and unsettling.

Yet, the more time I spent around Danilo, the calmer I felt, and it became easier to mirror his softness and tenderness with my own.

For a highly intelligent, extremely focused and competent individual, he also exhibited a certain fragility that stirred my protectiveness and made me want to care for him. I felt that for all his accomplishments, he often seemed lost, overwhelmed or even bewildered by the complexities of the world and the people in it, preferring to spend long periods alone in the company of his beloved mountains, or wandering around in the dark searching for tiny invertebrates. I didn't exactly understand the inner workings of his strange and brilliant mind, but I felt a kinship with him.

We had spent New Year's Eve together in the warm beech forest above Mid Wairoa Hut, searching for long-legged taonga amidst the tree trunks and low-hanging branches while Emilie slept peacefully in the tent.

I was delighted to find several brown and gold specimens hiding in plain sight amidst the leaf litter, and Danilo was equally delighted to get down on his knees to photograph them.

The magic of the bush takes on a different quality at night. The last of the warm evening light faded away to reveal the velvety texture of true night, and wherever I turned the beam of my head torch, I could feel darkness flow through the trees behind me as smoothly as the river flowing through the gorge below.

Under that blanket of darkness, the night creatures awoke. A ruru/morepork called forlornly in the distance. Hundreds of tiny insects emerged from their hiding places and hopped, flew, scurried or slithered into the night. The circadian rhythm of these nocturnal insects mean they are inactive during the day and hunt for food at night.

Safe from the burning heat, yet warm enough to still be active, the wētā and cave wētā Danilo was searching for spent their evenings either eating lichen, moss and leaves or licking nectar from flowers, although as omnivores, they wouldn't turn down an easy meal if they discovered a decomposing fellow invertebrate.

Time passed quietly, broken by one or the other of us sharing our observations and discoveries as more and more night insects woke up and went about their business. Danilo checked his watch: it was 11.55pm. Five minutes to midnight, the passing of one year into the next.

We kept searching until he called me over to admire a large, golden, native slug and the 'leaf vein' pattern on the back of its elongated flattened body. It looked just like a large yellow leaf, shimmering gently under the light of our head torches, its little eyes peeping shyly from translucent stalks.

It's midnight. Happy new year to a beautiful lady. I'm so happy to be here with you, he said.

There were no fireworks out here in the depths of the Wairoa Gorge, just the scattering of light from our head torches as we embraced gently. Happy new year.

Now, seven days later, these memories feel like a lifetime ago. I sigh and relax my body against the warm grass outside our tent, and the river sighs with me. The wētā, which I've decided is most likely a cave wētā since his antennae are quite close together and his legs are very long, has recovered from his dunking and wandered off under some leaves.

Emilie has grown tired of boat launching and circles back, still naked, to snuggle against my outstretched knees.

I love you, Mummy! she chirps, then in the same breath, *What's for dinner?*

The sacred lake with the clearest fresh water in the world is slowly choking with algae and goose shit. But you won't read those words on any tourism website, and to be honest, it was a surprise to me too.

Translated as the 'land of peaceful waters', Rotomairewhenua/ Blue Lake holds the title of the clearest lake in the world. We could see the bottom of the lake some 70 or 80 metres below its turquoise surface.

I wasn't expecting to see a thick mat of dried goose droppings covering its rocky shores, however. These large cylindrical droppings were from the Canada goose, an intruder from North America that has taken up residence in many high-country lakeside pastures, rivers, forests and tarns. They eat, breed and poop everywhere, fouling waterways and encroaching into habitat used by native bird species.

From our campsite on the island, we'd travelled seven kilometres through a narrow neck of beech forest that snaked along the base of the Mahanga Range, climbing higher and higher as we followed the river all the way to this special lake.

As the waters of Rotomairewhenua are sacred to Ngāti Apa ki te Rā Tō, who traditionally used the lake for bone-cleansing ceremonies to prepare the spirits of the dead for the long trip north to their spiritual homeland of Hawaiki, people are asked not to swim, drink or wash their clothes here.

The water tank at nearby Blue Lake Hut was empty, so we backtracked to fill our bottles from the river flowing out of the lake, trying not to think about the bones or the goose poo, before pushing on.

Emilie wasn't happy about it — she wanted to stay at Blue Lake Hut, and I almost did too, but recent changes to DOC's pricing system meant my annual Backcountry Hut Pass didn't cover this hut. There was no Paywave out here and, since I didn't have any cash to pay the $20 bunk fee, we were going to walk up to Lake Constance and stay in our perfectly good tent.

My pack was too heavy to hang around explaining myself in the face of angry protests and tears, so I walked off, Mother of the Year, picking my way over an old avalanche path and hoping Emilie would follow me soon.

After a short, sharp climb that brought us into the rocky boulder fields surrounding Rotopōhueroa/Lake Constance, we were friends again. It's hard not to want to feel the comfort of your fellow human when you're taking in awesome scenery, painfully aware of being a tiny insignificant speck amongst a huge, expansive landscape.

Whereas Rotomairewhenua is soft and blue and beautiful, Rotopōhueroa is deep, dark and imposing, a giant amongst alpine lakes. Measuring some two kilometres long and up to 700 metres wide, the lake fills the post-glacial basin of the upper Sabine Valley almost all the way to the base of the rugged Waiau Pass.

Ahh, Waiau Pass. I'd been whispering its name in my head for days, tormenting myself with feelings of fear and anticipation.

Pushed up between the towering bulk of the Spenser Mountains and Mount Franklin, the ragged scree slopes of Waiau Pass link Nelson Lakes National Park with Canterbury's Lewis Pass. We had to cross it if we wanted to keep walking south.

Of course, I'd read blogs recounting tails of wicked weather and zero visibility, icy rockfaces and unstable scree slopes, which had forced many others to turn back. I read that one walker had fallen to his death somewhere around here.

My eyes lingered on the jutting grey fortress looming in the distance, a giant slab of mountain barring our passage. Somewhere amongst those countless spikes and spires was a point just marginally lower than the rest. I say marginally because, at 1870 metres, this alpine pass is the second-highest point on Te Araroa.

The crossing is described as 'suitable for experienced parties only', the track itself as 'rough and rocky', 'climbs and descends very steeply in places', 'long and exposed with little shelter'. To top it off, 'Weather conditions can deteriorate rapidly, and icy snow conditions can be experienced at any time of the year.' I hoped that by this time we could call ourselves experienced.

Once across the pass, we would follow the Waiau Uwha River downstream through a wide, grassy valley until we eventually linked up with the St James Walkway, 56 kilometres of relatively flat valley walking that would take us to the tiny settlement of Boyle Village and yet another box of oats, nuts, chocolate and couscous.

Once we get across, it's all easy walking, I told myself, visualising my strong legs picking up the pace on those flat grassy trails, Emilie happily trotting ahead or behind.

First, though, we needed to navigate the rockface that loomed beyond the end of this gigantic lake. The following morning, we'd be getting up at the crack of dawn to give ourselves enough time to skirt around the sheer bluffs and slippery slopes surrounding Lake Constance, enough time to walk right up to that jagged scar of track running diagonally up to the pass. And I'd be watching the weather like a hawk for even a whiff of ominous cloud, although we'd been on such a good run for the past week.

That evening, after I settled Emilie into her sleeping bag, I lay back and watched the sky turn from dark blue to purple and then to black. I closed my eyes and said a little prayer to Papatūānuku: Please protect us girls as we pass through one of the more wild and dangerous parts of your domain.

The morning came with a wisp of mist that swept over Lake Constance and disappeared high over the mountains, revealing a bluebird day.

Our early-morning start left us both a bit ragged. Emilie spilled her mug of hot chocolate on my sleeping mat and, in return, I burnt the porridge while dosing up on the jagged fumes of instant coffee.

But before long we were panting our way up the first scree slope above bluffs overlooking the lake, just as the sun emerged slowly above the dark ranges and turned the waters from black to brilliant blue.

Forced to focus on placing my feet securely on the narrow track, I was captivated by the vegetation — the shining white and yellow faces of mountain daisies, the pinkish white of tiny snowberries, and the fearsome speargrass with its huge yellow flower spike emerging from the centre of a dense rosette of needle-sharp spines. The steep descent to the lake head was fringed by more flowers. Large mountain daisies jostled with clumps of golden tussock as we followed the path's dusty zigzag down to the water's edge.

With the lake behind us, Waiau Pass looked higher than ever, rising almost vertically from its base to that imperceptible notch in the jagged ridgeline far above our heads.

There was no point in worrying about it now though. I fed Emilie a muesli bar and a mouthful of water and made sure my InReach satellite device was accessible, should I need it.

Just one bit at a time, slow and steady, using your hands and feet, I instructed Emilie, and off she went ahead of me, climbing the impossibly steep scree slope in the direction of the next orange marker.

I soon saw that she was a natural at scaling what, to me, felt like an impossible climb. She was skipping up ahead like a mountain goat as I stumbled and scrabbled with my heavy pack, feeling as though every step took me two steps back as the loose rock swilled underfoot. On one side, the ground dropped away while on the other loomed a vertical and unstable scree slope.

Soon I reached some larger rocks and felt like I was making progress. The grassy floor of the Upper Sabine Valley was far below us; the sun reflected off the surface of Lake Constance like a gigantic mirror, and before long we reached a rocky terrace where the path was firmer underfoot.

I was sweating and thirsty as I dropped my pack to swap my woollen beanie for a sunhat. Even though it was still early, the sun had already burned off the morning mist and taken the cold bite out of the air.

Emilie dropped her pack too, then we both watched in frozen horror as it toppled slowly and started to roll back down the slope. I put my hand out to stop her running after it, and by some miraculous stroke of luck, the pack's trajectory was offset by a rock. It wobbled onto its side and stopped rolling. Trembling, I retrieved it, and we resumed our climb up to the pass.

Once we were up there, the ground flattened and widened and we felt safe again. We shed our packs again to clamber up a rocky outcrop to a high point where we sat and absorbed the expansive views. Behind us, Lake Constance had diminished to a shiny smear and before us, sheer rock gave way to a deep valley with a silver sliver of river trickling through. Up there, rubbing shoulders with ancient giants, we paused to add two small pebbles to a large rock cairn that passing walkers had built upon this lookout point.

We did it. We made it up to Waiau Pass.

As we wandered on, a shower of insect confetti erupted from underfoot, hundreds of alpine grasshoppers in vivid shades of green and brown propelling themselves wildly forwards, sideways, any way to escape being squashed by our trail shoes. Even when the alpine scrub gave way to sheer, slaty, rock scree and the occasional lumpy vegetable sheep, there were still grasshoppers.

There was snow too, remnants of the winter cloak that once covered these mountains. We found a thick patch of it on the shady side of the pass and Emilie was in her element.

While she shaped handfuls of crunchy old snow into balls, I slathered peanut butter on our crackers, reflecting that this was possibly why we were going to win the award for slowest trail walkers ever.

We seemed to find an excuse to stop and gawk and play or take photos at every possible opportunity, but I don't think either of us would have wanted it any other way.

I didn't care about covering long distances or shirking on food supplies to save the grams. This journey wasn't about stamina or speed. It was about soaking up as much of Mother Nature's beauty and wonder as she was willing to share with us. As long as we were warm enough and our bellies were full of something, we were happy just being out there. And right then, building a snowman with my little daughter at some 1700 metres, surrounded by jagged mountain ranges, eating peanut butter crackers topped with squares of stale chocolate, there was no place in the world I would rather have been.

Twenty-seven kilometres from Lake Constance, we were back on flat ground again, stomping through the long grass beside the Waiau Uwha River with the dark blue peaks of the St James Range and Spenser Mountains reaching up to the sky on either side of us.

We were walking through the grassy high-country plains of the St James Conservation Area, a place that was once extensively grazed by sheep and cattle. But since the station was purchased by the New Zealand government in 2008, all that had kept the exotic grasses in check were flocks of equally exotic pests including Canada geese, rabbits, hares, deer and wild horses.

That's why the grass was up to Emilie's shoulders and, in the early morning, every slender blade was covered in a freezing dew that had already soaked through our trail shoes, socks and shorts and was trying to infiltrate our raincoats.

We were on our way to Anne Hut after a night of camping in the long grass beside the Waiau Uwha River. But I'd forgotten how the cool air from the mountain ranges that towered above us would roll down and settle on the valley floor overnight, covering everything in a thin white blanket of frost, so the biting cold took us by surprise.

It was the coldest morning we'd had so far, colder than Lake Constance or anywhere in the Richmond Range. Even the damp and misty Tararua Range hadn't bitten as cold as this. We stomped our feet and blew on our freezing fingers in the icy dawn. The sunlight that kissed the tops of the high hills was still an hour away from reaching us.

Even rugged up in long pants, merino hats, gloves and waterproof jackets to fend off the long wet grass, the first part of the day's walk was a traumatic affair with Emilie wailing dismally beside me.

Emilie wasn't interested in the history of this place. She didn't care that our taxes contributed to the $40 million drawn from the government's Nature Heritage Fund to pay for our public enjoyment of this special piece of high-country land.

She wasn't even fazed by the irony of this land being labelled a conservation area when in fact it seemed to be a safe haven for pests and predators, like the lithe-bodied stoat we'd seen zig-zagging through the grass earlier that morning, or the huge hare that lolloped ahead of us.

According to Emilie, long grass sucked, her feet were wet and she hated tramping.

I had a more pragmatic approach. Perhaps we'd been a little gung-ho in breaking camp before the sun had risen over the dark flanks of the surrounding mountains and absorbed the worst of the moisture; perhaps I should have insisted she wore her waterproof over-trousers as well as a rain jacket to shield her from the early morning dew. Perhaps these tracks just weren't made with 120-centimetre-tall people in mind.

Once upon a time, adventurers crossing the Waiau Pass would stumble down the mountain to find themselves up against the fence posts and wires of private property spanning a whopping 78,196 hectares. They'd need to ask the landowner for permission to walk through the land and access the wild, mountainous country beyond, including gems like Rotomairewhenua and Rotopōhueroa.

Now, trampers and trail walkers can cross the main divide and link up with the iconic 66-kilometre St James Walkway as it meanders through pastoral land, beech forest and sub-alpine regions into the Lewis Pass area in the northernmost reaches of the Canterbury region.

The scenery was such a contrast to the alpine wonderland we'd travelled through only a few days ago. The mountain daisies and fragile herbs had been replaced by exotic grasses and weeds, purple foxglove, dandelions and flowers that would have been more at home in a cottage garden.

Once cropped short by sheep and cattle, these forgotten pastures now flourished mostly unchecked, and it was easy to see how the dense, thick mats of exotic grass smothered and outcompeted our native plants.

It made me worry that out there, in the relative isolation of our backcountry, nature was fighting a losing battle.

With the sun spreading across the wide valley floor, our socks were drying out, our raincoats had been stuffed in our packs and we were making good pace across the flat ground.

As my legs powered along the trail, my body eased into autopilot and my mind began to wander. The swaying grass heads reminded me of our block in Tasmania. Usually, we had let the grass grow almost to knee height before the farmer next door would come with his tractor and turn it into golden hay bales. He'd take a few for his troubles, and we'd keep a few to store in the barn.

Emilie spotted the wild horses before I did, a small herd with shaggy manes and tails grazing on the far side of the valley. I wished they were closer so we could admire their lithe bodies and elegantly curved necks, gently flared nostrils and dark, intelligent eyes.

I'd had a horse on that block. A 14-hand grey pony, to be precise, and her name was Tequila.

She looks like she's had too much of it! the instructor at my pony club exclaimed when I announced my horse's name, perched high on her back and beaming with pride. I had no idea what it even meant, just that it sounded pretty.

Tequila was my childhood dream come true, a gentle old grey mare. She was so gentle I could ride her bareback, and we would disappear together for hours on long rides through the nearby bush, following old four-wheel-drive tracks and trails through the eucalypt forest.

I loved lying on her wide, flat back as she carried me along, leaning forwards to pat her neck as she wandered beneath the trees. I would imagine myself as a wild bush girl with only my horse for company, travelling to faraway lands.

One time, Tequila startled me out of my reverie by stumbling into a rabbit hole, sidestepping with shock before coming to a standstill as I slid helplessly off her back and hung ungracefully under her thick neck. A less tolerant horse would have shaken me off and bolted, but old Tequila just stood there blinking in the sunshine, her lower lip drooping in the way that had prompted the pony club instructor to suggest she'd had too much to drink. She waited patiently until I'd installed myself on her back again, and off we went.

She was my pride and joy and my best friend, through the good times and the bad. I wept into her neck over some childhood hurts, her mellow, horsey scent soothing my sobs.

I'm not sure what happened to Tequila in the end. After my mother left, my father got rid of our various pets and animals and I suppose Tequila found a new home, hopefully with another family and a child who loved her as much as I did.

Memory is such an unreliable witness. I screwed up my face and tried to conjure up the images, wondering why some scenes were so clear while others remained a murky blur at the edge of my subconscious. I can almost smell the warm, horsey scent of Tequila's neck, feel the ropey strands of her mane, yet I can't place my mother's face in that house, at that time. Even as a nine-year-old child, obsessed with my pony, was I so oblivious of her distress, or, like so much else, did I just block it out in order to survive?

I don't even remember why I didn't join my mother and brother the day they left, failing to register my mother's fear and apprehension as we played the game of peeking through the curtains waiting for my father to get home, before piling into the old van and hitting the accelerator.

Instead, I stood beside my father and watched them disappear over the hump at the end of the driveway, my anger and disbelief fading into something beyond numbness. Silence settled over the two-storey brick and batten house my parents had built with their own hands.

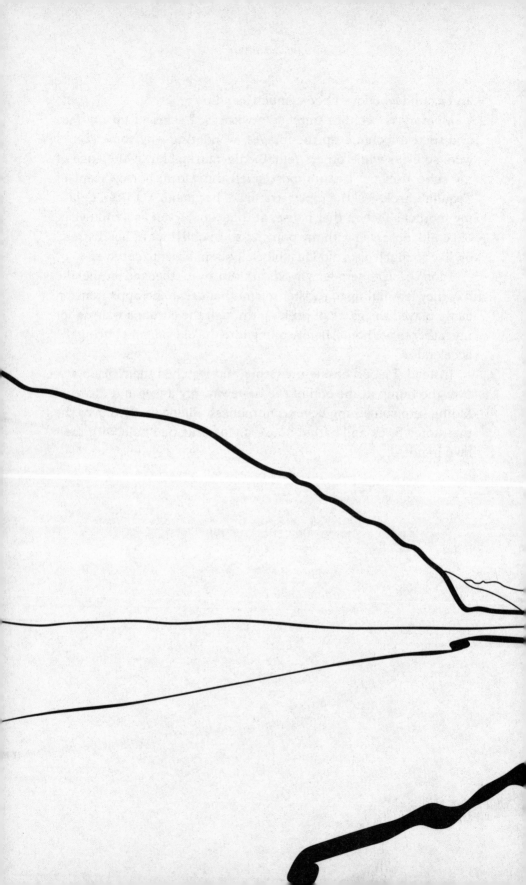

Chapter 10

Hope River

Te Araroa
Day 76

I'M LYING NAKED IN THE sunshine with one foot dangling in the river, just me and Emilie and the cow. The big smooth rock underneath me is cupped like an armchair, holding me up in its dark embrace.

The river is surprisingly warm, at least after the icy waters of the St James and Nelson Lakes regions. I suppose it has risen from the warmer hills of the West Coast and taken its time to wind down the valley to where we are now.

Emilie is naked too; she was happily submerged in a pool formed by huge river rocks until she spotted our new neighbour. Now, she's not so sure. It's hard to feel completely comfortable when an animal of that size is nearby.

The cow is indifferent. She's enjoying cropping the lush grass on the riverbank in the afternoon sun. Her pendulous udder swings under her round, red and white flanks. She seems to be on the opposite side of the river to all the other cows, but that doesn't seem to faze her as she munches her way towards us.

It's probably having a baby and wants some peace and quiet, Emilie decides, noting the rounded belly. I think she just looks like a big fat cow, and the farmer should fence their bloody stock out of the river so I can fill my drink bottle.

I'm not in the best mood, although it's hard to say why as I lie here by the river with the warm sun kissing my bare skin. We've just spent two nights at Boyle Village with a side trip into the spa resort town of Hanmer Springs to indulge our bodies in the hot pools, much to Emilie's delight. We're both still clean, our clothes have been washed and I've tried to restore nutritional balance by feeding us both up on broccoli and blueberries, in between the obligatory pies and ice cream.

But right now, my head hurts, I can feel a cold sore burning its way through my lower lip, and my back and legs are protesting from the weight of yet another resupplied food bag. If only I could tame the cow to carry our packs, then we could just get on and enjoy walking this stupid trail.

Dark, dark and darkness. I'm sick of myself, sick of my weak body and sick of these miserable thoughts. Why can't I just be happy, excited, on an adventure without a care in the world?

The group of 20-something-year-olds we shared the Boyle Village Education Centre bunkrooms with the previous night seemed enthusiastic about life. I wish I could drill open my head, cut out the sections of trauma-damaged brain, insert a big dose of serotonin and dopamine and all the other happy chemicals and just get on with things. Instead, I feel like a short, chubby, grumpy and unfriendly old woman who has no place amidst these taller, fitter, younger trail walkers.

I don't know where this bad mood has come from. It just blew in, like a nor'westerly wind, filling my head with a kind of nervous agitation. I'm probably getting my period, if my slightly swollen belly and tender breasts are anything to go by. Maybe something has triggered my PTSD and I'm recovering from another dirty dose of adrenaline and cortisol as the dark clouds of depression are closing in.

I'd stopped taking the antidepressants that I'd worked so hard to score all the way back in Palmerston North, partly because my mood had flattened off, leaving me numb, and I wanted to give myself another chance to feel my feelings.

I've always been sceptical of the pharmacotherapy revolution's promise that we can tame the spectre of trauma with a simple pill. My therapist said as much himself, although he was quick to remind me that antidepressant medication has its time and place. Feeling is healing, he would tell me. Repression is depression. However, there's no magic pill or quick fix to help the body and the mind heal from trauma.

Strategies such as psychotherapy (talking therapy) can help

people to acknowledge what's happened to them so they can take care of the wounds they're carrying inside. But I've found it very hard to talk about childhood experiences that I can barely remember, especially when my body seems so reluctant to let them go. Other practices such as yoga and mindfulness help people reconnect with their bodies and identify the physical sensations they feel inside. I suppose these techniques help people to manage the overwhelming feelings of pain, rage, sadness and shame that so frequently come crashing over them like waves on a stormy shore.

For many survivors of trauma, the healing process is a long and winding trail, without any track markers to show if you're going the right way. Even with the most talented of therapists, there's no set guidebook to help you heal from trauma. Everyone must walk their own path, in their own time, their own way.

After the dizzying heights of Waiau Pass and the wildness of the Richmond Range, the wide, calm valley flats of the St James and now the Hope River felt like a bit of a comedown. Since I no longer had to pay such intense attention to where I put my feet, my brain had resumed its restless search through my memory warehouse, and I guess it had found a few skeletons.

Maybe another dip in the river would help shake things up. I slide off my rock, breathe in, breathe out, squat down until my shoulders are completely underwater. Now it's cold, so cold, but after the initial shock it feels amazing.

I stand up, feeling the familiar warm tingle spreading through me. That's better. That will keep the ghosts at bay.

After washing the mud and dried blood from sandfly bites from our legs, I fill our water bottles and we wander back up to the little green shelter where we're sleeping tonight.

The younger trail walkers are long gone, leaving us in the dust, and we have Hope Halfway Hut all to ourselves.

Emilie is a burst of energy, skipping around in her matching pink thermals, demanding instant chocolate mousse for dessert. Why not? Let's treat ourselves. It saves me having to carry it any further.

Two days later, we walked through an impressive grove of red beech on the way to the wide valley of the Hurunui River. The sun shining through the canopy of the towering beech trees onto the carpet of green moss below should have been pretty, but my knees and shoulders hurt, and I just wanted out of this goddamned forest.

I'd like to say my mood had improved as we moved, but I'd be lying. There had been a dark cloud around me ever since Boyle Village and I struggled to understand why. But I knew there was no point trying to engage in cognitive thought, because you can't think your way out of trauma. Instead, I needed to allow myself to feel, to experience these intense emotions and let them out. Bottling them up deep inside was only making me sick, just like before Te Araroa, when professional burnout had thrown fuel on the ever-simmering embers of my fragile mental health and my body and brain had combusted in a fiery flare-up.

Perhaps Te Araroa was an analogy for our long walk through life. For some, their packs were light, their legs were long, and they seemed to cover ground with ease. For others, their emotional burden was so heavy it periodically brought them to their knees, and so there I was, grovelling in the leaf litter with the growing realisation that I couldn't do this any longer.

I'd lived with the debilitating symptoms of chronic depression and complex post-traumatic stress disorder for over 20 years, but only recently, with the help of my state-funded therapist, had I been able to actually put a name to what I was experiencing.

After so many years of unexplained symptoms, I was both relieved and devastated to receive a mental health diagnosis of not just one but two conditions.

It meant that I wasn't simply a crazy, sad, bad, angry human being, but one suffering from mental health disorders that warped my thoughts and hijacked my feelings. It was helpful to name these conditions, my therapist said, because then I could learn about them and take steps to manage them, so they no longer ruled my life — just like someone who was diagnosed with diabetes or high blood pressure.

I learned that trauma leaves both emotional and physical

imprints on the body, even years after the traumatic events had passed; that to protect me from my trauma, my sympathetic nervous system had automatically activated my body's fight, flight or freeze response. But because the traumatic events had been too overwhelming, too much, or had gone on for too long, my brain was now stuck in high alert, forever sending out panic signals long after the threat had passed. It was like a tired old soldier left behind at the sentry post, on guard for so long that he no longer remembered how to stand down.

So, what do I have to do to make it stop? When do I get better again? I beseeched my therapist.

His face grew solemn as he repeated what I imagine he must tell so many people. *There is medication you can take to help counter the depressive symptoms, but when it comes to trauma, it's a grey area. Your brain may be permanently damaged. What we can do here is try to rewire your neural pathways and try to access the emotions that you've buried deep inside of you, to help your brain feel safe again.*

What the hell would I want to do that for? Those emotions are tied to memories I can't even remember. You don't understand how hard I've worked to forget!

I guess no one said that the healing process would be easy or feel good. It was just something I needed to endure if I wanted to find peace within myself. So I kept on walking, with Emilie chattering away a few paces behind me, even though I would have preferred to just flop down under one of those giant beech trees and cry myself to sleep.

Eventually, we left the shade of the beech forest for the wide, sunny grasslands of the Hurunui River valley. This long, straight valley followed the line of the Hope Fault all the way from Lake Sumner, whose far shores we'd skirted earlier in the day, to Harper Pass at the base of the Southern Alps.

We took a break to swim in the Hurunui River, trying to ignore the patches of dried cow shit slopped over the rocks beside the crystal-blue water. It was cold, bitingly cold, eating straight through my skin and into my bones.

Emilie wanted to stay and play beside the water, but I was hungry and sore, and a tugging sensation in my lower belly reminded me that I needed to change my moon cup before blood started running down my legs. I didn't want to dig a hole and squat in the grass to empty its contents. Instead, I badly wanted to get to the hut, which apparently was less than two kilometres away, shed my pack, use the long drop, wash my hands and knickers in the sink then go and lie down. Worse still, I'd lost my pee-rag, a little square of bright orange microfibre cloth that I used to keep myself relatively clean and dry. Out in the bush, one of the few things that sets a rich person apart from a poor one was several square centimetres of fabric, and I was stewing about losing mine.

Come on, Emilie, let's go.

No, I want to stay here.

But Mummy needs to get to the hut. My back is really sore.

I want to play here.

Fine, I'm going. Just follow the orange markers until you find the hut.

Not the best parenting, leaving your seven-year-old child beside a swiftly flowing river and storming off across the narrow swing bridge.

After 100 metres, having blown off a bit of steam, I stopped.

Breathe.

I'd forgotten to breathe.

Stop being an arsehole.

I wasn't an arsehole. I was just . . . a tired mother with an empty bucket and no pee-rag.

The path beneath my feet was soft and spongy with red and brown beech leaves and framed by bright moss-covered rocks. The beech trees were smaller here, a dense canopy with dappled sunlight shining through. I stood quietly, breathing with the forest and watching a tiny black-and-white tomtit, which was watching me back. I could hear the gentle swaying of the wind in the tall branches, the cheeping of little forest birds and the distant melody of the river. Sucking in another deep, calming breath, I inhaled the sweet, earthy aroma of the beech forest. I am here. I am safe.

In a moment, I'd go back and get Emilie. Apologise. Talk to her gently. Promise her a game of cards and a biscuit at the hut. Just let me catch my breath.

A movement behind startled me, but it was just Emilie, wandering along the path with hiking poles swinging in her hands. She was in no great rush to catch me up, my calm, peaceful, strong-willed little girl. Soon she was beside me.

Oooh Mummy look! A tomtit!

It was 1.3 kilometres and a climb of some 60 metres away from the river flats and to the terrace where Hurunui Hut was supposedly waiting quietly to welcome us.

At two steps per metre, or maybe even three at our slow, shuffling gait, 1.3 kilometres was perhaps 2600 steps. After a 16-kilometre day, Emilie was rambling along unhurriedly while I was staggering like an overweight tortoise as my huge pack crushed me to the ground. Damn, why was this goddamned pack still feeling so goddamned heavy?

We'd resupplied at Boyle Village two days earlier with another heavy sack of food. In it was six days' worth of couscous, a block of cheese, a jar of peanut butter and another of honey, two boxes of Vita-Weat crackers, gingernut biscuits and a big bag of porridge oats cut with dried sultanas and coconut. I'd also bought fresh broccoli and carrots from the store in Hanmer Springs and an extra canister of gas for our small stove.

I no longer felt in nutritional deficit as I had at Mount Angelus, but the weight was insane, and it wasn't working. Once we made it out of that section, I'd need to rethink our food supplies. Either that, or we'd have to walk faster, instead of at the pace of a seven-year-old, I thought to myself. I shot a sideways glance at Emilie, who was digging in her pockets for another Fruit Burst, her little lips moving soundlessly as she told herself a Bush Baby story.

After maybe 2000 more steps, my resolve was crumbling. I realised I was staring wildly through the trees and willing the hut to appear — the slope of a roofline, the loo, anything, just please let me stop walking.

I pulled myself together. Huts don't like desperation. I swear they get up off their piles and scuttle away through the trees when they sense a desperate tramper drawing near.

And you know what? I came round a corner and there it was . . . squatting in a grassy clearing, the red and green outline of Hurunui Hut.

Over the next couple of days, we wandered further up the Hurunui River, and I realised I was thinking more about my father. Maybe the horses on the St James Walkway led me there. Maybe that was the reason behind my dark mood on the track to Hurunui Hut.

As a little girl, I tried to idolise my guitar-playing, folk-song-singing father with his talented hands and dark humour. I remember how those hands created child-sized canoes for my brother and me by planing strips off an old wooden door. They'd also made delicate mechanisms for handmade wooden trucks, excavators and front-end loaders.

You don't get much thanks for being a parent. After the back-breaking task of building a house, I imagine he also dug the post holes and strung the fencing wire for the field my pony lived in and built the huge barn that held our hay.

I remember how those fingers plucked the sweetest chords out of a steel-stringed guitar, and his voice — husky, mellow, evenly toned — rose and fell as he sang the songs that later influenced my own musical tastes. 'So Long Marianne', 'Bird on a Wire', songs by Leonard Cohen, Simon & Garfunkel, Joan Baez, Eric Clapton and more.

Eventually, he gave up on guitar-playing and carpentry and focused on his drinking. With my mother gone, I seemed to bear the brunt of his bad moods.

Cut it out, you filthy little whore, he raged as my head spun with the effort of standing upright.

The cheese sandwich and apple I'd inhaled only moments earlier now decorated the toilet bowl, a kaleidoscope of reddish green hunks of apple skin standing out amongst the pale yellow of the masticated bread like flower petals in a puddle, all coated in swirls of mucus.

I'm 13 years old and getting really good at this bulimia thing.

My head is swimming but my stomach is clear, and now my father's abuse comes as a thick dark cloud around my ears, black and blue like day-old bruises.

He's onto his third glass of cask wine, and the bathroom backs onto the lounge. I hold down the flush button as long as I can to drown out his voice then escape out the back door, over the fence to Gerry's house.

Anger churns in my guts, anger, rage and hate, spurred on by fear. The panic button has been activated, and my ears are thick with the white noise of my heartbeat. How I hate him, hate him so much. I wish to return home and find him dead, choked to death on a glass of that cheap red wine. If only I had the guts (and the physical strength), I could fight him, push him down, show him what it's like to be taunted and humiliated, maybe shove the remnants of the bloated goon bag down his throat and watch him asphyxiate slowly.

These thoughts energise me as I grit my teeth and storm through the streets. Gerry's house is empty; the gang must be at the skate park. I should find them. Maybe there'd be a joint going round, or a beer stolen from Gerry's mum's fridge, or at least a cigarette, because I was all out of mine.

Only a day earlier, Gerry and I had succeeded in getting some bloke to buy us a pack of smokes — a pack of Peter Jackson 20s for five dollars. We'd loitered outside the dairy for over half an hour, our purple bank note turned down by a couple of potential punters, before achieving success. Half a pack of cigarettes had helped me through a bad day at school — the mean girls had bummed a couple of durries then left me alone while they made someone else's life hell for a change.

I caught the bus to school from the bottom of our street, an early-morning bus crammed with eastern-suburb school kids in different-coloured uniforms. Almost always, taking over the back seats, would be this huge, ugly bitch and her cronies who cat-called me as soon as I stepped onto the bus, trying to hide under my strands of pink-and-red-dyed hair. She'd busted me smoking behind the bus stop near our high school one afternoon and now we held an uneasy truce at the cost of a few cigarettes.

Right now, I need more than a smoke. The adrenaline that's carried me this far is wearing off and I feel lonely and desperate. Big feelings, scary, overwhelming, soul-crushing feelings, are circling and threatening to overwhelm me. All that's left is the burning shame of being an unloved child, a horrible, worthless, defective creature cast out by her parents and society.

I prefer to harness the red-hot energy of my anger to get me through the day, otherwise I know where this is going to take me . . . my forearms still sting from the shallow red lines I'd drawn in blood late the previous night. When you're engulfed with this kind of pain, your mind turns to thoughts of escape by death. The best way to self-soothe is to take your artist's tools to the canvas of your body, transforming the mental anguish into physical pain that will eventually soothe and subside. I was becoming an expert in these tricks, my artwork decorating my upper arms and legs, my equipment a simple steel blade painstakingly hacked out of a cheap Bic razor.

Only a week earlier, I had locked myself in the bathroom late at night, desperate to put an end to myself, and tried to write an angry letter to my mother in my own blood to tell her all the reasons I was going to kill myself and why I hated her for leaving me behind. While it seems to work well in movies, blood is not really a great medium for written communication, so I used a pen, defiantly signing off with a red smear. My letter complete, I ran a bath, weeping uncontrollably, praying to have the courage to press down hard on my wrists with my makeshift razor blade. Just then, my father arrived home from the pub with what clearly sounded like female company, and thumped on the bathroom door yelling, *Hurry up and get to bed*. It was a rude interruption to my sad suicidal ritual, and I hurriedly cleaned up any blood smears and slunk into my bedroom to cry myself to sleep.

I can see the outline of dark figures twisting and writhing, hear the crack and snap of boards on concrete. The boys are at the skate park. Jake is passing a joint around, rolled from his father's stash, and I slump down beside him and inhale gratefully. It's cut with tobacco and tastes like shit, but as the haze settles over me, the demons in my head retreat behind a cloud of smoke.

It's hard to reconcile these scenes with my overall memory of childhood. It was supposed to be a happy childhood — home-schooled, travelling Australia in a bus, our block, exploring the bush and playing with my older brother. It sounds idyllic, wild and free.

But the details are sketchy. Most of the time my brain refuses to recall much more than a random collage of images. Memories are reduced to a handful of scenes, sharpened by old family photos.

My body told me something else. My gut was heavy, and my throat closed over when I tried to think back on my early years. There was this sensation at the base of my spine as though a fist was clenched tight around my spinal column, squeezing my ribs.

I could feel an inner battle heating up as my body and brain fought one another for control. Don't think about it, don't go there. There's nothing there to remember. But my body hurt and I could feel that familiar, dirty, tingling sensation rising up from my core. Soon, it would paralyse me completely and cease all cognitive thought, enveloping me in a greasy, sickening static of grey noise and inertia.

Now, in this valley, I reminded myself to keep breathing as I focused my attention on my feet. The track was climbing steadily across grassy sections and through beech forest, going around gorges to avoid crossing the river as we followed it to its birthplace at the base of Harper Pass.

My strong thigh muscles bunched and released, channelling movement from my feet, up my calves and deep into my glutes. My arms and legs were tanned from many weeks spent outdoors. I was strong, I was carrying my heavy load up the mountain, my breath was flowing through me all the way to my feet. The ground was reaching up to hold me, a solid, reliable base to absorb all of my uncertainty.

The runty beech trees were being replaced with reddish orange Dracophyllum, tree daisies and leathery, dark green flax. We were getting close to the little orange shelter of Harper Pass Bivvy on the north-eastern fringes of the Southern Alps.

I tried again, fishing inside myself for clues.

Finally, my body released something else from the mist of my memory.

I'm still 13, living in Tasmania with my dad in that shitty red-brick rental with no garden and no trees. I'm in my room when the acrid smell of smoke filters down the corridor. Something is burning. My father is yelling. It's my fault because I'd left the kettle on the stove and all the water had evaporated. The harsh smell was the metal burning on the bottom of the kettle.

You might not think that the destruction of a shitty, second-hand, stovetop kettle is a big deal, but it was enough to make my old man flip his lid. He's yelling at me, and I feel two foot tall. My shell-shocked teenage brain responds with dizzying speed. Fear, shame and humiliation are transformed into anger of my own and I yell back at him, a dangerous move with potentially deadly consequences, but I don't care. I'm flooded with my own rage.

He lunges at me, but he's already half-cut on that revolting cask wine, and I'm out the door in my bare feet, leaping down the front steps and out onto the street.

I'm not safe yet because he's coming after me with terrifying speed, puffing and blowing like an angry bear. I turn and run as fast as I can. For a moment he's gaining on me, but I can go for longer, even with my cut-up feet.

I run all the way down the street, across the park, into a cul de sac and down a laneway until I'm in a part of our neighbourhood I've never been to before. I keep running until I find a payphone and I call the police . . .

An errant tree root wrapped around my foot and I counter-balanced, trying to shake myself free of this mental quicksand. I paused with my heavy pack and waited for Emilie to catch up, an opportunity to swoop her up in a bear hug and feather her with kisses.

Emilie, Emilie, a manifestation of love and joy. May you never experience the stinging shame of being an unloved child. A kiss for Emilie and one each for the many iterations of my child-selves, all beautiful girls who deserved to be loved.

I'm capable, most days, of gracefully bowing my head when these internal storms rage through me, I have the experience and knowledge that no matter how terrifying and destructive these feelings may be, if I just sit still and do nothing, eventually they will pass. The trick is to just stay still and keep breathing, resist the overwhelming urge to get caught up in this twisted energy. Let it burn through you and fade away.

One of the most beautiful things about walking Te Araroa is that you get to wander through an ever-evolving panorama of New Zealand scenery, watching the landscape change slowly before your eyes.

Over the past few days, we've gradually emerged from the towering forest of mature red beech and into the sub-alpine, following the Hurunui River all the way to its birthplace at the base of the Harper Pass.

The drier forests of the east were transforming into the lush jungle of the west, as mountain toatoa, lancewood, broadleaf and mountain ribbonwood replaced beech trees. The riverbanks were thick with harakeke, moss and ferns with the occasional tree daisy and Dracophyllum popping through.

Soon we'd climb up and over the modest 962-metre pass through the mighty Southern Alps and down onto the West Coast, following the course of another majestic river as it meandered out to the Tasman Sea.

Our diversion would only be brief, as Te Araroa soon bounces east again over Goat Pass, just long enough to enjoy some lush West Coast jungle with huge tree ferns popping out of a thick canopy tinged red with flowering rātā.

First, we spent the night in the delightful orange shelter of Harper Pass Bivvy, its slightly tilted flooring making us feel like we could fall off its narrow bunks and roll right out the door.

Emilie tried to claim the lower bunk, but I told her she was dreaming. I may be her personal slave, pack mule, chef, entertainer and everything else, but no way was she taking the bottom bunk. Also, there was no way I could even fit on the top bunk, wedged up there barely a foot from the ceiling.

She griped and moaned for a while, but I stood firm. It was the top bunk or she could set up her sleeping mat on the sloping floor.

She abandoned the fight and stormed down to the creek after having attempted to slam the hut door on me. I say attempted because the heavy old door didn't move fast on its rusted hinges; it just creaked a bit and swung open again.

A wave of tiredness crashed over me, sucking me down into another patch of mental quicksand. I was tired, not just of this walk, my pack or my aching body — tired of seven and a half years of single parenting an awesome yet sometimes exhausting little human. Sometimes it felt like a whole lot of work for not much thanks, with no one to even offer you the best bunk.

And the expectations. Where's my breakfast, why haven't you set up my bed, where are my pants, can you tell me a story?

What is this, an all-expenses paid, fully guided tour of New Zealand? One which is clearly not living up to her expectations, a fact of which she isn't shy to remind me.

My storytelling powers have taken a dive on this section, possibly due to my dark mood and the fact I've run out of things to say.

For example, today she'd told me three stories and I didn't even tell her one.

I did try to talk to her about the birds that we were seeing, while she tried to talk to me about Our Generation dolls. At one stage, hot and frustrated, I explained to her that I wasn't really interested in hearing about dolls.

Well, I don't care about your stupid birds! she retorted, stomping off in front me.

So much for instilling a love of nature in our tamariki, future guardians of the planet.

Anyway. I took a deep breath and tried to be the adult in this child-sized room. Maybe a nice hot cup of tea and five minutes peace would help me feel better. But to do that, I needed to venture down to the creek to fill the pot with water and risk being spotted by an angry forest nymph.

I peeked out and saw her, and my heart melted.

She'd stripped off her clothes and was lying belly down on a rock in the sunshine, messy plaits dangling in the water.

Then she stepped into her paddling pool to submerge herself in the clear water before returning to the warm rock. Her little lips were moving all the time, although the sound of the water running over rocks drowned out any sound.

She skipped over to me, wanting her plastic dinner bowl so she could float it in the rock pool. She was a forest mermaid who lived on an island in the middle of this stream and was gathering her hoard of treasure and jewels. All bad vibes had been forgotten as she absorbed herself in her play.

I boiled water and made tea, then installed myself on a flat rock beside the river where tiny native bluebells were shimmering in the sun. Mount Drake towered above us with wisps of cloud moving rapidly over his head. It was surreal to think that we were going to walk through the Southern Alps the following day, crossing Harper Pass to the West Coast and the birthplace of the mighty Taramakau River.

Emilie came over to tell me she was actually a rare and endangered mountain stone mermaid, and I needed to pretend that I was a weary old explorer.

That I can do, my dear.

She asked if I could share my crackers and peanut butter, so I fed her some, although she told me she'd prefer Nutella.

Given that the sweet little bivvy was perched on a precarious angle and its tilted floor meant I'd probably roll straight off the narrow bunk I'd fought so hard for, I briefly toyed with the idea of setting up the tent on a flattish spot just across the stream, but I simply couldn't be bothered. So, much to Emilie's delight, we pulled the hut mattresses off the bunks and arranged them on the floor. Why hadn't I thought of that in the first place, instead of trying to fight her for the best bunk?

Hours after falling asleep, I awoke with a gasp from a bad dream. I crawled out of the tiny bivvy to pee in the cold night air, squatted, and scanned the dark ridges and lumps of the horizon for any signs of life.

Apart from the silver shimmer of starlight reflecting off the rocks, there was nothing there, nothing to hurt me. Yet my heart was still hammering in my chest.

The night was still, apart from the slightest breeze whispering through the clumps of tussock and rattling the spiky leaves of the tree daisies around our bivvy. The cold pricked at my skin, goosebumps dimpling my thighs.

Once back inside the shelter of the bivvy, I rearranged my sleeping bag, snuggling deep into the warm down.

I was tired but I couldn't sleep. My mind, restless, wandered and roamed. Back to the evening of my thirteenth birthday.

When the police car arrived, they didn't take me home to my father as I had feared they might. Instead, they took me to some big, old house on the city fringe where I stayed with some lady and a bunch of other kids for three days until my dad came to pick me up.

I screwed up my face, but I couldn't remember anything more, nothing about the kids or the lady or even the house — just a deep sensation of sadness, loneliness, guilt and shame.

What had happened to my father after the police dropped me off? Why hadn't he come to pick me up? Was he still angry at me about the kettle?

As much as I hated him for his harsh words and feared his quick temper, I also wanted very much for my father to love me and be proud of me, as I saw the fathers of some of my friends do. I was trapped and conflicted by my anger towards him and my desire to be loved by him. And it wasn't as though I could just get out my mobile phone, call an Uber and go stay in a hotel. There was nobody to turn to and no place to hide. I was completely and utterly dependent on my father, and it scared me.

I didn't understand his dark moods and terrifying rages. I felt helpless and incompetent because nothing I said or did or achieved seemed to please him.

Maybe part of me thought that if I stayed with him after my mother left, then I would somehow take her place and be the sole recipient of his love and attention. Instead, all I got from him was his rage and discontent.

How does a child cope with feeling chronically afraid and rejected by their only caregiver? What can you do with all that pain and hurt and the feeling that, no matter what you do, you're simply not good enough, unworthy of being loved? Such huge feelings must go somewhere.

Simply by observing him, my father taught me how to transform my pain into rage. For many years, my anger served me well, a powerful driving force propelling me through life. Then it faded into a terrible paralysing numbness, as though I were a ghost simply masquerading as a human being.

But enough is enough because I can't live like this anymore. Curled up on my side with Emilie's bum pressed against my belly, I wept silent tears into my sleeping bag.

Poor little me, and my poor old dad.

I confronted him about the kettle incident later in life. He said when the police came round he'd been in a really bad way.

They'd tackled him to the ground before taking him to the psychiatric ward at the hospital, where'd he'd spent a few days sobering up before being released and coming to get me.

I felt really sorry for him then, sorry for my thirteen-year-old self, sorry for the whole darn mess we'd ended up in.

There was a rustle in the undergrowth, and it sounded big. My heart had already bolted into my throat before my rational brain took over, reminding me there were no snakes in New Zealand, no bears or wolves — at the most you might stumble across an angry possum or a rutting stag. But then the harakeke bush opened and gave birth to a weka, and I couldn't help but laugh.

He peered around, his stump of tail working up and down, looking for all the world like a little bush chicken. These large flightless birds have a famously feisty and curious personality that often brings them into contact with humans, but I wasn't expecting to see one up here, at over 900 metres elevation on the way up Harper Pass.

The weka clearly wasn't expecting to see me either, but he didn't seem too worried about it. He stretched his stumpy wings and scratched nonchalantly at the ground, angling his handsome brown head to fix me with one beady red eye. Emilie stomped up to join me and we stood still and watched until he melted back into the undergrowth.

I've always been enchanted by encounters with wild creatures. Growing up in Australia I had many opportunities to share a magic moment with its raucous birdlife, charming marsupials and myriad frogs and lizards. I was, however, terrified of the huge hairy spiders that lurked in cracks and crevices, their long legs capable of propelling them in any direction, including towards me. When I first returned to New Zealand, I found the relative quietness of the bush somewhat disconcerting and yearned for the familiar sights and sounds of my childhood.

The encounter with the weka brought back memories of camping in Wilsons Promontory, a national park that spans a large coastal wilderness area along the southernmost part of the Australian mainland. Colourful flocks of parakeets swarmed the trees around our campsite and huge monitor lizards basked in the heat of the afternoon sun. But the most memorable was the wombat. He appeared at dusk when the deep blue of the sky was fading into pale pink and orange hues, that magical hour when the creatures of the night began to stir.

Looking for all the world like a cross between a little bear and a giant hamster, he emerged from the dark smear of bush and waddled across the grass with the air of a busy old man, pausing here and there to nibble on choice shoots of greenery.

I was fascinated and took a step closer for a better look, moving slowly and quietly like I'd been taught to move around wild animals. But the wombat didn't seem to care; he was deeply absorbed in his feeding and oblivious to the small girl standing beside him. I can even remember the sensation of the coarse hairs on his back under my palm, for my five-year-old self couldn't resist reaching out to stroke him, ever so softly.

How I wished I could join him on his evening ramble, greeting all the wild creatures of the night as they emerged from their slumber, until dawn peeped over the horizon, and we would return to his burrow to curl up together and sleep. Maybe he had a mate and baby wombats at home, and I could help raise them, keeping them warm while their parents went out to feed.

Somewhere I have a photo of myself aged two, brown and naked amidst a litter of newborn puppies. My mother says she ran all over the house searching for me after discovering my room empty and rumpled bedclothes, only to eventually find me curled up in the barn with our dog.

When we first came to Australia, we lived out in the whops of central Queensland in the Glenwood house my parents built with their sweat and tears. Our blue heeler, Penny, watched diligently over my brother and me, once killing a huge snake that had crawled into the shade of the concrete slab under the house where we were playing. In typical Queensland style, the house was raised off the ground on stilts, a design engineered to counter extreme weather conditions, floods and infestation by the myriad pests, which, given the opportunity, would chomp their way through wooden weatherboards.

When the heat of the day drove us from the baked brown grounds, we would seek respite on the cool of the concrete, and the snake sought respite there too. Quick as a flash, Penny leapt on the snake and broke its back, her jaws clamped on the thick coil of muscle behind its head. I don't remember what happened to Penny either, loyal companion that she was.

At some stage, we sold that house and moved to the cooler climate of Tasmania. My parents bought a Toyota Coaster bus, which my father converted into a campervan, using his impressive self-taught carpentry skills to fashion bunk beds for my brother and me, as well as a double bed that transformed into a dining table with booth seats.

For over a year we lived a nomadic lifestyle, travelling all over Australia in our bus, home-schooled by our parents with the bush as our teacher and playground. Without the pressures of building a house or running a household, my parents seemed happier too. With bikes on the back and two Canadian canoes strapped to the top, that big white bus felt like a palace, at least to us kids.

My parents had bought our home on wheels with the proceeds of another house they had built on the banks of the River Derwent in a place called Old Beach, some 35 kilometres from Hobart.

Rising in Tasmania's Central Highlands at Lake St Clair, the Derwent descended more than 700 metres over some 200 kilometres, flowing through Hobart before making its way past the back of our house on its way to the Tasman Sea. By then, its dark waters were slow and sleepy, and my brother and I would play in it with my dad's homemade canoes, much to the horror of our neighbours, who apparently came running over to our house to alert my parents that two little kids were adrift, alone, on the river.

Once upon a time, the banks of the River Derwent were covered in thick native bush and occupied by the indigenous Palawa people, who gave it the name timtumili minanya. When we lived there, before the housing boom, remnants of that native bush were only a block or two away, offering an easy-to-access playground that my brother and I would bike or walk to with another dog, Jessie, in tow.

Maybe that's why I loved being out amongst the mountains, despite the discomfort of my heavy pack and dirty clothes. It didn't feel foreign or alien to me at all — in fact it was quite the opposite: I felt safe and at home.

Sometimes aspects of the New Zealand landscape evoked a strange nostalgia, although I'd never set foot in many of these regions before. I suppose the shapes and colours of those unique plants reminded me of my early childhood in Tasmania, a cousin from the days of Gondwana — especially the giant tree ferns that looked as though they'd survived since the Jurassic period.

Another amazing species we share with our Australian neighbour is Dracophyllum, a strange spiky-leaved plant that grows in all shapes and sizes, from sprawling alpine shrubs to small trees that look as though they belong in a Dr Seuss book. There are 61 different species of Dracophyllum, and my favourite is *Dracophyllum traversii*, also known as mountain neinei or pineapple tree.

On the way to Harper Pass, I found myself face to face with a particularly handsome specimen. Perched on outstretched arms of flaky brown branches, the clusters of broad, reddish-purple grass-like curved leaves looked like dramatic hairdos at the ends of long, bendy necks.

The overgrown track was crunchy underfoot with hundreds of fallen Dracophyllum leaves, curled and brown in death, and silvery green fronds of *Astelia nervosa*, mountain astelia, were brushing against my legs as I walked by. Here and there popped the brilliant white of gentians and the yellow faces of mountain daisies.

As we slowly descended from the sub-alpine scenery of Harper Pass into the dense West Coast jungle, the forest reached up to embrace us in a swirl of green on green, every shade in the spectrum.

A thick carpet of moss and lichen-covered twisted tree trunks and clumps of bright green hook grass (*Uncinia uncinate*) framed the narrow path, the tiny, barbed, fish-hook extension on the seeds catching on my unshaved legs and woolly socks.

A huge, gnarled trunk twisted off into the canopy and I followed it with my eyes, trying to identify it by its leaves. This time the host tree was a giant broadleaf (*Griselinia littoralis*) with leathery, bright lime/apple-green leaves. Its thick trunk provided a home to smaller trees, and a huge lichen perched like a fancy lettuce, dangling moss and other epiphytes.

The sight of all this quiet symbiosis brought tears to my eyes. Everything seemed to have a place, an equal opportunity in the competition to survive. I found myself wishing to crawl into the arms of this huge tree, to sink my roots down deep and be absorbed in this wonderful orgy of living and dying.

I wondered if similar thoughts had come to the Māori travellers and early European explorers who made regular crossings of the pass, on what was once a well-trodden path linking the east coast to the west through one of the lowest points of the mighty Southern Alps.

Emilie's voice brought me back to the task at hand. We'd come upon a steep washout where part of the slope had slipped away, leaving a deep gash in the hillside. Down below, one of the many side streams that fed into the Taramakau gushed around river boulders. We needed to tread carefully so as not to slide down the mud-soaked shingle bank and into the gully below.

Emilie went first, her walking poles clicking against the exposed rocks, little red trail shoes finding stable footing on the narrow zigzag across the steep slope. I watched her go, admiring her courage and self-assurance. For her, it was just another challenge, a fun diversion from the monotony of walking.

Her strong little legs carried her down to the stream and in one leap, she was across. Then it was my turn to follow, leaning into the slope as my big thigh muscles bunched and released. The slip wasn't new; other walkers had been here before us, but out there in the green jungle flanked by dark blue mountains, we could have been the only humans in the world.

Hurunui River.

Chapter 11

Deception River

Te Araroa
Day 83

RIVERS ARE DANGEROUS. New Zealand makes up for its lack of savage and poisonous beasts with an ample number of rivers, streams and waterways, which emerge from its high mountains and eventually flow out to sea. You won't get poisoned or ripped to shreds by wild animals, but you could drown if you're swept away during an ill-timed river crossing. The Mountain Safety Council website says: *Rivers are a significant hazard in the New Zealand outdoors, and you'll come across one on most tramping trips.*

By this point, rivers had become an inseparable part of the track. We'd been travelling up them, down them and through them, wild camping beside them, filling our drink bottles from them, swimming in them. At times, the tracks had given up fighting through dense vegetation and left us literally walking along the riverbeds, picking our way across slimy rocks and shifting shingle. There were wide slow rivers meandering around bends; swift streams hastily rushing through frenzied rapids; wide braided waterways and deep cold torrents carving their way through unforgiving rock. No matter how they looked, as a tramper, it had been drummed into me to treat rivers with respect. Rain and snow melt can cause rivers to rise very quickly, transforming a calm stream into a thundering torrent of treacherous brown water.

With its boulders the size of small cars, when the rain sets in there's no way in hell I'd like to be here in the bed of the Deception River with its steep-sided chasms of sheer rock. Tumbling steeply down from its source on the slopes of Mount Franklin, just north of Arthur's Pass National Park, this 17-kilometre river travels through sections of deep gorge before widening out as it flows into the Ōtira River, one of the main rivers on the West Coast.

Right now, boulder-bashing our way up the river, everything is okay. We've received news that a big front is moving through in the next couple of days, but we'll be out of the river by then. I've checked and rechecked the short-range forecast on my satellite phone, and it shows nothing but sunshine for the next two days, although I squint up at the sky every now and then just in case. Right now, the thought of rain seems absurd as the sun burns down upon us.

The track sidles along beside the Deception until it gives up and we hit the riverbed. Only the occasional orange triangle, dangling precariously from a scrubby tree hanging off the far bank, gives us a sign of encouragement that we're still on the trail. Not that we have many options — its either upstream, downstream or face an impenetrable wall of brilliant green bush.

We jump, hop and step from rock to rock, criss-crossing the river, admiring its deep pools and giant boulders. The river is beautiful and, in mid-January, its flow is low, deceptively low. As terrifying as it would be, part of me would love to witness the almighty floodwaters that managed to roll these behemoths of boulders downstream.

Signs of carnage from previous deluges still adorn the banks — a broken tree trunk with roots twisted like an outstretched hand, huge branches wedged between even vaster rocks.

It appears the force of the river is washing lesser rocks downstream, until I look again and see the round, shiny, blue-grey black of whio — not one, but four beautiful creatures.

We stand in the shade of the riverbank, watching the group deftly navigate a swift rapid, swirl in the eddy then, defying gravity, paddle their way back upstream. Mid-flow, one of the whio hauls to the side to dabble in the white water, sounding his nasal, whistling call then sliding underwater with the grace of a scuba diver before bobbing back up again. These ducks thrive in clean, fast-flowing waters where they feed off the many tiny invertebrate species like the mayfly and dobsonfly larvae we've inadvertently scooped up while refilling our drink bottles.

A couple of nights earlier, Emilie and I had witnessed the

magical metamorphosis of a newly hatched mayfly clinging to a rock on the riverbank beside the discarded shell of its chrysalis.

We were wild camping under the trees on a soft carpet of beech leaves on one of the terraces beside the Taramakau River after a long hot day following the river downstream. We'd reached the large, red shelter of historic Locke Stream Hut around 3pm, but its dark, unwelcoming interior and pungent smell of rat piss saw us shoulder our packs and continue walking downstream. Someone had scratched a new name on the hut door — Rat's Nest Hut — and I wasn't in the mood to stick around to find out more.

As the kilometres passed and we wandered further down the widening river valley, the thick tangle of jungle that coated the mountainsides gave way to drier beech forests, scrubby matagouri, golden tussock and dried grasses, so we decided to pitch our tent.

The sun had drained from the sky, but we weren't ready for sleep. Instead, I took Emilie on an insect-spotting tour within the beech trees. We stepped away from our tent into the darkness of the beech grove, shining our head torches up the rough trunks and into the low canopy, hoping to find some long-legged insect treasures.

Our torchlight reflected off a tiny golden button, the carapace of a native cockroach, the delicate curved legs of an orb spider and the strange, curving, crawling form of a millipede.

Emilie was unimpressed, until we found the wētā. It was a nymph, its tiny, semi-translucent body dwarfed by its long, twitching antennae and neatly folded legs as it clung to the underside of a branch just above my head.

Pick me up, Mummy, I want to see it too! Emilie demanded.

I complied, hoisting her solid little body onto my hip. As she was nearly half my bodyweight, this didn't last long, and our entomology session dissolved into giggles.

A few more minutes' searching revealed nothing more exciting than another pair of cockroaches; clearly the insect diversity had declined along with the vegetation, so we headed down to the river.

I love the magic of the night. As a child in Australia, I was always a little afraid of the dark, my overactive imagination conjuring up spirits of the Dreamtime — during which, according to Aboriginal belief, the world had been created — mixed with mythical beasts from my storybooks.

I felt a little tingle of excitement. The absence of light seemed to heighten all other senses, noises were sharper. I could hear the tinkle of broken water above the hum of the river and feel the sensation of the warm night breeze on our faces. Somewhere far away, a ruru was calling.

We squatted down on the riverbank, playing the torchlight over its rippling depth. A flash of movement in the shallows revealed tiny fish, probably one of our secretive native species that feed at night and hide during the day.

Then we spotted the mayfly. It was holding onto the side of a large river boulder, fragile pale wings unfolding into the night. We could see it had only just emerged from the safety of the chrysalis that was glued to the rock beside it.

Mayfly nymphs live in rivers and streams, their torpedo-like flattened bodies and short legs helping them cling to the underside of rocks even in fast currents. After many months of aquatic life, the nymphs are summoned by some inbuilt biological urge to leave their watery home and venture above the surface, climbing out onto whatever solid surface is nearby.

Then they shut down and undergo the amazing process of metamorphosis, emerging as an ethereal-looking winged insect. Just like a tragic fairy tale, the beautiful adult version only lives a couple of days before it succumbs to exhaustion and dies. Living only to experience a night of passion that hopefully results in a successful mating and egg-laying session, the adult mayfly has no mouth parts and neither feeds nor sleeps during its short life. It sounds like a risky existence, but this strategy must work for the mayflies, as these delicate creatures are part of an ancient lineage of insects that date back to the days of the dinosaurs.

Looking around carefully, we discovered more and more of these shimmering little creatures clinging to rocks and river stones, their fragile wings pointing up from elongated bodies.

Somehow, we'd managed to stumble into the perfect place at the perfect time to witness a magical transformation for this community of mayflies.

All my aches and pains were forgotten as I crouched in the darkness, absorbed in this wonderland. I hadn't planned to camp here, hadn't watched and waited for this special day when hundreds of native mayflies would swarm together for one night of passion. Our timing was pure luck, and the magic and privilege of witnessing one of Mother Nature's many wonders was not lost on me.

By the time we stumbled into Arthur's Pass, two days and 30 kilometres later, Mother Nature was demonstrating another of her almighty spectacles. The weeks of fine weather had finally given way to fierce winds and driving rain as a big front blew in off the Tasman Sea and settled right over the top of us. Weather warnings had been issued for parts of the West Coast and Canterbury and we couldn't walk any further in those conditions.

As the nature of trail walking is to keep moving, I felt like a caged animal that had been forced to stay in one place for too long.

There were options, but I wasn't sure what to do.

Hope you girls find somewhere dry to wait out the rain! No good walking in this weather! xx Danilo messaged me.

He'd dropped off our food resupply box for us a few weeks ago, and Emilie was delighted to find a little bag of chocolates amidst our standard fare of porridge oats and pasta.

It was only enough to last us the 45-kilometre section from the Waimakariri River to Lake Coleridge, maybe three days' walk from here, and the forecast was dire, maybe a week of heavy rain and swollen rivers.

We couldn't walk and there was no point sitting in a cold, damp hut until we ran out of food. I thought about trying the backpackers at Arthur's Pass, but it would be expensive — plus I'd have to interact with people, which after eight days of solitude, I didn't really feel like doing.

It seemed surreal to be there in Arthur's Pass, a mere two-and-a-half-hour drive from our home in Christchurch, our friends, civilisation. I knew we'd be welcome to crash on a friend's couch or take over their spare room, but I was loath to return to the concrete jungle of a city after months in the bush.

Thankfully, luck was on our side in the form of an offer from some lovely souls, again through Instagram, to stay in their holiday cottage in the tiny settlement of Cass, a short drive or a long walk down the road from Arthur's Pass Village.

It was so humbling to think that somewhere out there, people were watching our progress and cheering us on. I checked our Givealittle page. It was sitting at almost $12,000 in donations, more than halfway to our goal of raising $20,000 for the Mental Health Foundation and Federated Mountain Clubs of New Zealand. I was stoked to think that the journey of a mother and daughter across New Zealand had won the love and support of so many people, and somehow it helped me feel less isolated and alone.

I opened the weather app Windy.com and watched the green, yellow and red swirling colours marking the front that was slowly bearing down upon us. It was a good time to be sitting tight for a few days but, for no apparent reason, the need to divert from my plans and find an alternative to trail walking until the wild weather passes had triggered something. I could feel the confusing and unhelpful fog of panic bubbling in my gut and taking over my brain.

Stop it, I hissed at myself, *I don't need this right now. For fuck's sake, it's not hard, we just need to find somewhere to stay.*

But it was so difficult to think straight when my frontal cortex had shut down and adrenaline was pulsing through my body. The spiral of self-doubt exploded into action. What was I doing, stupid woman, mother, dragging my damp child through the wild, in search of what? A peace and clarity I could find while watching mayflies in the dark but couldn't manage to bottle and keep with me.

The physical sensation of being slowly dipped in a bucket of wet cement is so hard to shake. It's as though every cell in your entire body is begging you to curl up in the foetal position and gently rock yourself, moaning, aching for the soothing and comfort that never comes. In the past, I'd tried to find the words to explain the debilitating symptoms that accompany post-traumatic stress disorder, but I was usually met by blank faces or pitying expressions that left me feeling even more distressed and isolated as I struggled to hold myself together.

I'd tried to tell my work colleagues about my condition before I gave up and threw in the towel.

It seemed there was no place for mental health in that workplace. Despite the politically correct posters put up by the human resources department and the slogan 'It's OK not to be OK', my experience of advocating for myself as someone living with post-traumatic stress disorder felt like a socially ostracising, professionally humiliating experience at best.

Only when I left that concrete jungle on Christchurch's Hereford Street did I realise what an immense pressure it had put upon my soul. I walked away, a single mother with no job to go to, and I felt as free as a bird.

As I sat there in that little cottage, watching rain lash against the windows, the memories of the shame and isolation crashed into me like a punch in the stomach.

I was suddenly transported back to that tiny sixth-floor meeting room, shoulder to shoulder with my colleagues yet feeling like a social pariah, trying to arrange my features into a calm expression and swallow down the giant scream that was welling up inside.

I had hoped my face wouldn't betray how distressed I felt. Loser, loner, weirdo, outcast. The words didn't echo through my head as much as throb deep inside of me.

What are you doing here? You didn't go to the same school as us. You don't have a nice family like us. You don't shop at Kmart like us. You don't join in shallow conversations about Netflix like us.

They didn't say these things out loud, but I was so sure I could read it on their faces, see the judgement in their eyes. Or maybe I was just crazy, going crazy, sick, broken, weirdo.

What's wrong with you?

I didn't know what was wrong with me.

My head was full of static, so loud I couldn't think let alone speak, except to rehearse the words that would help me avoid scrutiny. I wanted their eyes to pass over me as quickly as possible so I could become invisible again. But the huge stone in my guts was digging in under my ribs, I was slowly petrifying as my lungs collapsed under the pressure.

Gotta get out of here, gotta get out of here, something screamed from deep inside. Instead, I opened my mouth and hoarsely said, *I'm working on the community board newsletters this week and hope to send them out by Thursday, so if you have any content that you'd like to include, just let me know.*

I twisted my features into a smile, kept my eyes fixed on the desk of that small, claustrophobic meeting room she made us all squeeze into each Monday morning, launching into the working week without as much as a hello.

I didn't realise I was having a panic attack. Or that my hyper-vigilant nervous system was stretched to breaking point. I didn't realise the debilitating feelings of being alone and broken stemmed from having a brain scarred by childhood traumatic events, none of them my fault. I just knew I was different and that I felt so terrifyingly unwell.

I guess I always felt a little bit different from other people. After all, my unconventional childhood seemed to set me apart from my peers.

Where are you from? Where did you go to school? people would ask, and I'd give an awkward laugh and try to explain my nomadic roots.

People don't really want to hear all that. Our brains are designed to categorise people, sift through information and place it into neat little boxes. Safe, unsafe. Familiar, unfamiliar. Psychology books explain that this is why we gravitate to the people who we feel most comfortable and familiar with, and I guess I stood out amidst this cohort of middle-class, white Canterbury mothers.

But there's another narrative. My therapist also explained how my traumatic experiences had rewired my brain and altered my perception of the world and those within it so that I viewed almost everyone as unsafe, unfamiliar. My child's nervous system, stuck on overdrive for so many years had created an adult brain that continued to interpret everything through the lens of fear and distrust, and instead of being rose-tinted, my glasses were black.

I cried in his office once that penny had dropped, to think that my intense, ongoing distress at feeling rejected and cast out from society was all an artificial construct created by my stupid, trauma-damaged brain.

An old white truck rumbled into the driveway and pulled up outside the house, windscreen wipers working frantically. It was Barry, the old bloke who had given us a lift to Cass from Arthur's Pass. He was the sole permanent resident of this tiny settlement, which really is just a couple of ramshackle houses beside the railway station.

Barry was a retired railway man turned chicken farmer, and he'd come to see if I wanted to join him for a ride into town. I could see Emilie's curly head silhouetted against the passenger seat window — she'd taken herself off to Barry's place an hour earlier, all dressed up in a fancy pink princess dress she'd found in a thrift shop. It was almost as if the dress had been made for her and left waiting for her to find it on the $2 rack at the Salvation Army store in Greymouth. We'd visited the town, having hitchhiked from the road end of the Taramakau River in order to spend a couple of nights with our dear friend Ken before heading up the Deception River into Arthur's Pass.

I'm delivering some eggs then going to the pub, he announced, wispy white hair sticking out from under a chequered cap. *You girls want to come along for a ride?*

Emilie was up for anything, and I was down for a beer, anything to distract me from my dark thoughts.

Plus, I liked Barry, he seemed like a good bloke.

Over a pint at the Bealey Hotel, Barry told me he'd left home and worked for the state-owned railways at the age of 16. Eventually, he'd found himself living in the one-man town of Cass, on the outskirts of Arthur's Pass National Park, its little red box of a railway station made famous by a Rita Angus painting.

Barry must have liked the solitude as he'd stayed on in Cass, responsible for the highest section of the track linking Christchurch on the east coast to Greymouth on the west. Now in his seventies, he spent his time pottering around this quiet piece of the world, looking after the settlement and his chickens and occasionally rescuing displaced persons like us.

A few days earlier, when the storm had first struck, I'd received a message from Deb, a kind soul who'd offered for us to stay in her family bach. She lived a few hours away but Barry knew where the keys were, and she'd rung him and asked him to pick us up.

So, we'd wandered down the road, rain whipping our legs and dripping off the hoods of our rain jackets, until a white ute slowed to a halt and out hopped Barry.

He'd insisted on lifting my heavy pack and we'd all bundled into the front, Emilie installing herself beside him, full of chatter at meeting a new friend.

You're walking the length of New Zealand! Barry had exclaimed as we'd tried to explain ourselves. *Bloody hell, that's a long way. Why don't you come on over to the shed once you've settled in and we'll have some lunch? There's sausages on the barbecue.*

We didn't have to be asked twice. Barry's residence was an eclectic combination of Kiwiana and country living, the self-containment of someone used to living the rural life.

He'd transformed one of the old railway sheds into a bar and had poured us drinks with all the solemnity of a bartender — a beer for me, apple juice in a tall glass for Emilie.

Onto my second pint at the Bealey Hotel, I grinned across the table at Barry, who was being entertained by Emilie in her frilly pink fairy dress — he was her new best friend after he'd ordered her an ice cream sundae complete with chocolate sauce, fresh strawberries and a paper umbrella. Emilie had also figured out that Barry had a TV at his house, with cartoons, as well as a pantry full of cake and biscuits.

I felt like Cass wasn't such a bad place for two trail refugees to be.

In retrospect, I could understand the overwhelming feelings of anxiety that had gripped me that morning.

The sudden change of plans, the uncertainty, the sense of displacement had all pushed buttons deep inside of me. After several months of spending our days outside, negotiating the track or zoning out with the scenery, it was a shock to the system to stop moving and be stuck inside.

I felt better for recognising and naming my body's physiological responses. These sensations might have felt uncomfortable, but in time they would pass, just like this storm.

I gazed out of the window of the big empty pub and watched the churning torrent of the Waimakariri River far below. Swollen with rainwater that had rushed down from the craggy peaks and dark valleys of these huge mountain ranges, the river had transformed from the deceptively mellow braids we'd wandered past days earlier into a raging flow. But as quickly as it rose, it would fall again, its ever-changing channels weaving between islands of gravel. Maybe I could learn something from the river and allow myself to gracefully bend and flow as we journeyed along the great unknown of Te Araroa.

Goat Pass Hut at the head of Deception River.

Chapter 12

Craigieburn Forest

Te Araroa
Day 88

AS SMALL AND HARMLESS AS they may seem, mice have no place in the New Zealand ecosystem. Not only do these introduced mammals prey on our native insects such as wētā and eat the eggs of our native birds, they are also a tasty treat for bigger and nastier predators such as stoats.

In the South Island beech forests, mice fatten themselves on beech seeds, and the stoats fatten themselves on mice. Once the mouse population is depleted, the hungry stoats start hunting birds, with devastating consequences.

That is why I'm going to kill this defenceless little mouse.

I explain my logic to Emilie, but she isn't having a bar of it. Melissa doesn't need any convincing. As our resident ecologist, she knows only too well the devastation wreaked upon our natural environment by introduced pests — although as a botanist, the destruction of our native flora species is her focus.

Well, hurry up and do it then, she says, as Emilie and I play a serious game of tug of war over the metal billy that contains the hapless mouse.

No way! I want to keep him! Emilie exclaimed, tugging the billy from my hands. *Hello, Mousie!*

I hunt around for something to do the deed with — a rock or a hammer to knock the poor thing on the head before I bury it, but other than a handsaw for the firewood, all I can find is a huge axe.

This is becoming comically stressful. As Emilie refuses to part with the billycan, I feel my mojo slipping away.

After several days waiting out the rain as ladies of leisure in Cass, we'd reunited with Melissa, who'd driven up from Christchurch to join us for the 45-kilometre walk from where we'd left Te Araroa at Arthur's Pass to Lake Coleridge.

It's 11am and we're outside the old and decrepit West Harper Hut in the Craigieburn Forest, where we had stopped for lunch and discovered the mouse. Perhaps rustic is a better description for this historic hut with its axe-cut beams, canvas bunks, dirt floor, open fireplace and rusted sheet-iron roof.

We'd stepped inside the hut for a look around when I spotted the mouse. He was huddled forlornly on the windowsill and didn't bother moving when we came close for a better look.

All hunched up with his fuzzy flanks quivering and surrounded by green crumbs, he was showing all the signs of being a very sick mouse succumbing to a slow death by poison bait.

Ugh, let's get him out of here, I said, thinking of the stench his rotting corpse would leave behind in the already dank and unwelcoming hut.

I took a metal billy from one of a collection of cooking utensils above the big open fireplace and gently nudged the mouse inside.

Now where to put him . . .

You can't just let him go, Melissa pointed out, which was true, as perhaps a ruru or some other animal would gobble him up and also succumb to a slow and painful death.

He's dying. It would be kindest to put him out of his misery, I said, convincing myself as well as Emilie that this was the right thing to do.

I remember being a little girl of her age, living on that block in Tasmania with the grass growing long, and how our two cats loved hunting for fieldmice. I hated to see any animal being hurt and would chase the cat and prize the sodden mice from its jaws. If they showed signs of life, I'd smuggle them down to the barn and hide them away in a shoebox with a little piece of bread and a bottle cap of water, checking on them multiple times a day to be sure they were recovering.

Now, I could see Emilie dreaming up mouse rescue plans of her own, as she wandered around the hut with her nose in the billycan.

Love, please give him to me.

No! He's mine. I'm going to take him home and call him Mousie.

249

But sweetheart, he's a pest.

Then I'll call him Mousie Pestie.

I look beseechingly at Melissa, who is rolling her eyes.

I think we can just knock him on the head and bury him over here where the ground is soft. Then we can keep going.

I use the blade of the axe to cut a hole in the moss-covered ground and wrestle the billycan off a protesting Emilie. *Go and play by the river, we'll be there soon.*

I'm going to knock the mouse on the head with the back of the axe and drop it into the hole, I tell Melissa, hunting around for a flat rock. I need to put the mouse on the rock before I donk it, otherwise the blow will just get absorbed by the soft moss.

I tip the prostrate mouse onto the rock and pick up the axe, but you know what, I just can't do it.

Ahh fuck. Can you do it?

I don't want to do it! Melissa says.

But we've wasted 30 minutes of walking time messing around with this mouse, so once she sees that I'm completely useless, Melissa steps up to the challenge.

All right, give me the bloody mouse. She raises the axe while I cower and cringe, then lets it drop with a sickening thud.

It's horrific. The axe misses the mouse completely and strikes the rock, which flips up like a seesaw and sends the poor mouse flying.

Bugger, Melissa says.

The next blow is more accurate, but Melissa, ever the scientist, picks up the mouse by its tail to examine it. Dangling from her hand, its little face now a mess of blood and tissue, the mouse is most certainly dead, and I'm feeling traumatised.

I try to save face by quickly burying the mouse without any help and lay a few leaves on its grave.

Emilie comes storming over, her eyes full of angry tears. I don't blame her. I suggest she find a few leaves and flowers to decorate Mousie's grave, but she chases me away with teeth bared and goes to pick blossoms from a flowering hebe.

After departing from the resting place of Mousie Pestie, our solemn procession pushed on along the Harper River towards Hamilton Hut. The track followed the course of the river though a forest of beech trees, the understorey of their dark canopy thick with bright green ferns, mosses and lichens.

As we walked, Melissa gave me a private ecology lesson.

While the river had returned to its usual flow, the obvious signs of recent flooding were everywhere, including right under our feet.

A few days earlier, the driving rain, which had kept us huddled in Cass, had swept through these parts, swelling the side creeks and turning the river into a raging brown torrent.

Swathes of dead sticks and tangled branches were strewn across low sections of the track. Pools of water covered thick layers of rotting vegetation. And then there was the mud — deep brown pools of goop just waiting to suck the shoes off our feet.

Emilie said we had to practise our mud ballet. We must make our way over a rotten branch that was protruding from the goop like a slimy balance beam.

Actually, she was talking to Melissa, as I was dead to her while there were other more exciting, shiny people around to chat to. The fact that Melissa had swung the death blow meant nothing to Emilie. It was I, her own mother, who had taken Mousie Pestie from her arms and sentenced him to death, and for that I would be ignored . . . at least until it was snack time. For now, there was mud to cross, and Emilie went first, demonstrating her technique and the benefits of weighing only 30 kilograms. Melissa followed with her leather tramping boots and knee-high gaiters, then I stepped out with a misplaced foot and sank up to my ankle in icy cold muck.

I overcorrected myself to avoid falling face-first into the muck and toppled slowly into a big clump of silver-green spears, my trail shoe still firmly stuck in the bog. Face down in a deeply intimate moment with the vegetation, my heavy pack slid up my back and over my head, effectively pinning me down.

For fuck's sake! my cries were muffled by a mouthful of slender silver-green leaves.

That's Astelia grandis, Melissa explained to Emilie, *or kakaha, also known as the bush flax or bush lily. See how the ribs are kind of reddish and right now its flowering — you can see the little clumps of green flowers.*

The others talked amongst themselves while I recovered my composure. I had a mucky brown thigh to match my mucky brown shoe and various smears and smudges across my face and arms.

Fortunately or not, the track soon meandered across the river, and I could wash both my feet.

Further on, a swing bridge spanned the confluence where Hamilton Creek flowed into the Harper River, and 10 minutes later we pushed through a grove of baby beech trees to find the big red and brown structure of Hamilton Hut.

We were delighted to see it, but as soon as we'd unlaced our damp footwear and strung our filthy socks on the washing line, we realised the sandflies were delighted to see us too.

The warm humid weather and thick grass around the hut had created a haven for sandflies, which feast on the juicy limbs of hapless trampers.

We slapped and scratched, donned spare socks and long-sleeved tops, groaned and cursed before giving up and retreating inside the dark sanctuary of the hut.

It was a shame, because I would have loved nothing more than to drag a mattress outside and flop around in the sunshine on that wide wooden deck. Instead, we stayed indoors, preparing our sleeping quarters for an early night.

The following day, we pushed on down the Harper as it swelled and widened, sucking up a dozen more side creeks before it finally joined forces with the Avoca River that rushed towards Lake Coleridge and the end of our trip with Melissa.

Only half an hour after leaving Hamilton Hut, the track faded away completely, leaving us to rely on our topo maps and imaginations.

With the river on our right, we slopped through bright green marshlands that gave way to deep muddy pools and hidden streams, fought through thickets of matagouri and picked deer trails through the beech forest. Every so often an orange marker would appear, a sign of encouragement that we were going the right way.

Melissa showed me how to bush bash like an ecologist. While I envied her boots and knee-high gaiters, I tried to make up for it with enthusiasm and willingness to explore, including sinking up to my thigh in a surprise bog hole, much to Emilie's delight.

We discovered a mosaic of native plants including wispy native grasses, cushion plants and mosses making their homes amongst the rocky, braided riverbed. Here and there were clutches of tiny native broom, a distant relative of the pea family that's often gobbled up quickly by browsing herbivores like deer and goats. We also encountered clear streams brimming with fragile aquatic plants and tiny native fish.

Many hours and multiple river crossings later we staggered off the floodwall next to Lake Coleridge and into a gravel carpark close to where the Harper River flows into the brilliant blue depth of the lake. I was so glad Melissa had been there to help me haul a reluctant Emilie across the Avoca River as its multiple braids had been deceptively swift and strong.

But after Lake Coleridge we would come to another river that was impossible to cross, at least on foot. The mighty Rakaia is one of the largest braided rivers in the South Island, rising in the Southern Alps and flowing some 150 kilometres to the east coast shores, cutting directly across the path of the trail.

Waiting in the carpark was my friend Nadia, who had agreed to drive us to the trail head on the other side of the Rakaia, then join us to walk the almost 70-kilometre section through the Hakatere Conservation Park. Nadia was another tramping mum and we'd shared several fun adventures with two of her kids, Amber and Zayne. The mood was jubilant as we all piled into her van, and the jubilation increased when she pulled out a couple of ciders that had been waiting on ice.

Hakatere Conservation Park covers nearly 60,000 hectares of rugged mountain country between the Rakaia and the Rangitata rivers, another fast-flowing monstrosity that we had no choice but to drive across somehow. The trail notes recommend booking a local shuttle, but I hadn't been that organised. We still had at least six days of walking ahead of us before we hit the Rangitata, if the weather held out.

Having farewelled Melissa, we set off into the Hakatere with Nadia, leaving the far bank of the Rakaia and slogging our way up a punishing 600 metres of elevation in the midday heat. Upstream, out of view, lay the massive river valleys of the Mathias and Wilberforce, two main tributaries of the Rakaia, which drain the Lyell and Ramsay glaciers of the Southern Alps near Whitcombe Pass.

As far as the eye could see, there were only dusty rolling hills covered in tussock and flax and speargrass with the occasional stunted hebe. There was nothing to offer us even a moment's respite against the burning sunshine.

It's all well and good to imagine strolling the hills on a summer's day, but to get up into them you need to put in the grunt work, and the short, sharp zigzagging track from the head of the gully to the saddle was a killer. My strong brown calves screamed in protest and my back ached under the weight of my freshly loaded pack. Emilie was also wilting — she was never a huge fan of hill climbs and especially not in that heat. Nadia still managed to exude the freshness and enthusiasm of a busy mum who'd left the kids at home and was out for an adventure.

We flopped around on Turton's Saddle, catching our breath and admiring the expansive views across the Rakaia, which had opened up in wide braids far below. With the big climb behind us, we enjoyed wandering through the high country, grasshoppers scudding away from under our feet and the click and whir of cicadas echoing in our ears.

Appearing a greyish-gold monotone from a distance, close up these open plains were actually a kaleidoscope of colour and movement. Golden tussock blended with the reddish purple of stunted Dracophyllum, the bright green of cushion grass and the yellow and white faces of mountain daisies. Tall, viciously spiked flowers emerged from the occasional clump of deadly looking speargrass. Tiny beetles were exploring their tiny kingdom and flimsy-winged crane flies drifted past on the breeze.

We were in a high, hanging valley, skirting around the bluffs with the wind at our backs. To our left, the rounded flanks of the Black Hill Range had shed their olive-grey cloak to emerge capped with grey scree; to our right we could see the head of Godley Peak looming some 2087 metres into the sky.

The track sidled downhill until we came around a bend and the landscape opened up to reveal the tiny blip of A Frame Hut on the golden tussock flats below.

It was big empty country all around until the following day, when the track entered a narrow gully that led us into the low flanks of the Taylor Range. Squeezed into a rocky gorge crowded with matagouri, we were forced to either walk up the stream or fight our way through thick groves of fierce spikes. At one point, the track seemed to completely disappear until I managed to spot an orange marker a few hundred metres upstream.

Sometimes it felt as though the agreement between the Te Araroa Trust and DOC was limited to the paper it had been signed on, as scantily used connections like this one were not regularly maintained. It was as though some DOC workers had flown over in a helicopter and thrown out a handful of orange markers, figuring that the gung-ho Te Araroa thru-hikers would do the rest themselves.

The track had vanished, and our options were limited, so we stepped into the stream. It was icy cold and surprisingly fierce. My trail notes didn't mention anything sinister about Round Hill Creek, but after an hour of fighting we'd only made our way 800 metres further upstream. Occasionally, a promising animal trail cut a narrow gash of track through the scrub, then petered out and we were forced to return to the creek.

The gully turned into a gorge where the water raged over slimy rocks. Emilie was losing her mojo and I was losing mine too. The recent rains must still have been draining out of the tussock basin, which is why the creek was so fierce. The steep sides forced us to cross and cross again, linking arms and packs as we stepped out into the middle of the whitewash, feeling the pure weight of fast-flowing water against our tired legs.

We were making slow and frustrating progress. I looked up at the bluffs crowding in on us. Scaling them to find an easier path high above the river wasn't an option. Finally, we'd had enough of fighting the river and decided to give the matagouri a turn. Also known as tūmatakuru or wild Irishman, matagouri is a thorny bush or small tree with wickedly long spines that early Māori used as tattooing needles. I don't have any tattoos, but I did have a deep gash below my knee from an earlier encounter with a particularly nasty specimen.

A track, maybe even the actual track, led us out of the creek and up around a bend, until it dead-ended in a sheer drop. Cursing and groaning, we looked down at the river flats only a few metres below us, separated from us by a dense jungle of thick spikes.

While they posed an impenetrable if not suicidal barrier at chest height, I learned that these gnarly bushes were fairly benign underneath. As long as we brushed any fallen daggers out of our way, we could effectively drop to the ground and commando-crawl our way under a dense thicket of matagouri.

I had difficulty convincing my comrades of this interesting fact, so I demonstrated it to them instead. It helped that some beast, possibly a wild pig, had broken this trail before me, so I could slide downhill inside my tunnel of matagouri, dragging my pack behind. Apart from a spiked palm and earth-smeared elbows, I emerged, victorious onto the river flats below.

It worked! Come on down!

Emilie came next, complaining at first, but then having fun, because tunnelling through the undergrowth is so much more fun when you're little. We waited for Nadia to emerge, hauling her green backpack. Us – 1; Matagouri – nil!

This new way of travelling was fun until I got myself wedged under a stubborn branch.

I'm stuck! I yelled, face down in the undergrowth.

Where are you? called Nadia, who had chosen to stay in the creek.

I heard her splashing up the stream until her eyes locked with mine as she peered up through a tiny hole in my spiky jail. We simultaneously burst into loud peals of laughter, and she dragged me out, pack and all.

We made progress upstream and the creek finally dwindled to a more manageable size as we stumbled closer to its headwaters. It seemed to rise from the wide flax- and tussock-covered basin just below Clent Hills Saddle, water oozing out of the ground and trickling down to form a stream.

As the landscape opened up again, the sky was closing in. The short-range weather forecast on my satellite beacon showed cheerful little emoji clouds giving way to rain and possibly snow. Snow! The prospect seemed ridiculous given the baking hot temperatures we'd endured the previous day. But still, this was the high country, and the Southern Alps were looming nearby. As we climbed higher, the matagouri gave way to clumps of speargrass, Dracophyllum, sprawling mounds of mountain daisy and tussocks.

Once we were up on the saddle, the scree-coated flanks of unnamed peaks loomed into the cloud. A thin scar of track cut across a dark grey scree slope and dropped out of sight. Words like barren and volcanic floated through my mind, although the only thing volcanic there were the cone-shaped peaks and wispy, steam-like cloud.

We hadn't seen another soul for days when suddenly a figure emerged out of the mist, tailed by a small white blip. He moved towards us with surprising speed, powering across the same ground that we'd slipped and slid along. He was a local hunter and his little white terrier was called Nip.

When we caught up with him again 30 minutes later, he was lying on the ground peering through a huge hunting scope, Nip wagging her tail at his side.

Would you like to see a tahr? he asked Emilie. Her eyes shone as she nodded in response.

Somewhere on the far side of these seemingly barren and empty hills was a shaggy, reddish-brown, 100-kilogram animal, completely oblivious to our little group. Introduced in 1904, Himalayan tahr have made New Zealand's Southern Alps their home, venturing down the slopes to feed amongst the alpine grasslands before returning to their lofty bastions of rock and crag.

Without the specially equipped footwear of the tahr, whose hooves can grip smooth rocks and lodge in small footholds, our own progress down the steep, shingly slopes was painfully slow. Once back on the lowlands, we found ourselves pushing through a forest of giant chest-high tussock, sheltering the biggest speargrass specimens I'd ever seen.

Suddenly, Nadia fell forward with a scream, and my heart lurched into my throat. Had she tripped and impaled herself on the razor-sharp spines of the speargrass? Almost — she had twisted her ankle and could barely walk.

We were less than two kilometres from Double Hut, but it might as well have been 10. Nadia's face was twisted in pain as she tried to weight-bear on one long leg. As if sensing the unfolding drama, the wind whipped up, funnelling through the wide gap between the mountain ranges. Grey banks of low cloud were marching in, obscuring the mountain tops. Soon it would start to rain.

Shall I set up the tents? I asked Nadia. *It's really exposed here. Can you walk at all?*

Without her pack, leaning heavily on both hiking poles, she could limp along. At least the trail had widened out into an old four-wheel-drive track without too many obstacles. I squatted down before her pack, gritted my teeth and hoisted it up, looping the straps over my shoulders. A backpack and a front pack.

Together, we hobbled the remaining distance to the corrugated-iron shelter of Double Hut, pain and shock dissolving into giggles once we were safe inside. The rain arrived only moments later, then turned to snow overnight.

The warm wind blew across the top of my beer bottle like a wind chime. I was onto my second bottle and, although lukewarm, it still tasted bloody good. I raised my bottle to the sky to thank Peter, a retired farmer who had found us wandering down the dusty road outside his house and invited us in for a cup of tea and a bite to eat. He'd sympathised over the story of our cold night spent in the old musterers' hut and told us of the ragged ridgelines he'd followed while herding his sheep, before sending us on our way with beers for me and a tin of peaches for Emilie.

There was no sign of the recent storm that had kept us confined to the freezing darkness of Double Hut two days earlier while snow had blown outside. Nadia had left the hut in the early morning to hobble out to Lake Heron carpark where her husband would pick her up, while we spent the rest of the day huddled in our lightweight sleeping bags watching dark clouds sweep by.

A long, cold day had dragged into night, then transformed into a bright, sunny morning, sending us scuttling out of our rusted tin shelter and into its warm rays. Nine hours later, we were still walking, fuelled by the surprise treat of cake, human connection and a bottle of Speight's.

Holding my half-empty bottle up to my mouth like a microphone, I joined Emilie in a rousing chorus of 'Let It Go'. I hate that song, but she loves it and I was trying to encourage her to cover another couple of kilometres before pitching camp.

We were moving through the Hakatere Conservation Area towards Lake Clearwater, two tiny slow-moving specks against a gigantic open landscape of rolling olive-brown hills with ragged scree-covered tops. It had been a long day and the edges of the sky were beginning to fade from brilliant blue to a dark purple- and pink-tinged sunset. It was big and beautiful and brilliant, especially while I was enveloped in the warm bliss of beer. But what I loved most were the gentians, their bright white blossoms standing out against the dirty gold of sunburned grass and scrubby tussock.

There was a fragility to those blossoms that seemed out of place in that stark landscape, yet those tough little flowers would continue to bloom for another few months.

The ghostly whiteness of their rosette, tinged with a soft yellow, seemed ideal for a funeral flower. I'd never been to a funeral, although I had seen dead people and, on several occasions, tenderly prepared their bodies before they were taken away to a funeral home.

I was 21 the first time I saw a dead body and, despite the seriousness of the situation, my first reaction was an overwhelming urge to giggle.

I was on a two-week practical with students from my nursing college, gaining the work experience needed to earn our diploma. Fresh from our theoretical exams, we had a list of items we needed to practise in the flesh, ranging from intramuscular injections to care of the deceased, and our facilitator had just come to tell us that he had a body for us to prepare.

Stunned and horrified, we traipsed into the small hospital room to examine our charge, an elderly gentleman with tufted white hair, who had finally passed on to the next world. Our job was to prepare his stiffening body by removing his hospital gown, washing him, changing his sheets and dressing him in clean attire. And at the end of it, our facilitator would tick off another item on our checklist — care of the deceased.

It was a serious business, to be carried out with the utmost respect, but somehow my adult brain had scurried off into the depths of my subconscious and emerged with the warm and pleasant memory of morning cuddles with my grandfather. My brother and I loved to sneak into my grandfather's bedroom in the mornings and creep up beside the bed, whispering loudly, *Poppa? Are you awake?*

He would fake a snore and we would tiptoe closer, stifling our giggles as we reached out to peel back one eyelid. Once we were really close, he would launch upright with a roar before locking us into a tight embrace. I adored my grandfather. He was so much fun and never yelled or made us feel small, making him one of the few loving male figures from my childhood. Sadly, he'd recently lost his battle with cancer.

As I looked down at someone else's grandfather, I couldn't help feeling bubbles of joyous anticipation rising in my belly and thinking that perhaps he might just be faking it and, as the motley crew of nursing students closed in on him, he would also erupt from his death bed with a cheerful roar.

My grandfather's death sent shockwaves through me that plunged me into the dark hole in my life that nothing seemed to fill — a hole now full of regret for not spending more of his last days with him. His death was so sudden, unplanned, no one thought he would leave us so soon — although I suppose all the signs were there. He'd faded away from a massive cancerous growth that took root deep in his bowel, and by the time the specialists got to him, they decided he was too old and frail to operate on.

I remember visiting him and my grandmother for a long weekend. Actually, I had left Emilie with them and taken myself to a yoga retreat in the hope of finding something to soothe my soul. Afterwards, I was getting ready to drive the three hours back home when my grandfather called to me from his room. When I went to see him, keys in my hand, he told me, *Never mind love — I'll tell you next time.*

I had lain on the bed with him for a few moments, locked in my own struggles while he was locked in his, then driven away.

A few days later, my grandmother rang to say he'd passed away early in the morning. I felt like something had been ripped out of me.

Can I come? Can I see him? I'd asked, but he had already been taken to the funeral home and when I rang them, they advised against it.

He died hours ago love, and his body is really far gone, the attendant said. *Besides, he's being cremated in the morning, so we haven't bothered embalming him.*

He'd always said he didn't want a funeral, didn't want the fuss, so there was no opportunity to say goodbye, at least no official way. He just disappeared from our lives, possibly the only man who'd made me feel special and loved.

When you grow up, there will be a line of boys around the block waiting to knock at your door, and I'll be waiting for them with a big stick, he'd tell me when I was maybe nine or 10, and I'd laugh, lapping it up. And when Emilie arrived, oh, how he loved that baby. Even when he was too frail to get out of his chair, he would sit and play with her as she pushed toys into his hands. I only wish he could see her now.

I stopped walking and felt the waves of emotion crashing over me, staggering a little — and not just because of the beer. A low, keening moan swept away on the wind. The intense feeling of loss ripped through my body and suddenly I was just so very tired.

Emilie was 50 metres behind me, swiping at the gentians with her hiking poles and singing to herself. I tried to resist the urge to cut the emotion in half, block it out, stop it from hurting me.

This habit of emotional dissociation was useful when you were a terrified teenager in foster care, but it's no good for you anymore, my therapist had warned me. *You can't keep pushing it down inside of you, that's what's making you sick. To process grief, you need to allow yourself to experience it, let it flow through you and away from you.*

But it hurts! I protested, fighting the giant lump that was stuck in my throat like a stone. What would this stupid, over-qualified 30-something-year old psychologist know about grief?

Yes, it's supposed to hurt. Just keep breathing and it will pass.

Fuck it. Grief is such a heavy burden. I threw down my pack and leaned back against it, stretching my aching legs along the parched dry ground. I was tired of running away from my emotions. Bring it on, then.

A dark shadow loomed over my tightly clenched eyes.

Hi Mummy! Shall we sing some more?

Somewhere just beyond the tight squeeze between Dogs Hill and Mount Guy ran a tiny creek with flat spots to camp. We could hear the tinkle of running water, but any access was thwarted by thick stands of matagouri — and I was in no mood to mess with it. We dropped our packs by a rocky outcrop that promised to offer some protection should the wind pick up during the night and wandered up and down forlornly, searching for a way into the creek.

Peter, the retired farmer who'd showed us such kind hospitality, had suggested we camp here, beside Paddle Hill Creek. *There's a good wee spot on the far side of the creek*, he'd told me, and after 50 years of mustering in this area, I was sure he knew it all like the back of his hand.

Emilie found the access point, and we gratefully filled our water bottles and cooking pot from its fresh, cold source. We'd got a special treat for after our dinner of couscous, dried vegetables and soy protein — the tin of juicy peaches donated by the lovely Peter.

I was still thinking of death and dying and other facts of life as I set up our little yellow tent, using a rock to force the red tent pegs into the ground. Amongst many things, the theoretical side of my nursing qualification touched on Elizabeth Kübler-Ross's five stages of death, dying and grief — denial, anger, bargaining, depression and, finally, acceptance. I was good at the first four but always got stuck on acceptance.

In the quiet of his big house, Peter had told us that his wife of 55 years had passed away on Christmas Day. Less than six weeks ago. I couldn't imagine how difficult it would be to come to terms with such loss. It was so hard to sense the enormous burden of someone's grief and not be able to do or say anything to help take it away.

Even after years of working in aged care in my early twenties, where death was just part of the curriculum, I still struggled to separate my own emotions and would often wander home after my shift blinded by tears.

But sometimes just being there beside someone as they move through their grief is the best gift you can give. I don't know if we helped Peter in that moment, but when we saw him again the next day, I thought he looked happier.

We followed the trail out past Lake Clearwater and skirted along the high banks of Potts River, a mighty waterway that flowed into an even bigger river system — the Rangitātā.

As usual, the end of another section was accompanied by a strange sense of coming down, of quiet reflection, a moment of pause to savour the sensation of living wild before re-entering the chaos of society.

Because, wedged up against the banks of the immense river valley of the Rangitātā, which trampers are advised not to walk across due to its sheer size and sometimes impassable river braids, we had to hitch a ride some 135 kilometres downstream, across the closest vehicle bridge and up the far side of the river to the flanks of the Two Thumb Range.

Rising from the towering fortress of the Southern Alps, this time from the Clyde and Havelock river valleys, the greyish silt-laden waters of the Rangitātā River carry millions of tiny particles of sediment through its wide, shifting, shingle braids as its flows some 120 kilometres southeast across the Canterbury Plains and out to the sea.

As the river rises and falls, fed by springs, streams, wetlands and melting glacier ice, the river braids change course again and again, criss-crossing a wide gravel bed that takes hours to walk across, if one dared to attempt such a crossing. Because even if you manage to ford its deep, swift braids and treacherous pools of quicksand, if it starts raining upstream in the mountains, the river can rise dangerously and without warning.

I had the phone number of a shuttle company, but there was no mobile reception out there. But right then, I was too tired to really care. It was past 4pm and the sun was burning the narrow asphalt road that crossed the Potts River, winding its way further upstream to service the giant private stations of Mt Potts and Erewhon. I'd probably get mobile reception once we walked the six kilometres to the tiny settlement of Lake Clearwater, but for the moment, I was completely content just lying in the shade with the cool breeze caressing my bare feet.

Emilie didn't have a care in the world either. As soon as we'd reached the road, she'd dropped her pack and headed for the water, where she lay in a shallow pool, slathering thick grey river mud on her golden skin. A farm truck rumbled past in a cloud of brown dust, but she was oblivious — although I wondered if I should have flagged them down. I hadn't arranged a ride to anywhere, so we were hoping for a lift into Lake Clearwater or Mount Somers, if another car ever came past these ways.

After another half an hour of lazily batting away the flies, I rose and dragged Emilie out of the water. It was time to go, since we only had a bag of dried nuts and half a cup of couscous for dinner.

Luck was on our side in the form of a big white campervan, which pulled over and happily welcomed two smelly girls aboard. Suddenly the vast landscape that we'd been wandering through for many days was falling swiftly away behind us in a cloud of dust, and I felt a twinge of sadness to be leaving it behind. The elderly couple dropped us at Lake Clearwater village, and a moment later we spotted Peter in his pickup truck — he said he was having a look around to check if we'd got there safely, and now he'd drive us wherever we wanted to go.

We raced to the local dairy to stock up on double-scoop ice creams, insisting on buying one for Peter too.

Make sure you come back to visit me! he said 40 minutes later when he dropped us in the town of Geraldine.

I reflected how the kindness of Peter and so many others had helped keep us going over the 1500 long, hard kilometres we'd walked since the start of Te Araroa. We were smelly, dirty, hungry and tired but, that evening, our hearts were full.

On the far side of the wide river flats of the Rangitātā, the mountains jutted straight up out of the ground like an impenetrable grey fortress. We were attempting to sneak into the back door of the Two Thumb Range via Forest Creek, stumbling over silt-smeared grey boulders as we followed its icy braids deeper up the valley. My head was throbbing from the self-inflicted wounds of over-indulgence, and I wasn't in the mood for this at all. I had learned the hard way never to try to outdrink Jan, a veteran tramper, nature lover and president of Federated Mountain Clubs, who had welcomed us into her home in Geraldine the previous night. After a happy, clean and well-fed Emilie had been put to bed, Jan and I had sat up drinking, chatting and listening to her wonderful music collection until the wee hours, and I was paying for my folly.

After a couple of painfully slow hours' walk upstream, the broad braids of Forest Creek began to squeeze between sheer-sided bluffs. On our left was the privately owned stronghold of Ben McLeod Station, punctuated with a series of authoritarian signs warning against even thinking of camping there, while on our right was a steep slope of native bush that eventually gave way to scree-smeared tops.

We pottered along, searching for a place to pitch our tent. Each step seemed to be vibrating up my legs and shaking my alcohol-abused brain against my skull. We saw the squat stone shelter of a hut across the river, but it was privately owned by the local station, on the wrong side of the tracks. A further 15 minutes stumble upstream revealed a grassy patch under a grove of beech trees that was just wide enough for our tent.

The next day we would climb almost 1000 vertical metres until we emerged above the bush line into the open tussock and alpine herb fields at the head of Felt Stream, before crossing Bullock Bow Saddle and making our way to Royal Hut.

As I lay back on my sleeping mat and closed my red-rimmed eyes to the harsh daylight, I thought of Peter and how our conversation about death and dying had evoked memories of being a trainee nurse.

It was back then that I'd first had the flashbacks. I was standing in the elevator with my colleagues when a deeply buried memory exploded in front of my eyes. It was exam period and the air was thick with anxiety as students tried to recall the past 12 months' worth of pharmacology, microbiology and pathophysiology. We were a combination of young folk, like me, and older women, like my friend Asanatu, who were transitioning to a formal qualification after years of working as healthcare assistants.

I was quietly confident about the biology examinations but worried about the pharmacology test with its stringent minimum grade of 80 per cent. Then, from out of nowhere, a graphic image exploded into my mind. It was more than just an image — its sensation and emotion all crashed over me like a tidal wave. In shock, my head whipped back with such force that it bounced off the stainless-steel wall of the elevator.

Vicky-mama! What are you doing? Asanatu hissed, strong and solid beside me in her colourful African dress. Originally from Sierra Leone, she'd come to Australia through the refugee resettlement programme and was now on a mission to become a qualified nurse. She'd adopted quiet little me early in the school year, buoying me with her wicked sense of humour and warm demeanour as she demanded my native English skills to help with her assignments.

I had no idea what I was doing. All I knew was that something terrifying was happening to me. Despite our brief studies of mental health nursing and two-week practical experience within local mental health wards and facilities, I had no understanding of trauma, or flashbacks, or even post-traumatic stress disorder. Wasn't that something that happened to war veterans, or survivors of horrendous civil conflict like my dear friend? And there I was, days away from gaining an important qualification that I'd worked so hard for, and my world was crumbling under my feet.

Somehow, I managed to get through that day and the rest of my examination block, but I was haunted and deeply ashamed by the vivid memory that had forced its way into my conscious mind.

Now, my therapist would say these flashbacks are part of a process called re-emergence, which is when your body begins to release memories of traumatic events experienced long ago.

To help you survive in the aftermath of trauma, your brain and body place the terrifying memories into a 'deep freeze' to allow you to continue functioning in day-to-day life. You can show up to school, to work, perform your duties and appear, for the most part, like a completely normal individual, even though you're convinced that something is deeply wrong inside.

Then, after a while, when life calms down and starts feeling safe again, your body decides it's time to release the memory so you can heal.

But bodies don't always have a great sense of timing.

After gaining my Diploma in Enrolled Nursing from the technical college, I signed up for the Bachelor of Nursing programme at university, as did several of my colleagues, including Asanatu. Armed with our diplomas, we could breeze straight into the second year of the three-year qualification, and I knew that all I wanted was to emerge as a credible, successful person with a university degree.

I guess I thought that everything would magically change once I graduated, and by pursuing the learning I'd always loved, I would somehow become the person I wanted to be. I'd never thought I'd become a nurse — veterinarian, zoologist or marine biologist were part of my childhood dreams — but I had always wanted to go to university and now there I was.

Through my second-year studies I read excerpts of the *Diagnostic and Statistical Manual of Mental Disorders* (better known as DSM-IV), an ominous tome with a classification system that enabled medical professionals to diagnose serious psychiatric disorders.

Phrases like *patterns of unstable and intense interpersonal relation-ships, persistently unstable self-image, periods of low mood, inappropriate intense anger and feelings of detachment or estrangement from others* screamed at me from the pages.

I'd glance nervously around the room to see if anyone else seemed to be identifying with these diagnostic criteria and decided to keep quiet.

After all, it was only 2005 and Australia was still in the dark ages in terms of concepts like mental health awareness and wellbeing. The DSM-IV refused to accept PTSD as a clinical diagnosis until the late 1980s, and research in this area mostly focused on war veterans, not traumatised children or rape victims. It would have been social suicide to draw attention to myself and call out my doubts over my fragile sanity — or so I felt.

Perhaps it would have helped if I'd had someone to talk to. After all, I'd been effectively on my own since the tender age of 16, rattling in and out of different share houses until finally securing a lease on my own little flat in north Brisbane.

After shaking off the drug addiction that had overshadowed my teenage years and the shady people associated with it, I had few friends and virtually no adult mentors. The hangover of humiliation, shame and resentment from being placed in foster care meant I had little contact with my immediate family.

Still feeling emotionally bruised and battered in the aftermath of another failed relationship that had ended with the termination of an unplanned pregnancy, I was working night shifts at the hospital and attending university during the day.

I was so proud to be there, rubbing shoulders with professors and academics, real people, so I thought, people without the dark and shameful baggage that clattered along behind me. This was my ticket to a better place.

Less than six months into the course, I dropped out — out of university and out of my first job as an enrolled nurse at a prestigious private hospital. I didn't turn up to work, stopped going to school and fell into a deep hole of depression, loneliness and self-loathing.

I found myself living in isolation with powerful emotions that ravaged me day and night. I couldn't escape the all-pervading sense of doom and shame and self-loathing that had taken over my life. It was as though the fiery rage that kept me going through my younger years had been smothered into damp, smouldering ashes and now all I felt was grief.

At the ripe old age of 21, I felt I had seen it all. I no longer had the strength to keep going and wanted my miserable life to end.

I had big problems, but nowhere to turn. I guess at some stage I rationalised that maybe I should seek medical help, and, after swilling back enough vodka to give me courage, found my way to my local medical centre. The doctor took one look at me with my dishevelled hair and swollen red eyes and told me kindly to just take a seat in the waiting room because help was on its way.

Within 10 minutes an ambulance arrived, and two male attendants gently but firmly ushered me inside. The hospital was only a short trip away. I knew this because I worked casual shifts there sometimes. But the ambulance drove past the emergency entrance and pulled up outside the psychiatric ward.

Once inside, the metallic clunk of the automatic doors locking behind me meant there was no way out unless someone with authority let me go. I sat there on the cold blue seats opposite a girl with bandaged wrists, who was rocking herself in the foetal position. Despite the generous dose of alcohol in my system, I sobered up real quick.

I'd learned enough from my nursing studies and practical experience to understand that this place was not going to be the answer to my problems. I'd even worked the occasional paid shift in the mental health unit and seen its patients in their various states of medicated stupor.

As a trainee nurse I'd felt traumatised after witnessing an older lady receive electric shocks (electroconvulsive therapy) for something called treatment-resistant depression. As a student nurse, my job had been to record her blood pressure and pulse rate then accompany her into the treatment room, where the anaesthetist put her to sleep before applying electrodes to her head.

The sight of her prostrate body arcing off the procedure table burned itself into my brain, as did the sound of her silent weeping once she woke again. I had wept too, reading her case history during the hours I had to sit by her bedside, monitoring her heartbeat until she woke up.

She was an older mum whose kids had left home. She had struggled with depression for years and no medication seemed to help. She'd stopped eating and attempted to take her own life, so her husband had agreed to place her under a Mental Health Order, so she no longer had any say over what treatment she received.

There was no fucking way I was going to let that happen to me, so when a psychiatrist eventually came to see me, I lied and told them everything they needed to hear in order to let me go home.

I was just overreacting, having a bad day, had absolutely no thoughts of killing myself whatsoever and was sorry to have caused them any inconvenience. All I needed was to go home and rest.

Once I walked back out of that cold, white-walled prison, the heat of relief flowed through my tired body like sunshine.

Outside the tent, Emilie was floating sticks down the river that washed tight against the bank below our campsite and she wanted me to play too.

I dearly wanted to be left alone in peace to nurse my aching head, but I dragged myself outside and lay on my belly in the mossy grass, snapping dry beech twigs into boat-sized pieces and dropping them into the water. They bobbed and dipped in the current and were swept swiftly away downstream. I imagined they were little ships laden with my sadness, courageously setting sail and carrying all my grief away.

The A Frame Hut in Hakatere Conservation Park.

Chapter 13

Two Thumb Range

Te Araroa
Day 98

I'M LYING ON SCORCHED GRASS at the head of Bush Stream, deep in the Two Thumb Range, that eastern spur of the Southern Alps. We're some 1300 metres above sea level in this wide, tussock-clad basin, yet the only views are of even higher peaks looming all around. Behind me is the reddish rusty shelter of Royal Hut and in front of me, just below my outstretched toes, is the stream. In its infantile state, Bush Stream is a mere knee-deep flow of crystal-clear water, a cooling respite after a long, hot day. You'd never think that further on it roars down from the ranges in a whitish-grey torrent before joining the mighty waters of the Rangitātā.

The last few droplets of water are evaporating from my bare skin as the sun kisses my flat belly and strong, curved thighs. We're the only humans around in this huge empty bowl at the head of the valley, and I've joined Emilie to bathe in the stream. She is still splashing, a happy little forest nymph with her wet braids dangling in the water, and I'm lying here in a warm glow of exhaustion with my mind as still as the sky overhead.

Earlier, as we'd staggered slowly up out of the riverbed away from Forest Creek to Bullock Bow Saddle, memories passed through me like morning mist. As I climbed higher, I focused on feeling my thigh muscles clench and release, inhaling and exhaling with every step until I was in a kind of yogic trance. The memories flowed more freely, ghosts and images. Some memories were as ephemeral as morning mist lifting from the forest canopy. I tried to grasp at them, calling up the images in my mind's eye, but they dissipated like wisps of cloud.

Other memories remained trapped in a frenzied repeat reel, a mix tape like the ones I would record as a sullen 13-year-old from the alternative/indie Triple J radio station, back when my big black stereo boasted a record player, double tape-deck and AM/FM radio. My mind lingered over certain memories like a scratched record, warping and distorting.

It was leading me down a maze of disconnected neural pathways, tangled and interconnected like the network of roots under a forest floor. It didn't really matter. I knew where it wanted to go. I just wished it wasn't trying to go there right then, when my pack was so heavy and the bloody slope so steep.

I just wished I could be certain that once I allowed myself to recall these memories, they would somehow be released and leave me in peace. I was scared, you see, scared that it was going to hurt and I wouldn't be able to cope with it, the way I couldn't cope when I was a frightened child, or a terrified, angry teenager, or a broken young woman in my twenties.

But I guess up there was as good a place as any, especially when I'd just hauled 16 kilograms of food, water and gear up a 1000-metre slope. The sun was beating down and the rocky ground reflected the heat back into our faces. We were way above the tree line on the barren plains of the saddle. Except barren isn't the right word because the wide-open space was home to hundreds of alpine grasshoppers, and between sprawling carpets of light green moss and reddish lichens I could see the bright yellow glow of scree buttercups (*Ranunculus crithmifolius*).

I wish I had known that all this beauty existed back when I was fighting my way through life. I wonder if my teenage self would have cared about the alpine grasshoppers or the delicate petals of the buttercups. Would she have marvelled at the turquoise blue sheen of the alpine tarns, watched the antics of the resident pair of paradise ducks, or dropped down to wait for a shy skink to emerge from a clump of tussock? Maybe if someone had brought me out here, shown me some love and told me how much they believed in me, things might have turned out differently. Maybe I wouldn't have wasted so many years punishing myself and feeling like a dirty, broken, worthless human being.

After all, I didn't ask to be raped. It had nothing to do with the choices I'd made. I was just a dumb angry kid, on the run from the authority figures who were trying to take over my life. What sort of animal rapes a 14-year-old anyway, getting hard and forcing his cock inside a terrified girl with barely any breasts and a soft, pubescent body? Fuck him.

I wasn't the angry, antisocial, attention-seeking and manipulative creature that the social workers wrote about in their poorly worded reports. I was a girl on fire with pain and anger, a raging inferno that destroyed everything in its path to protect the mortally wounded creature behind. A girl who had to fight for herself because no one else was in her corner, who grew into a woman who was tired of battling. A woman whose hypervigilant nervous system was stretched like an old rubber band, ready to snap.

As my mind raced, my body responded and a hot fist clenched around my gut and belly. I could feel the panic erupting until I caught myself and remembered to stop struggling against it.

Breathe in, breathe out, focus on the buttercups, listen to the breeze blowing across the tussock, feel the soothing heat of the afternoon sun. The tight knot that burned inside me was releasing, I was releasing, water was flowing freely down my face and onto my sweat-stained shirt.

Once in Tekapo, we swapped our packs for mountain bikes and rode all the way through to Twizel, covering 55 kilometres of gravelled pathways in a matter of hours instead of days.

Over the past few days, we'd caught glimpses of the mighty peak of Aoraki/Mount Cook as it towered above the other snow-topped spikes and spires of the Southern Alps/Kā Tiritiri o te Moana.

It felt surreal to have spent the past few months wandering beside the jagged 500-kilometre spine of this mountain range, then to find ourselves staring directly up at its most famous peak, separated from it only by a wide blue expanse of glacial waters.

I thought about the Māori proverb: Kia tuohu koe me he mauka teitei, ko Aoraki anake — if you must bow your head, then let it be to a lofty mountain. The mountains we'd passed through on Te Araroa had bent, broken and reformed us, but they were modest challenges compared with the grandeur of Aoraki, sitting head and shoulders above the other peaks at a lofty 3724 metres.

From our lunchtime bathing spot on the eastern side of Lake Pūkaki, we were a mere 50 kilometres from the base of the alps and the glaciers that carved their way out through steep valleys.

But this was as close as we'd get to Aoraki, because the mountain bike trail we were riding along snaked away east around the end of the lake and continued through to Twizel.

The icy waters of the lake closed over my swollen feet as I looked up at Aoraki, the Cloud Piercer, then bowed my head.

Hours later, while sitting outside our cabin in a pleasant little holiday park, we met a man who had enjoyed a special relationship with this part of the Southern Alps — mountaineer Jim Wilson.

I was sitting on the sunny deck in my faded red sports bra, enjoying a tall glass of the strongest beer the Four Square supermarket had to offer, when our neighbours arrived.

At first glance, the small group of octogenarians looked like a bunch of grandpas on summer holiday — until we noticed their attire of tiny bike shorts, cotton shirts and their serious-looking e-bikes.

Emilie was busy demolishing a big bowl of cherry tomatoes, corn chips and hummus, but when Jim's group turned up, she immediately sprang into action.

Emilie loves 'oldies', her term for anyone who looks even remotely over 50, and Jim, with his twinkling blue eyes and bushy white Santa Claus beard, was the perfect target.

After introducing herself with all the charm of a curly-haired cherub, she soon had him up and skipping around the garden. I sat and chatted to his friends and watched as Jim and Emilie borrowed the peg basket off the communal washing line and filled it with leaves and petals, which they then scattered with salubrious joy. Emilie had found a kindred spirit in a body 70 years her senior.

Jim told Emilie he had climbed 'that mountain' over there, and as her eyes opened like saucers, he shared a few tales from his climbing days, including joining legendary New Zealand mountaineer Sir Edmund Hillary to climb Mount Everest.

We told them about Te Araroa and they told us about their e-bike adventures, including this reunion of four 80-something-year-old friends biking sections of the Alps2Ocean Cycle Trail all the way from Mount Cook to Ōamaru.

I went to sleep thinking about how liberating it must have felt to journey into the wilderness of these mighty mountain ranges and summit previously unscaled peaks, 50-odd years ago when the world was such a different place.

The next morning, Jim and his friends gave us a warm and encouraging send-off as we tried to look strong and confident under the weight of our heavy packs.

I'd visited the Four Square again for fresh bread and vegetables to top up the food supplies to last us the next 100 kilometres through to Lake Hāwea, and was already regretting the extra weight. I told myself we'd eat it soon enough and in a few days' time I'd be grateful for the additional food, especially once we got into the mountains again and were slogging up the three big saddles between Lake Ōhau and Lake Hāwea. That's when the days would be long and slow.

First, we would climb up Freehold Creek to cross an unnamed saddle into the Ōhau Range in order to reach the tangle of thin blue lines on my topographic map that marked the mighty Ahuriri River, the largest unbridged river crossing on Te Araroa. The thought of attempting this river crossing on my own, with Emilie, sat heavy in my mind. I tried to push it away as we walked out of Twizel, following the highway for four kilometres before taking a gravel path that skirted around the side of Lake Ruataniwha and followed the Ōhau River to Lake Ōhau itself. There were lots of distractions with Emilie chattering away and rabbits scattering under the trees, but as soon as silence fell, the thoughts would resume.

Quite a few trail walkers reported having difficulty crossing the wide blue braids that drained directly from the Southern Alps. But if the rain held off for the next few days, then the river levels should remain low. After all, it was March and the end of a long hot summer. If we got there and the flow was too high, there was a bridge some five kilometres downstream, an inconvenient detour, but at least we had options.

Options — and yet the anxious thoughts rolled around in my

head and gripped my spine in a cold vice. What if the river looked fine but I lost my footing and we got swept away and had to pack-float ourselves to safety? What if I really was a bad, irresponsible, selfish mother for dragging my child all this way, to then lose her or traumatise her in a near-drowning? Surely I knew how to read a river well enough to judge whether it was crossable or not — or had I just got lucky this far? What if . . .

Fear settled in like a dark fog, not just about the river but about the unknown hills we were about to walk through. And not just the hills, but also what came after. We had recently celebrated our 100th day on Te Araroa and hoped to reach Bluff, another 500 kilometres away, by the end of April, but then what? I still didn't know what the future would bring.

There was something very peaceful about the simple existence we had going on right now. Something comforting about knowing we were just tiny specks amidst a huge landscape. I had no desire to return to work. What work? How could I take the artificial constructs of a capitalist workplace seriously after living and breathing nature all this time? How could anything humans have created be more marvellous or worthwhile of my energies than what Mother Nature had got going on right there? Why would I willingly walk back into the chains of a mortgage and all the other financial trappings of modern life when I could stay here in the hills?

Except I had a daughter who wanted to go back to school and develop her own place in this world. How could I balance both our needs? No matter which path I chose, would I ever be free from the darkness that seemed to follow me around wherever I went, even across high mountain passes and swift rivers? Maybe that was the real issue here, after all.

How should I reset my trauma-damaged brain so I could experience the peace and calm I so badly craved? And what would life look like if I couldn't fix it? Would it even be worth living? Because if Te Araroa had taught me anything so far, it was that I didn't want or need a better job, a fancy house, or a bigger car or anything I could not carry upon my back. I just wanted a strong body and a calm mind, so I could experience the sanctuary of peace and joy, wherever I went.

It worried me that I had no answers to such huge questions.

The 500-metre climb up Freehold Creek to the saddle took us through tall stands of beech trees that grew progressively shorter and stumpier until we finally emerged above the tree line and turned to admire the brilliant blue expanse of Lake Ōhau far below.

Having spent the past few days passing through the highly modified drylands of Tekapo and Twizel with their swathes of wilding pines, exotic trees and other grassland weeds, I was touched by the beauty of this patch of sub-alpine wonderland.

Up here, everything felt familiar, like we were back amongst old friends. I could see the reddish-gold fingers of Dracophyllum, upturned spikes of speargrass, broad silvery-green straps of mountain daisy amidst wavy clumps of tussock. Juicy white snowberries popped out from beds of green and red leaves, and we paused to fill our mouths with their faint sweetness.

The sound of water seemed to be everywhere as it seeped out of the mountainside and filled the gushing stream that flowed into Freehold Creek and out to the lake below.

Slow and steady, we sidled across the base of a rocky scree slope to the start of a different creek that was also emerging from under the mountain, and would hasten and swell as it flowed for 15 kilometres before joining the Ahuriri River.

We followed the shallow valley for a few more hours as the sun rose overhead, the landscape an inverted triangle of golden tussock and dark grey scree that had slid down from the jagged teeth of the surrounding peaks.

The occasional splash of orange from the poled markers rose above the tussock and speargrass to mark a route that had dwindled into a narrow goat track following the true right of the creek.

The earth was hard and unforgiving underfoot and my calf and thigh muscles twinged and contracted with every step. I could feel the ache in my back, nowhere in particular, just a generalised pain as though I'd been gently beaten with a lump of wood until my muscles had turned to pulp then frozen solid again.

Emilie was starting to lag. She didn't do well in the heat, and there was no escaping the fierceness of the sun in this high, exposed, treeless area.

I wasn't sure where we were trying to get to that day. I had hoped we would make it to the banks of the Ahuriri to scout out the best place to cross, but there were still seven kilometres to go, and I was losing the will to go on.

Why can't we go play in the stream, Emilie whined from behind me. *I'm hot and my feet hurt.*

I couldn't blame her. After wind had swept down the valley and whipped up waves on the glassy surface of the lake late the previous afternoon, we'd decided to climb part-way up the hill towards the shelter of the beech trees. Despite the forcefulness of the wind, no rain followed.

We'd spent the night in our tent halfway up the Freehold Creek track, camped on a flat piece of ground right beside a conveniently placed, if not slightly random, picnic table with sweeping views across Lake Ōhau.

In the morning, we'd been up at the crack of dawn. Our tent fly was completely dry and the air was warm and still, although the sky was an eery shade of brilliant pink. Pink skies in the morning are a tramper's warning, someone had once told me, but I couldn't remember what warning it signified and, anyway, I just needed to get across that river, then the rain could do what it liked.

We need to walk twenty kilometres today so we can get to the riverbank, then we will check out the river levels and either walk across it or walk downstream to the bridge then back up again, I had explained to Emilie, wanting to prepare her for a long day on her feet.

But there had been little point trying to strategise with a seven-year-old, especially one who was rolling around on her sleeping mat and pretending to be baby.

Mummy, imagine you woke up in your tent and you heard a noise and when you looked around you found a baby, she chirped, completely caught up in her game.

I sighed. What would I do if I looked around and saw a baby, another bloody four kilograms to tote up the 500-metre climb to the saddle? But I knew my part in this game.

Oh, wow, a little baby! I cried, leaning over her as she gazed up at me, wide-eyed and gap-toothed, endorphins flowing between us.

Goo goo! Gah gah! she cried and pulled me into a warm embrace. I have so many photos of Emilie as a baby, her wide-open mouth always ready for kisses. How nice it would be just to lie here all day and snuggle a warm squishy baby and kiss its soft cheeks, and maybe even go back to sleep for a while until the bruises behind my eyes from chronic exhaustion have faded away.

But the child was wriggling out of my grasp and the tent was flailing as she rolled around, and the sleeping bag that I'd half-packed was oozing out of its stuff-sack, and I still hadn't had my coffee.

Emilie! Emilie, stop thrashing around please. Can you go and fill the pot from the stream so I can make our breakfast?

Awww! Do I have to?

No, of course not, just stay here and relax and I'll do everything for you. Would you like your nappy changed? Shall I breathe for you? This sent her into spasms, the mirth bursting out of her in joyous peals of laughter.

Oh, Emilie. I remember the first time I heard your voice, the angry yowl of a newborn baby so rudely disturbed from your warm sleep. I was 41 weeks pregnant and wondering if the giant watermelon that had taken over my body would ever shift, when my midwife sent me through to Rotorua for a scan.

Nothing drastic, just a check-up to see if everything is fine, she assured me, so I wedged myself into the old white station wagon and drove an hour and a half up the highway. I didn't think that the next morning I'd be making this drive again, this time to the hospital with a hastily packed maternity bag in the back seat. It wasn't on my mind because I was planning to have a home birth, in the safety and comfort of my own tiny living room, within the warm waters of an inflatable birthing tub that was all ready for the first signs of labour.

I wanted a water birth, with soft music and candles to help calm and soothe myself and the baby. I would practise my yogic breathing to ease each contraction and help deliver my own baby from my body, with delayed cord clamping, of course. I couldn't say I was excited about the birth part, but the more I read about home births, the more confident I felt about getting this part of the process out of the way so I could meet baby Emilie and hold her in my arms.

Ahh, you may laugh at my optimism, but I was young and naive and still desperately wanted to believe that I was in control of this process.

The midwife took one look at the scans and called the hospital. *There's not much fluid left around the baby, plus she's a big girl and not in the best position. I think you'll struggle to get her out and it looks like she needs to come out now, before she gets distressed.*

Fuck, fuck and fuck. I knew the position had been an issue earlier in my pregnancy as I'd spent evenings trying to follow my midwife's advice to lie upside down to encourage the developing foetus to turn. From my precarious position balanced on an ironing board that I'd leaned against the couch, I'd pondered what was becoming of my life.

I was 28 years old, single, heavily pregnant and unemployed, although I was two papers into a Master of Business Administration that was proving as boring as it was expensive. I had a diploma in nursing, an undergraduate degree in journalism and a CV with a collection of interesting media and public relations roles from Australia and Southeast Asia.

At a quick glance, it looked impressive, especially the covering letter, but I knew there was a different story. Graduating with my journalism degree at age 24, I had already proved my aptitude for writing with a string of published by-lines gained from many months of unpaid work experience, but I'd struggled to hold down jobs for very long. The initial high of being accepted into a new gig would soon be overtaken by boredom and bitter depression, which saw me fading away from my duties before jumping ship to new challenges or running into conflict with various authority figures.

My relationships seemed to follow a similar pattern. Sometimes, in painful moments of clarity, I could see and understand how the walls of self-defensiveness that I'd been building and reinforcing since I was a child had me trapped within a fortress of my own making.

I hid behind anger, sarcasm and aloofness because these helped me feel big and strong, instead of allowing my softer emotions like fear, sadness and tenderness to break through.

It wasn't that I was confrontational. Instead, it felt like conflict sought me out. A critique from a senior editor or a comment from a manager could instantly fill me with a buzzing, paralysing fear that turned to anger before I even had the chance to register what I was feeling. I just knew I felt so hurt, so wronged, so misunderstood that I had to fight back the urge to lash out and defend myself.

When the anger faded, the dark hole loomed inside of me, full of guilt and shame and the knowledge that I wasn't good enough to be there, that I wasn't like them, that if they knew I was a former foster child who had been raped and left for dead, then the gap between us would yawn even wider and I would be shunned and shamed.

Somehow all of that triggered a form of primal panic deep within me that I couldn't even begin to explain. I didn't want my bosses to know I was crazy! I really wanted to be a journalist, to write the stories of people who had no voice to call their own, to help explain their fears and deeper feelings in a way that brought our society closer together.

It took so much energy to hide how bad I was feeling. I didn't know what was wrong with me or where to turn. How could I be both a talented journalist, capable of networking with chief executives, diplomats and foreign aid workers, as well as an emotional cripple? I didn't understand what brought on the groundswell of emotion that washed me away in its flood before dumping me, spent and stranded, in some strange new territory, often trying to pick up the pieces of whatever I'd just destroyed.

But I thought all that was going to change because I was having a baby. I was going to become a mum, just like my mum, someone warm, calm and gentle. My memories of my own childhood were little more than a dark tunnel that I didn't dare venture into very deeply, full of scabs and raw patches of skin that stung if pressed. The gentler memories of my mother had long been overshadowed by the sting of what I perceived as her rejection of me, abandoning me to an uncaring father and later, the foster care system. It was better simply not to go there at all, or to select just the pleasant memories to portray in snatches and glimpses, like static on an old TV screen.

One memory that came to mind was more of a sensation than a

vision: the feeling of my mother rocking my brother and me to sleep. She would get us to lie on our bellies, head to one side, and place one hand on each of our backs. I loved her rocking me, so much so that when she gently raised her hand, I would continue rocking myself. When I was a little kid, wild, barefoot and home-schooled in the bush, my mother always seemed calm, that's what I thought I remembered — calm and available to do yoga or crafts or sewing and other activities with us. I am sure I adored her passionately, deeply, although, as is probably the nature with most children, my parents just kind of faded into the background. They made up the set, but the main characters were my big brother and me. He was my playmate, my love, my best friend, perhaps I even considered him my property and part of myself. That's why it had hurt so much when we separated and grew distant, not just physically but as people. He turned into someone I didn't understand and didn't like — a hulking, angry, uncommunicative human being. My mother was critical and judgemental, as though she didn't like the person I had become. My clothes, what I ate, the way I spoke, the music I listened to and the company I kept, none of it was up to her standards. I felt betrayed and abandoned, by my brother, my parents and Emilie's father.

But I didn't need any of them anymore because I would have a baby.

Emilie arrived at 10:35am, just in time for a leisurely brunch, although after 20 hours of excruciatingly painful induced labour that ended in an emergency caesarean, I had no appetite.

After the irritable anaesthetist had got his needle into my spasming back, they'd draped a curtain over my lower half so I couldn't see them cutting me open, although I could still feel them tugging and pulling with surprising force.

As a student nurse, I had watched an elective caesarean, and noted the excited anticipation on the faces of the husband and wife, before recoiling at the force the paediatrician used to tear out the residual uterine fibres. Apart from that, everything had seemed very calm and controlled: a horizontal incision in the skin, then a vertical incision in the muscular layer to expose the birth sac, which was pierced and a slimy-looking red baby lifted out. A quick check-up by the doctor and nurse, then baby was wrapped in a white towel and brought around to the delighted parents. In contrast, everything that could have gone wrong seemed to have done so for me, but I was beyond caring — I just wanted Emilie to be okay.

I heard her angry roar as they pulled her from my belly and felt the familiar tingle rise up inside me with surprising force.

How is she? Is she okay? I called, but I couldn't see anything, only the nurse's back as she held the baby away from the operating table. Everything was a blur with blood and shock pounding in my ears. *What are you doing? Give me my baby!* I yelled at her, fighting to move my semi-paralysed body.

As they placed Emilie on my bare chest, I gazed in a mixture of wonder and horror at the tiny, wrinkled creature with her thick head of black hair matched by the black eyelashes that framed her closed eyes. She was the size of a doll, a perfect little doll, her peachy shoulders covered in a soft downy layer of hair, her soft little arms and the tiniest clenched fingers. As I stared, she hunched her body like a caterpillar and extended her chin, inching her way towards me with her rosebud mouth opening and closing like a goldfish.

Oh look, she's doing the breast crawl already, exclaimed the nurse, *she's ready to take her first drink*. At the time, I had no idea that this was an automatic reflex that all babies are born with, and felt delighted and terrified at the sudden weight of responsibility, plus the 3.65-kilogram baby, on my chest.

After the trauma of birth, everything was easy with Emilie, or as easy as being a single mother to a newborn baby can be. At the time, it was terrifying and overwhelming, yet she latched on almost immediately, had an insatiable appetite, never suffered from reflux, slept, and in general was a happy and calm little baby. I couldn't wait to take her home and tuck her into bed with me.

Even in the hospital, as soon as they wheeled me back into my room, my neatly sewn-up belly still smeared with iodine, I popped her into bed beside me. The nurses were unimpressed and warned me of the dangers of co-sleeping, but I had read literature, which showed sudden infant death syndrome rates were lower amongst cultures where co-sleeping is the norm. I wanted to soothe her, attune to her, our heartbeats aligning just like when she was back in my womb. I made sure she was tucked up safely so I could touch, kiss, whisper reassurances and breastfeed her during our long nights together.

She was my little doll and still is, although the soft squishy body of the baby and toddler had been replaced with strong limbs and sharp elbows, one of which was digging into my stomach as she played in our tent.

Squash me, Mummy, squash me! she cried. For such a sweet-looking little girl, she loves a bit of rough play. We flopped and wriggled around in the tent together until I was worried that we'd puncture the sleeping mats, and anyway, we were supposed to be getting an early start to knock off some kilometres before the heat set in.

Right, that's enough. We need to pack up! How about filling that pot?

The baby was burrowing back into its sleeping bag, so I gave up and went to fill the pot myself. A miromiro, a quiet black and white ball of feathers, observed attentively from a nearby tree as I went about my morning routine. As I stirred milk powder and instant coffee granules into my cup, he hopped down onto the picnic table and bounced around the tent.

Emilie, your friend the tomtit is here to see you.

Nine hours later, we'd only covered 12 of the 20 kilometres to the riverbank when the roofline of a hut came into view. I stopped to check my map. There was no mention of this hut in the trail notes but there it was, a little tin shelter streaked with rust, tucked behind a rocky outcrop.

No way was Emilie going to walk past it and, since it was 4pm, I decided we might as well call it a day. We dropped down off the track to cross the stream then climbed the river terrace towards the hut, pausing to dump our packs before heading back to the playground of the creek.

More dedicated trail walkers might have kept going, but we had better things to do. I'd promised Emilie to help her build a fairy garden and kept my word, gathering pebbles and flowers and snowberries that she arranged on a flat river rock.

Let's get nudie, Mummy, and pretend we are river mermaids, burbles my little doll, so there we are, squatting by the burbling stream, the warm afternoon sun caressing our bare skin.

Later that night, two new friends emerged, although neither of us wanted to play with them. A pair of inquisitive mice were delighted to share their home with two weary trampers, and, as we struggled to get comfortable on the sagging wire bunks, the mice tore around the room, scaling the rough-hewn bunk frames and scampering across the exposed rafters. I had no desire to get into pest control mode, and anyway, Melissa wasn't there to help.

After leaning over to kiss Emilie goodnight, I snuggled down in my sleeping bag and closed my eyes, willing the warm glow of sleep to wash over me before the restless doubts returned.

Fear is a normal, hardwired and automatic response to perceived physical and/or emotional danger.

I'd been thinking about this since the early hours of the morning, after waking from a disturbing dream. Lying there in the dark, listening to Emilie's heavy breathing, I'd decided that there was a big difference between healthy fear and the unhealthy, insidious dread that accompanied my mental health condition.

Former American president Franklin D Roosevelt described this inappropriate fear well in his famous quote: *The only thing we have to fear is fear itself — nameless, unreasoning, unjustified terror which paralyses needed efforts to convert retreat into advance.*

In other words, the type of fear that transcends to a primal, paralysing panic. People often think that, in the face of danger, they'll swing punches like a boxer or run like an Olympic sprinter, but more often they just freak out and freeze.

That's what had happened in my dream that night. I needed to run, but instead I froze. My body slowed down like I was moving through wet cement, and then they caught me.

Do you know these dreams? The urge to flee floods your body like a shot of methamphetamine, but your legs turn to jelly and when you try to run, you can't.

You open your mouth to scream but nothing comes out, and instead you're choking on the thick, viscous slime of silence, clawing your way helplessly through heavy air as your attackers close in.

Except this time, I'd managed to wake myself up. I wrenched myself out of that nightmare world and back into the semi-darkness of East Ahuriri Hut, gasping and gagging as I fought my way out of my sleeping bag.

Once I'd assured myself that it was just us, all alone out here in the mountains, I ventured outside for a pee. I squatted amongst the tussock and stared up at the night sky, watching the glow of the moon emerge from behind a wisp of cloud. I thought about who else might be out there, looking down upon our tiny, fragile planet as it drifts by, watching the stars form, burn, then die?

I thought of my therapist's words, about how my nervous system was stuck on high alert for any whisper of threats, determined to keep me safe from harm. But I was safe. I didn't need those defences anymore. Behind the rage and anger that had helped keep me safe was a huge pool of grief that I needed to allow myself to feel, to process and to let go, so I could move on with my life.

Once I'd finished peeing, I went back into the little tin shelter. Emilie was breathing heavily in the semi-darkness. After climbing back into my sleeping bag on that sagging wire bunk, I lay and wept for a little while, silent tears running down my cheeks and into my hair. I wept for that scared little 14-year-old and all the other versions of myself that had followed me there, 1620 kilometres across New Zealand.

When the bright light of morning shone in through the cracks and chinks in the corrugated iron cladding, Emilie stirred. We had a big river to cross.

We saw the wide canyon of the Ahuriri long before the bright blue braids of the river came into view. It didn't look too dangerous, but it was hard to tell from a distance. From the river terrace, it looked little more than knee-deep, clear and blue, curling hard against the far bank before widening out and cascading over a broad rocky rapid and regrouping in a deceptively calm pool.

We climbed down into the steep-sided terrace and onto its shingle bank. It was much bigger up close.

If we'd been in a group, we could have linked our arms and packs and made our way through, but there were just the two of us. In fact, apart from a surprise encounter with a group of trampers who'd been descending from a night at the tarns, we'd seen no one this entire section.

These long periods of aloneness weren't quite what I was expecting from Te Araroa. As one of the world's long-distance hiking trails, it's usually crawling with trail walkers from all corners of the globe, but we were in the midst of a coronavirus pandemic and New Zealand's borders were closed.

Maybe in a different year we'd have teamed up with other walkers to attempt this crossing together, but right now it was just me and Emilie and the river.

We hung about, eyeing up the best possible spots before deciding to take the plunge. I made sure my phone and InReach were tightly secured in their waterproof sack in case we did end up taking a swim. Unclipping our chest straps, we threaded our arms behind each other's backs, and I took a firm grip of Emilie's pack. She was a full 30 centimetres shorter than me, so it was not the best fit and I didn't want to yank her off her feet in case she fell into me and knocked me off balance.

Are you okay, sweetheart? We can stop for a break on the other side and have some lunch, dry out our shorts. I was positive and up-beat, hoping she would be too as I encouraged her to walk with me into the freezing water. I didn't want her to start panicking, although part of me was amazed that she just followed my lead. I was pretty sure no one would have got me walking into a gigantic river when I was seven years old.

Baby steps, little steps. I was upstream of Emilie, sheltering her from the force of the current, digging my hiking pole in between the slimy rocks and leaning my body into it as my feet followed. I could feel the force of the water against my shins, my knees. It was almost up to my thighs. It was cold and clear and deceptively deep.

The sheer weight of water is an amazing thing — how something as fragile as a flake of snow, a droplet of dew on a spider's web, the damp kiss of morning mist can multiply into an element that carves its way through earth and stone.

Almost halfway across, and we were doing great.

It's so cold! Emilie whined.

You're damn right, it's like stepping into a flood of pure melted ice. First it stings, then it burns and then you go numb.

There, with the roar of rushing water all around us, the pebbles we had seen from high on the riverbank turned out to be sunken boulders covered in a slimy layer of sediment.

It would have been so much easier just to shuffle through the water, but these boulders were blocking my way. They'd created a channel that the water was rushing through, compressing the flow into an underwater funnel. I knew I had to step around this obstacle and through the bulk of the flow, but the river was sucking at my raised foot and pressing heavily against my leg, pulling me off balance.

Then both of my feet were firmly on the riverbed again and I was leaning into the current to counterbalance, pulling Emilie with me. I could feel her floating beside me, knocked off her feet, but the bank was so close now. With one more step, we were out of the current and across.

We made it! Good work baby. You did great! I pulled her out of the water and up onto the riverbank where we collapsed in the sunshine, feeling the sensation return to our freezing legs.

My heart was hammering in my chest, but I felt strangely calm, quietly proud.

We'd made it across the Ahuriri. All that stress and worry, but in the end, it hadn't been so bad. The largest unbridged river crossing on Te Araroa was now behind us. There was that one bit . . . but otherwise, it was okay. Perhaps we would make it to Bluff after all. And beyond.

Maybe it didn't matter that I didn't really know what our future held once we finished Te Araroa. Sometimes when you walk right up to the very things you are afraid of, you realise they aren't as scary or as impossible as you think. Fear magnifies everything.

We took off our shorts and T-shirts and draped them over the warm rocks. Emilie made for a sandy patch on the riverbank, decided to lose her knickers but kept her hat. I sat and watched, enveloped in a warm glow, as she crawled about in the sand, a little river nymph absorbed in her play.

It was hot down there beside the river, out of the wind. I lost the rest of my clothing and walked back into that freezing cold water, using my breath to help me immerse my body in its icy grasp.

Every nerve in my body screamed *no*! but something deeper said *yes* as I pushed myself through the initial discomfort and felt the addictive tingle of the running water caressing my bare skin.

I lay on my back with the rapids thundering in my ears like a heartbeat, a naked baby rocked in the cold embrace of the river.

We'd been racing the wind all day, shoved and buffeted on the way to Mount Martha Saddle and pushed and screamed at for a further six kilometres to Top Timaru Hut.

But there was no refuge for us at that little six-bunk shelter. It was packed full of trampers, judging from the assortment of tramping boots, trail shoes and hiking poles scattered on the deck, so we didn't even stop to look inside. Instead, we headed down to the creek with its wide, flat terraces — perfect for fair-weather camping but with no shelter from the gale-force winds.

The shallow valley had transformed into a deadly wind tunnel and we were struggling to stay on our feet and keep calm with this deafening roar all around us. Across the creek, a side-stream tumbled down from a short gully flanked with stunted beech trees. Up there. There would be a flat spot and some shelter up there, out of the worst of the wind.

We stumbled through the tussock and scrub, willing the ground to flatten out before our eyes. There was a spot on the far side of a beech tree that would have to do. Emilie helped me peg out the groundsheet then scampered off to collect rocks from the stream. I hoped the weight of the rocks placed over my pegs would prevent the wind from ripping them out of the ground.

We wrestled the inner of the tent into place and threw the

mustard-coloured fly over the top, racing to secure straps and pegs before the next gust of wind was upon us.

It was scary and exhilarating, and our hair was whipping around our mouths and into our eyes, but it felt like we were winning.

Quick, get in the tent! I told Emilie, who bundled herself inside, pack and all.

I paused to fill our water bottles and cooking pot from the creek, the wind whipping spray into my face, before joining her inside our flimsy shelter.

With the additional jerking and flapping of the tent, it was even noisier inside than out, but at least there was some respite from the invisible menace that had pushed and shoved us all day.

Since that morning, we'd covered the painfully slow and bitterly exposed 800-metre ascent from privately owned Tin Hut up the Avon Burn to the 1680-metre saddle. Mount Martha herself towered overhead at 1906 metres, mirrored by nearby Mount Melina at 1925 metres.

We'd squeezed in between them across the rocky saddle before picking our way down a steep, narrow scar of a track that zig-zagged across the scree-ravaged slopes to the head of Timaru Creek.

The wind was relentless, pushing us this way and that, with gusts sometimes so strong they pinned us against the side of the mountain. Emilie wasn't happy at all. The higher we climbed, the colder it became, and she was already rugged up in her raincoat, neck gaiter, gloves and woollen hat. The wind coming over the saddle behind us was incredible — freezing cold gusts of at least 80 to 100 kilometres an hour.

Emilie had already tripped and stumbled on the way up with the wind at her back and cut herself deeply just below the knee on a jagged gash of rock. Strangely enough, it didn't bleed much, although I could see pink flesh and white gristle through the open wound. I think the sight of her leg ripped open scared her more than the pain of the impact. I quickly covered her knee with a thick patch of plaster, offering cuddles, reassurance and a piece of chocolate.

But she'd lost her mojo and, by the time we reached the saddle and saw the steep and technical descent ahead of us, I had almost lost mine too.

On the way down, I kept expecting an extra-strong gust to suck her right off the side of the mountain and tumble her into the creek bed far below. I kept her close by me so I could grab her pack while we braced ourselves until the gust died out.

Once we were in the tent she was happy again, however, rolling around on her half-inflated sleeping mat, setting up our sleeping bags.

You can sleep there, Mummy, and I'll sleep here, she burbled, ripping everything out of my neatly packed backpack. I could feel the heat rising inside of me because I was sore and tired and I didn't want her to be making all this mess, with sticky, unwashed clothing everywhere.

The noise of the wind was getting to me. I lay on my side with my back to the chaos, fiddling with the cooker. It's not recommended to cook inside your tent, but there was no way I'd get a flame going outside in this gale, so I decided I'd try to avoid setting fire to my closed tent fly and cook in the vestibule.

I could have boiled water and soaked a handful of couscous, dried peas, dried mushrooms and tomato soup mix, but I couldn't be bothered fiddling around with all the different ingredients inside the tent just to create another bowl of bland trail slop. This had become a running joke between Emilie and me after I'd prepared dinner for her one night saying, as I handed her the bowl, *Here you go, a nice big bowl of pig slop!* From then on, those words never failed to transform any culinary complaints into rich peals of laughter.

That night, though, we were having gourmet pig slop, as I'd located two of our precious dehydrated meals: a chickpea curry for me and a spaghetti bolognaise for Emilie. I poured boiling water inside the pouches and sealed them back up. After 10 minutes, an easy, mess-free meal would be waiting for us.

I'd carried these dehydrated meals for almost 700 kilometres as emergency rations in case we ran out of food before the end of a section. I'd envisaged eating them huddled in a remote mountain hut, lashed with rain, but instead we were inside our little yellow tent, which might or might not make it through the night intact, so I guessed we might as well eat them.

As darkness fell, my head raced through all the possible scenarios. A pole will be snapped by the wind and rip the lightweight material of the tent to shreds. A peg will be ripped out and the fly will detach and get sucked out into the night. A branch will break off that tree overhead and crush us under its weight. I shouldn't have camped here, shouldn't have walked here, shouldn't be here. Stupid, stupid, stupid girl, woman, mother.

Stop. Just fucking stop it, I told myself. The voices dried up but the buzzing static of anxiety remained, 1000 tiny butterflies fighting their way out of my stomach and up my throat. I lay there and breathed deeply while trying to employ logical thought to our situation.

A common local weather pattern is for large fronts to sweep in from across the Tasman Sea and slam into the South Island's West Coast. The rain-swollen clouds push up against the towering rock wall of the Southern Alps and release their moisture, before transforming into powerful forces of hot air that roll downhill before eventually working their way out over the drier plains of the east.

As the wind races down from those high rocky summits, it speeds up in manic glee, building up pressure and transforming what might previously have been a calm and sunny landscape into a terrifying inferno of energy in motion.

That's exactly what was happening. We were in the eastern ranges of the Southern Alps and the wind was roaring down the rocky slopes and rolling around the shallow bowl of the valley, shaking everything in its path, including our little yellow tent.

It will blow out, I reassured Emilie. *We just need to wait.*

As the light died from the sky, the wind grew stronger and louder, huge gusts flattened the tent against my chest. I cuddled Emilie in my arms, forcing myself to breathe slowly, calmly, inhale and exhale until each gust died out and the tent bounced back up.

Tell me a story, Mummy, so I launched into a telling of 'Bush Baby's Stormy Night' and felt her little body relax against me.

Eventually, when it became clear the tent wasn't going to split apart or blow away with us inside it, Emilie fell asleep, snoring contentedly with my arm sprawled protectively over her chest. Somehow, I must have fallen asleep too, because when I opened my eyes again, dawn was spreading a gentle pink glow across the sky — a sky that was calm, spent, its rage and wrath blown out across the eastern plains.

Apart from a slight bend in one of the crossover poles, our tent emerged unscathed and so did we. There was no point hanging around, so we packed up our campsite and started walking, another 15 kilometres to Stodys Hut, 10 more to Pakituhi Hut and another 10 to the township of Lake Hāwea, where we planned to rest, shower and resupply for the next section. We'd been walking for 106 days and had only 466 kilometres to go on this crazy adventure called Te Araroa.

The undulating tussock trail down to Camp Stream Hut.

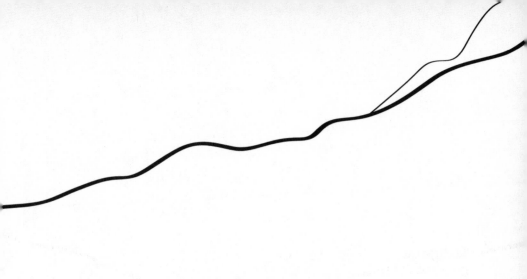

Chapter 14

Queenstown

Te Araroa
Day 114

LAKE HĀWEA IS BIG AND Lake Wānaka bigger, but Lake Wakatipu is larger than them both. We'd spent a week climbing up and down and up again over multiple spurs, ridgelines and passes as we made our way along the mountainous Motatapu Track. Alternatively baked by the sun and lashed by wind and rain, we'd stumbled on, reaching the high crests only to see mountains flanked by more mountains, like waves in an ocean of brown and grey.

And then we saw the lake. The brilliant blue expanse of Lake Wakatipu signalled many things: that we'd almost completed the demanding 50-kilometre alpine tramp between Wānaka and Arrowtown, that we were only days away from meeting up with friends to walk part of the Queenstown Lakes section together, and that we were only 400 kilometres from the coastal town of Bluff and the end of our Te Araroa adventure.

Only 400 kilometres. A few hours' drive down the highway, but at least a few weeks' steady walking through the valleys and mountains surrounding Queenstown, past Te Anau, through the foothills of the Takitimu Mountains and the notoriously muddy Longwood Forest until the trail finally emerges onto the southern coastline.

It was all planned, yet nothing was planned, as my mind was as empty as the huge, sweeping landscape and it refused to contemplate what life after Te Araroa could possibly look like. What would I do for work, where would we live, and what would the future hold? I'd love to go back to university, refresh my brain, have a career change, but I was scared of ending up in another awful workplace where my passion and creativity were stifled by bureaucracy. I just wanted to write, paint and go tramping as often as possible.

After five months of wandering through an everchanging panorama of mountains, rivers, forests and lakes, even the thought of going back to society seemed ridiculous. Why would we when we could be free out here? There were no bills to pay, no social standards to uphold. I could pee behind any tree I liked. Emilie could drop her pack and play with whatever took her fancy. We ate when we were hungry, slept when we were tired. Woke up with the birds. Walked until we decided to take a break. Bathed naked in rivers and streams. Washed our underwear and dangled it off our packs to dry in the midday sun, and walked with the breeze tickling our bare thighs and beyond. Who would want to return to a world where you must wear underpants, pee in a toilet and shower indoors?

I was still musing over all of this and many other things when we arrived in Arrowtown and handed over our dusty backpacks to the e-bike company. They'd offered us free hire of two e-bikes and a complimentary pack transfer, all the way through to Queenstown, in return for a review of their service.

Instead of a huge 30-kilometre day of walking along dusty trails, it would only take us a few hours to ride the gravelly bike tracks around the back of Lake Hayes to Lake Wakatipu.

The brilliance of the fluorescent lighting is burning my eyes, yet closing them only intensifies the throbbing in my head. I stare down at my dirty trail shoes. I'm lying on white sheets on a white hospital bed, a white blanket covering the cuts and scrapes on my hairy brown legs. I wouldn't usually wear shoes in bed, but when I lean forwards to untie the laces a searing pain shoots up my left arm and explodes behind one eye. I lie back and feel a wave of nausea wash over me. A nurse is at my side talking to me in words I can't understand, then fear snaps me awake again.

Where is Emilie? Where is my daughter?

She is with your friends, remember, she's at the hotel with your friends.

Friends . . . hotel . . . I try to make sense of the words, but the meanings disappear like mist. It hurts to think so I slip back into the dark fog that's surrounding me.

Later, another voice cuts through. It's the doctor, a man I'd consider handsome if I was in any state to do so. I drag my eyes up his body and onto his face, because he's telling me I have a minor concussion and they want to keep me in overnight.

I don't want to be kept in overnight. I'm banged up and dirty and I want to go home to my daughter, even if home is just a temporary concept, a room in a Queenstown hotel. I don't remember falling off the e-bike and slamming face-first into the unforgiving trail, ripping my forearm and knee open and twisting the ligaments in my shoulder on the rough gravel. Even with a helmet, the impact to my left temple caused my eye to haemorrhage within its socket and gave me a minor concussion.

Maybe if my brain had been working properly, I would have taken the doctor's advice and remained in hospital overnight, but I couldn't think straight, and my body was buzzing with adrenaline. I begged them to discharge me and returned to the hotel, where my friends Smash and Erin were looking after Emilie.

The next five days were a painful blur as my swellings peaked and began to subside. The tender skin around my eye transitioned from a deep, angry purple to a dull, greenish yellow, and my cuts and scratches faded to brown. Erin left and Smash stayed on, hanging out with Emilie who was loving city life while I lay in bed trying not to chase my fragmented thoughts.

The first few days of my concussion were surprisingly peaceful as my mind was empty of any cognitive thought. I lay quietly with the curtains drawn, drifting in and out of sleep. Even getting up to make myself a cup of tea was a strange and confusing experience, as I stared down at the cup in my hand, wondering what to do next. The thoughts and ruminations that constantly ran through my head were suddenly absent, and stringing a sentence together felt like a huge effort as I struggled to find the words.

As my swelling decreased, my mind slowly pulled itself back together. A great sadness washed over me as the gravity of our situation sunk in. Should we get off the trail, put the remainder of Te Araroa on hold until I recovered fully? But where would we go? Our house was occupied for another two months. The white walls of the hotel room were suffocating. It had gone from being a place of peaceful respite to a silent tomb.

I missed the calm, green surrounds of forests and mountains. If I was going to recover, then I had to get back into the bush that had become our home over the past five months.

Smash was walking Te Araroa northbound, having started her own epic journey in Bluff a couple of months earlier. Before my accident, we had made plans to walk the 60-kilometre section from Queenstown to Mavora Lakes together, and now, with my bruises all but faded yet my shoulder still sore, I decided to keep going. I told myself that if it got too much, Emilie and I could always backtrack to Queenstown and take a bus to a friend's house. If an emergency arose, we had our InReach satellite phone.

We decided to stock up on food and take the next section very slowly, with lots of time to rest and chill out in nature together.

The beauty of the Greenstone Valley with its tussock flats and beech forest distracted me from the dull ache in my shoulder and head for a while, but eventually my injuries won out. The painkillers and paracetamol just weren't cutting it. I was continuously sore and it was getting me down.

My shoulder hurt when I slept, and it hurt when I was awake. I still felt spaced out and Emilie's chatter had become intolerable as I struggled to keep up with her. But it was better than being in the concrete jungle of Queenstown with all its lights and action.

We'd walked barely two kilometres on the first day before setting up our tents on the wide grassy flats at the junction of the Greenstone and Caples rivers, then a further five kilometres on the second day before taking over the rustic, corrugated-iron shelter of Slip Flat Hut. Its four bunks, dirt floor and open fireplace became our home for the next two days, just me, Emilie and Smash.

We gathered wood for the outdoor fire, dragged the plastic mattresses outside onto the grass to lie in the sunshine and wandered down to the river to bathe. It was slow and peaceful and just what we needed.

We learned that Smash, who was 26, had lived in a tent in Australia for several years. A slender, short-haired gymnast, climber and a beautiful soul, she was mighty fine at stoking a fire. Smash lived with her own set of demons and I felt a connection with her and her history that only the children of trauma will understand.

Once you've experienced such darkness, the world becomes divided into those who know and those who don't. Those who haven't had a shared experience cannot be trusted because they don't understand.

After swallowing down a couple of codeine, which were doing very little to take the edge off, I lay in the late afternoon sunshine on my slightly sticky hut mattress, my mind wandering back in time to another version of myself, that 16-year-old girl-child chasing the dragon.

In a twisted kind of way, sometimes I think that soothing my broken soul with highly addictive opiates was a kind of self-medication, a way of suppressing my hyper-aroused nervous system and replacing my loss and grief with a toxic, chemical calm.

Because all opiates — whether scored on the street or administered by medical professionals — block pain, attach to receptors in the brain to help calm the central nervous system and create a sense of ease, happiness or, as I experienced it that very first time, an intense euphoric bliss.

But artificial highs don't last, the drugs are full of toxic shite and these chemicals rob you of your ability to feel anything. You might as well be dead.

Perhaps my personal prejudice against the zombification of opiates had piqued the interest of one of my journalism lecturers, who'd called me in to discuss an essay I'd written early in the course, or perhaps he was just horrified by my complete lack of a classical education or the fact that a student of journalism didn't own a TV. I can't remember the exact essay question — something along the lines of what television programme do you like, and why? An innocuous little question to introduce our first-year minds to the concept of media content analysis.

I didn't own a TV, and my home-schooling hippie parents didn't raise me with the habit of watching one, so I'd led with a quote from the darkly humorous Australian film *He Died with a Felafel in his Hand*, based on the cult novel by John Birmingham. There's a scene in the film where European vegetarian Anya (played by Romane Bohringer) arrives to inspect a room in a dingy Queenslander occupied by a bunch of flatmates from hell. When one couch-ridden, bong-smoking flattie explains the rules for the TV remote, Bohringer haughtily retorts that television is the opiate of the masses. I agreed and used my essay to denounce what I believed to be the mind-numbing, stupefying attributes of visual mass media.

Do you know where that quote really comes from? my lecturer asked me, before taking pains to explain the frequently paraphrased statement of German sociologist and economic theorist Karl Marx, *Religion . . . is the opiate of the masses.*

At 22, I was several years older and generations wiser than many of my first-year colleagues, but I had never heard of Marxism or sociology. I was intrigued.

My lecturer also explained that back in Marx's day, the impoverished, suffering poor used opium as pain relief to buffer them against a harsh and uncaring world. Marx had argued that religion's role was to provide a candle of hope, constructed by people to calm uncertainty over their place in the universe and in society.

I could understand what he meant. While still under the care of the New Zealand state, one of my last placements was with a Christian faith-based organisation that ran a residential care facility called Arndt House. I can't remember it very well, except that they were kind and caring, not punitive or derogatory towards the kids like some of the other facilities I was referred to when I exhausted the list of foster carers. Some of the girls and I went to the church choir services together.

While singing those hymns, my heart would fill with warmth and hope, something that had been lacking for a while in my young life. Even after the trauma of sexual abuse and all the dark experiences accumulated over the previous 18 months, I felt there was still light at the end of the tunnel for me, if only I could find my way there.

It was during my stay at Arndt House that I successfully detoxed off whatever shitty, cheap, badly cut drugs I'd been using and actively engaged with the social workers to plan out the next few years of my life.

This included returning to Australia, not to live with but to be close by my mother, a vital connection to a key member of my whānau that social workers noted I so desperately wanted and needed to restore. I would be attending adult classes to obtain my high school leaver's certificate and then working to gain entry to university.

Vicky would like to study art and psychology, my social worker had written in notes I'd found after sifting through that manila folder couriered to me from the government agency, Oranga Tamariki.

Services will need to be in place to support Vicky to readjust and reach her potential, the social worker had noted. *She is very fragile and prone to insecurities.*

I don't remember any services. I doubt any of them would have specialised in trauma. And I imagine my 16-year-old self wouldn't have felt safe enough to tell them anything. I tried to tell my mother about being raped but was left feeling that it was probably my fault. Just like going into foster care had been my fault, because I was an angry, aggressive, attention-seeking teenager who she said had wanted to destroy us all. I didn't talk to her about it again. Instead, I pushed it deep down inside of me with all the other memories and tried to deaden my rage and pain at being unlovable and unworthy with mind-numbing substances.

My father seems to be missing in these notes. Later, he told me he didn't know that I'd been in foster care. It didn't really matter. Back then, I didn't want to spend too much time dredging up the past. It hurt too much. Telling my story was an overwhelming, distressing ordeal in which my body always flooded with terrifyingly overpowering sensations. These days, I can either freeze up or disassociate as though I'm telling someone else's story, but when I was younger, the force of energy that would flood through me drove me into fits of rage and destruction, either towards myself, beating my head against walls or ripping out chunks of hair with my fingers, or raging against anyone who dared come close — social workers, counsellors, friends or lovers, or my mother.

My therapist explained that the sensation of overwhelm was the memory of trauma, lodged deep within my body, like a splinter causing a toxic infection. The trauma had interfered with my brain, deeply affected aspects of my functioning and damaged parts of my mind and my body. These unpleasant sensations were my body's response to the foreign body of the infectious trauma.

Sometimes he'd hop up out of his chair, straighten the creases in his chinos and draw me lines and graphs on his whiteboard, diagrams of the brain, maybe in an attempt to help me or himself feel better about the psychological processes at play. I wish I'd had him on my side all those years ago, postulating with his whiteboard marker and arguing my case with those CYFS-appointed psychiatrists, shutting down their pseudo-diagnoses of borderline personality disorder, oppositional defiant disorder and others.

But sadly, the simple telling of my story didn't release my body from the terrifying and destructive forces brought on by trauma. Not only did it upset me, but it also upset other people.

I quickly learned not to share my story, that in order to avoid the shameful sting of rejection from friends, colleagues, co-workers, classmates . . . and my mother, it was best to bury my secrets deep down inside of myself, remove myself from polite society and stay alone in my pain, anger, shame and grief.

It was hard work. People like to ask innocent questions during small talk as part of 'getting to know' each other, but questions like, *So where did you grow up? Where did you go to school?* or *Where do your family live?* triggered terrible feelings of guilt and shame. I would either tell them straight up and watch the subconscious recoil in their faces, or avoid giving a straight answer and watch as they moved on to chat with the next person.

Either way, I knew I was different, tainted, broken, bad, a miserable, angry and intrinsically unlovable person who, as sad as it was, probably deserved to be rejected by everyone she met.

My university lecturer suggested an alternative way of thinking that radically changed how I saw myself. He was one of my first formative adult mentors and I valued his friendship, even if it was unconventional. While my classmates partied it up at the student bar, he and I would sip our drinks upstairs in the staff lounge and discuss whatever was topical at the time. He asked me questions about my life, my upbringing and experiences with interest and intrigue, and never once recoiled in disgust.

Instead, he suggested that I could view my life as a trajectory where, through no fault of my own, I had started my journey lower down the social ladder and, due to my own determination and resilience, had risen high above the baseline to emerge head and shoulders above my peers.

Be proud of yourself, because you've come so much further than many people ever have, he urged me. He meant the ones partying downstairs with the security of knowing their families loved and were proud of them, and who had their basic needs met with spending money, food, maybe even the loan of a car to drive themselves to university or Dad's credit card to purchase brand-new textbooks, so they could focus their remaining energies on enjoying life and picking up a few key concepts at any lectures they managed to attend.

But I wasn't attending university to enjoy the beer and skittles. I was 22 and this was my third attempt at tertiary education.

After escaping what I considered a close call at the psychiatric lockup some eight months earlier, I had allowed myself to wallow in my latest episode of intense emotional dysregulation for a period, before picking myself up once again.

I had to get back into tertiary education and get somewhere in this world. This time I would choose a programme of study where I could do something I enjoyed, and I'd always enjoyed writing. As a kid, I loved writing poems and stories, even when I was little, I would create mini books for my Barbies, cut out of cardboard and stapled together, their multiple pages painstakingly filled with miniature handwriting.

It seemed a straightforward and completely logical decision, so I got back on the university websites and found the Bachelor of Journalism course at the University of Queensland. If I got my application in soon, I could start my studies as part of the mid-year intake.

My lecturer shook his head when I told him this story.

A love of writing is the worst reason to study journalism, he said. I didn't really understand what he meant until years later when my own creativity was stifled again and again by the confines of ruthless editors and politically charged newsrooms.

I threw myself into my journalism studies, slowly building up my fragile self-esteem as my good grades saw me receive accolades, such as the Dean's Commendation for High Achievement several semesters in a row. I even applied and was accepted for an exchange programme with a prestigious French university, the Paris Institute of Political Studies, known as Sciences Po.

I worked weekend and night shifts with the nursing agency to fund my studies and spent long hours in the library. I made tentative friendships with a couple of postgraduate students, but mostly I kept to myself.

During the course, journalism students had the option of attending a two-week unpaid internship with local media outlets. I stayed on for weeks, months, until one kind editor at *The Courier-Mail* put me on her books and made sure I got paid for any stories they published. I later became a regular work experience student at the Brisbane office of Australian Associated Press, the busy wire service that I eventually joined officially through their annual journalism cadetship programme, moving to Sydney to kick-start my professional life.

I loved my life in Sydney. It was so much more vibrant and exciting than Brisbane had ever been, and much warmer and greener than inner-city Paris where I'd spent almost six months living in a tiny one-bedroom apartment while taking classes at the freezing-cold historic buildings occupied by Sciences Po. I had a close circle of friends, including my dear buddy and flatmate Greg, and we worked hard and played harder.

Alas, my dark moods, bouts of depression and general dislike of authoritative figures made me a shitty employee and I was discharged from AAP before completing the full cadetship. This time, instead of falling into another pit of despair, I took a part-time job in production at the nearby *Sydney Morning Herald* and saved up for a one-way ticket to Bangkok, with the dream of going to work in neighbouring Myanmar.

Part of the reason for my dismissal from the wire service was that I'd apparently breached the terms of my contract by selling my stories elsewhere — stories, I argued, which I had researched and written while on holiday in northwest Thailand, and which had nothing to do with my current employer.

I had spent a couple of exhilarating weeks on the Thailand-Burma border, following up on a string of contacts given to me by a sympathiser of the minority groups fighting for freedom against the military regime. I had visited a refugee camp, been smuggled across the border into Myanmar in a small boat and been taken on a wonderful tour of the resistance army's military strongholds. I'd also ridden blindfolded on the back of a motorbike to the headquarters of a group of young freedom fighters, Burmese men and women around the same age as me.

Their stories were heart-breaking and compelling, raw and real compared with the staged press conferences and media releases of Sydney. I felt like a younger version of veteran war correspondent Christina Lamb as I typed up my notes late at night while the back-up generator hummed through the window of the simple motel in Mae Sot in western Thailand.

I had even emailed my boss at AAP to offer them these stories, only to receive a short, curt response. To cease and desist. Undeterred, I sold the stories to a dissident media outlet funded by NGOs, hoping naively that my words would bring a voice to the voiceless and some justice for those poor souls on the Burmese border, as well as the thousands of others trapped inside under the military regime.

I was still thinking about my arduous journey through tertiary education and the many doors that opened and closed for me as we parted ways with Smash at Greenstone Hut. I was sad to leave her — after so many days together she felt like a little sister and I wished I could have done more to help her on her journey, just as she'd helped me and Emilie. Now, it was just me and Emilie again, following the Mararoa River a further 40 kilometres through to Mavora Lakes and on to Te Anau.

Later that evening, we basked in the sunshine outside Taipo Hut following a quick end-of-day dip in the river, and I thought about my 16-year-old self and all the things I'd say to her if I only could.

None of this is your fault. You're not unlovable, worthless or broken. You were just a kid whose parents, for their own reasons, were unable to take care of you and give you the love, support and understanding you needed. What you are feeling is completely normal and it's okay to feel anger, pain, hurt and grief. Let me hold you tight in my arms so you can feel safe again — safe to cry, safe to feel whatever it is that's ripping through your little body. I love you and I will always love you and I'm always here for you, no matter what.

I turned to Emilie and wrapped her up in a bear hug, my half-naked little daughter, glowing in the evening sun.

I'm sorry Mummy hasn't been very chatty today. My head has been so sore. I'll call the doctor once we get to Te Anau and see if she can send me some medicine. And we'll find a nice little motel to sleep in overnight.

Will they have cartoons, Mummy? I hope so!

She was happy with that, my beautiful, loving, forgiving little big girl. Oh Emilie. How I wish with all my heart that you never have to experience this kind of pain in your warm and generous soul. I will do whatever it takes to love you and protect you from harm.

Emilie was hungry, so we headed back inside the hut and I spread peanut butter over our stale wraps. It had been six days since we'd left Queenstown, dawdling our way towards Te Anau. I rummaged through our supplies, thinking that we'd better start covering some distance over the next few days or we would run out of food.

A resupply box was waiting for us at a place called The Key, a mere blip on the map where the trail crosses a highway and heads deep into the mountains, but I planned to top it up with fresh vegetables and a few treats in Te Anau, a picturesque township on the outskirts of the glacier-carved Fiordland National Park.

It seemed that our thoughts and desires revolved mainly around food: eating it, wanting more of it, wondering if we had enough of it. We tried not to fall into the trap of talking about all the things we'd like to eat if we weren't walking Te Araroa, but it was hard work. When you're chronically hungry and craving big calories to match the energy you're putting out every day, food is foremost on your mind.

Over the next few days as Emilie and I staggered closer to Mavora Lakes, we were joined by another angel, a petite trail walker from the Netherlands called Eliene. She was also heading south, to Te Anau and beyond, and within 10 minutes of our meeting, Emilie was all over her like a puppy dog. I'm not sure if Eliene realised it, but I was so grateful for her company. The nagging pain in my shoulder and my bruised brain was contributing to my low mood and I was too preoccupied with my misery to laugh or joke much with Emilie.

On the other hand, Eliene had been walking alone for the past few weeks and had plenty of attention to give a boisterous little girl. We walked together for the next three days, Eliene sometimes boosting off ahead of us after lunch on her long slim legs, only to reunite with us at the huts in the evening. Emilie asked a million questions, about her food, her gear, where she had been, what she had seen, and was especially intrigued by Eliene's shiny pink hairbrush.

The older sister of several brothers, Eliene was gentle and kind, and Emilie was happy, which helped me a lot. Because by that stage, I was only just hanging on to get to Te Anau and ring my doctor for a fix of a different kind.

Slip Flat Hut in Greenstone Valley.

Chapter 15

Bluff

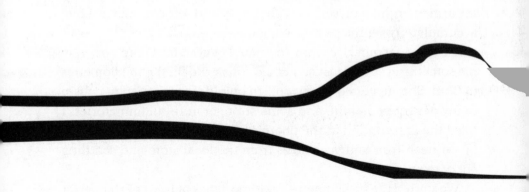

Te Araroa
Day 129

PAIN IS DISTRESSING. NOT ONLY does pain affect your body, but it also affects your emotions and your mind. It can cause anxiety and depression which, in turn, can make pain worse. Maybe that's why the heroin withdrawals of my younger years had hit me so badly. After the warm, soothing bliss of being high, the agony of withdrawals was relentless, trapping me inside the prison of my own head. And now, to a lesser extent, so was my shoulder. At rest, the pain reduced to a dull throbbing sensation, but raising my arm or reaching out to steady myself resulted in sharp stabbing sensations. While my back and legs were strong, I could barely raise my arm to undress myself, and all the joy and self-confidence I had accumulated over the past 1500 kilometres was slowly ebbing away.

Once we got ourselves into Te Anau, I begged my GP to prescribe me something strong just so I could finish the final 400 kilometres to Bluff. She suggested Tramadol, an opioid that is a distant cousin to my old friend heroin, and some stronger anti-inflammatories. I filled the prescription at the pharmacy in Te Anau before stocking up on fresh fruit and vegetables from the local store and scuttling out of town.

We started the 70-kilometre Takitimu Track at Lower Princhester Hut on an overgrown trail that led us up to an 800-metre saddle before descending towards the northern boundary of Waterloo Station. Here we fought our way through a field of giant tussock, which reached almost over our heads, our feet squelching through an orgy of boggy, mossy wetland.

As we climbed up and up into the foothills of the Takitimu

Mountains, fighting our way through the lush vegetation of the lowland forests, I marvelled at the difference the drugs made.

My pain was gone and my mood was buoyed, despite the weight of my resupplied pack. I could talk, think and laugh again as I chased Emilie through thick patches of fern. These Southland forests were dark and wild, and the tracks desperately overgrown. Above us loomed a solid mass of a mountain range that, according to Māori legend, is the remains of the upturned hull of the Tākitimu canoe.

A glimpse of red in the beech forest caught my eye — it was Eliene! We joined forces to race the oncoming rain to the next hut, singing loudly as the cold water lashed our legs and faces. Emilie's exuberance was overflowing after we discovered two other trampers setting up their sleeping bags inside, and she ripped open her pack to show them all her sparkly new hairbrush, a Tangle Teezer purchased along with my pain medication at the Te Anau pharmacy. It was a party of strangers, with one delighted, excited, pink-thermal-underwear-clad and sparkly-hairbrush-wielding child.

The following morning, Eliene hugged us both goodbye — she was going to boost ahead to the border of Linton Station, while we were aiming for the modest achievement of the next hut, some 10 kilometres away. My shoulder had stiffened overnight so I decided to wash down a second Tramadol with my cup of bitter instant coffee.

Memories of my 16-year-old self were still lurking in the back of my mind, and as I settled into the day's walk, she resurfaced again.

While the heroin itself left my body within a couple of weeks, it took several months for me to fully recover from the ordeal and maybe even years before I experienced feelings of pleasure or happiness again. It's hard to feel joy once you've felt heroin. It has a way of draining all the colour out of life, until everything fades to monochrome.

You're doing a great job, Mummy! Emilie burbled, interrupting my stream of consciousness. I smiled up at her little face, my tiny wahine toa, as she watched me try to navigate a stream crossing without getting my trail shoes wet. If only I'd had a crystal ball at age 16, or 17, or whatever I was by then, and I could have seen how much joy was waiting for me on the other side.

Emilie is the greatest joy of my life. Whatever the endorphins are that new mums experience when they look at their babies, they still make me melt inside when I look at her, kiss her soft cheeks, snuggle in close to her warm neck.

Thanks, sweetheart! You're doing a great job too.

All the messing about to keep my trail shoes dry was for nothing as we soon encountered a section of track that had turned into a deep bog, with no way over, under or around it through the impenetrable dark bush. Emilie managed to escape the worst of it by balancing on a rotten log that disintegrated under my weight, plunging me up to my thighs in thick mud.

Mummy has been eaten by a mud monster! Emilie crowed as I floundered out the other side.

Come here and give me a cuddle, Emilie! The forest rang with her squeals of laughter.

I scraped the worst of the muck off with a stick and we stumbled on, the path light beneath our feet. Eventually, the thick rotting vegetation gave way to a running stream where I could clean myself properly. It had been hours since we'd seen the sky through the forest canopy, and when we eventually climbed out of the river and up to the hut nestled in a clearing, the clouds were low overhead.

Everything felt damp, including the interior of the dark little hut, our packs, socks and shoes. I coaxed a fire to life in the open hearth and installed Emilie in front of it. She was an angel in her bright pink pyjamas, all rugged up in an equally bright yellow down jacket. She read excerpts to me from her book, giggling at all the funny parts. Snake and Lizard, what a pair of clowns. How could I ever be lonely with Emilie around? She is my angel, my brave, bright, beautiful girl.

As the light faded from the sky, the cold seeped into the tiny hut, even with the fire going. I was freezing, rubbing my thighs through my lightweight merino thermals and pulling on my woollen beanie and down jacket. It was the end of March, autumn, and we were in the deep south of the South Island. As much as I liked to fantasise about remaining out here in the hills forever, in just a couple of months this part of the world would be frozen in the grip of winter.

The following day, we would camp at the boundary of Linton Station, a huge, privately owned sheep and cattle station halfway between Te Anau and Invercargill, before climbing the fence and walking a further 25 kilometres to the road.

Greg was walking through the fields to meet us, a sturdy figure in a red woollen cap. We'd spent the past few days wandering through his stomping grounds in the foothills of the Takitimu Mountains and that evening he was taking us home to stay at his backpackers' accommodation in Tuatapere.

Thanks to the connectivity of social media, Greg had not only followed our journey southbound from Cape Reinga, but also some of our early tramping adventures when Emilie was four and five years old.

By the time we'd bundled into his car and patted his excited dogs, it was like we were among old friends.

Now in his fifties, Greg had spent many years exploring the mountains of Southland, Fiordland and beyond, back in the days before GPS systems and lightweight tramping gear. Over a glass of red wine that evening, we shared our love of time spent in wild places, as well as our personal experience with grief, loss and the black dog.

The following day, I left my heavy pack at the backpackers and we got a lift back to the trail. I felt like I was walking on air with only Emilie's little pack on my shoulders, crammed with lunch and plenty of water for the 24-kilometre day from Birchwood to Merrivale. Was this what ultralightweight trail walking should feel like, when you're not weighed down with food, clothing and gear for two?

The lightness wasn't just in my body, it was also in my mind. With my pain finally under control, I sang and chatted with Emilie as we boosted up 300 metres of almost vertical hillside, following a fence line through sheep paddocks until we reached the forestry plantation. We raced each other for short spurts up the ridiculously steep slope then collapsed, panting and giggling. We offered each other silly presents of dandelion blooms, bits of grass, dried sheep-poo pellets.

Emilie is an actress, a comedian, an entertainer extraordinaire. She loves reciting stories to me, her voice rising and falling as she imitates the different characters. I managed to join in and tell a story of my own making, much to her delight. Emilie is my sunshine. If you could bottle up her laughter, you'd have yourself a tonic of pure joy.

By this time, the native bush on the low flanks of the Takitimu Mountains was already a dark olive-green smear far behind us. After leaving the mountains, Te Araroa cuts through exotic forest and farmland, and all the land around us was a patchwork of bright green agriculture. Sheep, cattle, crops. Civilisation. Humans.

You don't realise the extent to which humans have altered New Zealand's natural environment until you spend time in our wild places. There's so little of it left untouched by the destruction of human hands and pest species. In some places, our forests are silent, there are no native birds singing in the trees, no large flightless birds bumbling through the undergrowth. Everywhere there is evidence of intruders: nibbled leaves and twigs, torn bark, a flurry of feathers from a bird carcass, hoof prints and droppings.

Scarily enough, sometimes it's the complete absence of certain plant species that signifies a forest is riddled with herbivorous pests. Mostly it's deer down in the lowlands, maybe tahr or chamois higher up in the mountains. Or goats, those opportunistic creatures that adapt so easily to a wide range of environments. These browsing animals can damage many different indigenous plant species including grasses, sedges, ferns, shrubs and trees, or eliminate highly palatable plant species.

Another opportunist is the possum, introduced from Australia to be hunted for its soft fur. With no natural predators to keep it in check, possum populations have exploded across New Zealand with devastating effects, including for our fragile native plants and old-growth forest canopies. These furry omnivores feed mainly on leaves but will also eat buds and flowers, sometimes devouring so many of the flowers that the plants never have a chance to set fruit. Or if they do, possums will also eat their fruits, as well as ferns, insects, land snails, native birds and their eggs.

In the undergrowth lurk rats, mice, stoats and their brethren, feeding on insects, lizards and birds. Emilie and I came across stoats hunting in broad daylight, the first time up a tree surrounded by screeching korimako, and the second time peering out of a hollow log.

We witnessed the destruction and damage of these pest creatures throughout Te Araroa. We came face to face with wild pigs in the Tararua Range, goats scaling the sheer sides of the Whanganui River, tahr in the rocky outcrops of the Hakatere, deer in the Greenstone Valley, feral cats creeping through scrub as well as rats, mice and possums making their homes in our backcountry huts.

Hunted to death in their native forests and with the bulk of their habitat burned and cleared to make way for farmland, New Zealand's native creatures and the wild places they call home face a bleak future.

It's hard not to feel a deep kinship for our charismatic native creatures and quirky plants, fungi and lichens. Over five and a half months, we'd walked amongst them, slept amongst them, fought our way through them, stepped over them, fallen into them, listened to their sweet songs and marvelled at our chance encounters with them.

We powered along a gently sloping forestry trail, following a series of trail markers as we traversed the tops of the Twinlaw forest. Road junctions snaked off on either side of the 4x4 track, but there were no forestry operations underway and overall, it was pleasant and easy walking. As we walked through a towering eucalypt plantation, it was eerily quiet. I hadn't expected to find native birds in there, but it still felt strange without them.

Eight hours and 24 kilometres later, we passed through boggy farmland, much to the interest of a herd of young cattle, then clambered over a stile to the road. Soon Greg would be there to pick us up and we would be able to enjoy another hot shower and ice cream from the local store, before making our way into the depths of the Longwood Range.

The Longwood Range lies between the high, rugged mountains of Fiordland and the low, expansive foothills and plains of Southland. With the Waiau River to the west and the smaller Aparima River to the east, these low ranges rise out of the landscape like an island, forming an isolated, irregular plateau around 10 kilometres wide and 30 kilometres long.

Its humps and summits are not high by South Island standards, peaking at a mere 870 metres, but when you're sliding down the muddy, boggy mountainside or clawing your way back up over roots and slimy, rotting vegetation, it feels much bigger.

We quickly realised that sections such as the St James Walkway, Greenstone Track and even Ninety Mile Beach were more like highways compared with the dense, wet jungle of the Longwood Forest. Coastal and westerly winds bring fog and drizzle to these low mountains nearly all year round, and the earth underfoot was oozing with water. Thick swathes of rotting vegetation gave way to dark swamps of viscous mud that threatened to swallow us up. We knew there would be mud, but this was something else entirely, wetter even than the storm-deluged jungle of the Tararua Range.

The rough track and wide swamps made for slow going. But I wasn't really in a rush, although I knew the only accommodation en route was the historic four-bunk shelter of Martins Hut, some 25 kilometres away.

The last hut of Te Araroa. The last wild forests of Te Araroa. Somehow, we were only 100 kilometres from Bluff and the end of the crazy adventure that had begun more than six months earlier, with sand whipping our bare legs at the tip of Ninety Mile Beach.

The thought of our journey's end filled me with an immense lethargy that was only partly caused by the thick mud coating my legs as I wallowed through the muddy track.

The stunted forest eventually gave way to windswept tops covered in harakeke, mountain toatoa and Dracophyllum. Beyond was the wide expanse of the south coast. Over there was the sprawling city of Invercargill and the rocky headlands we would walk around before arriving in Bluff. The dark mound on the horizon was Rakiura/ Stewart Island, a dream destination for trampers and nature lovers.

Emilie stumbled and was nearly consumed by a particularly deep pool of evil-looking black murk. But my Mummy reflexes were lightning quick, and I caught her, although my muddy hands stained her shirt. We held each other and started to giggle, because there was nothing else to do, there was no escape from the clinging, cloying, clutching mud.

Now you nearly got eaten by a mud monster! I told her as she laughed up into my face with her little button nose, wide smile and big brown eyes.

We sat down on some damp moss to scrape the worst of the mud from our legs, woollen socks and filthy and battered trail shoes. Somewhere back at home, there's a photo of me as a little girl, maybe three or four years old, completely naked apart from a pair of yellow floaties on my arms, and covered head to toe in thick brown mud.

Emilie reminded me about that photo. *Why, Mummy, why were you covered in the mud?*

I can't remember why, except that it was probably from a hot day playing in our dam on one of those Australian blocks, and I was smearing myself with mud because it felt cool and smooth and wonderful, and I was young and wild and free.

I thought about that little blonde girl with her bright blue eyes and joyous smile, and of all the things that happened to her on her long journey through life. How, despite the sadness and the trauma, she'd managed to fight her way through, a little warrior, a wahine toa, an old soldier, a bright little soul, who was still there inside of me and who still wanted to laugh, love, look after wild animals and feel at peace in wild places.

I looked at the bright little soul beside me, munching on a muesli bar, her strong brown legs smeared with mud and scratches. She was also a little warrior and I hoped this time spent out here together would give her the strength to navigate whatever challenges life throws her way. Perhaps one day she will come to crave the sanctuary of wild places, and I hope, with continued conservation efforts and education, there will always be a place for her to come where she can connect with nature's creatures and feel happy and calm.

She pointed up above our heads to show me the miromiro watching us from a tree. *Look, Mummy, it's my friend the tomtit!*

My eyes filled with water as a burning lump forced its way up my throat, but this had nothing to do with trauma. These were the sweet tears of joy, not grief.

I scooped my beautiful little daughter up in a warm embrace. I was filthy, damp and covered in mud with no chance of a shower that night, but there was nowhere else I'd rather be.

The historic timber slab shelter of Martins Hut was built in 1905 when gold-mining operations were in full swing in this part of the Longwood Forest. The solitary maintenance workers who lived out here alone in the thick, dark bush faced the task of ensuring fallen trees and raging storms didn't disrupt the steady supply of water required for downstream mining operations.

I wonder what sort of people thrived in this environment and whether they loved or loathed the thick wet jungle growing up around the hut, hemming in the sky with its dense canopy of leaves and vines.

This morning, I'm full of love and, from my lofty seat on the Martins Hut long drop with the loo door shamelessly wide open, this forest is one of the most beautiful I've ever seen.

The warm glow of sunlight is rippling through the tall, majestic trees, accentuating the brilliant shades of green, all the way from the bright tones of the ferns on the forest floor to the darker shades in the understorey. The clear sweet call of a bellbird rings out across the small clearing around the old hut.

I think I could be quite happy to live somewhere like this, surrounded by forest friends, tiny insects, birds, plants, everything to do with our natural world and nothing to do with people. Except that cutting myself off from other people isn't the answer anymore, nor is it the answer for modern society to distance and cut ourselves off from our wild places.

Human beings need the emotional security that only comes

with deep connection with one another. And I truly believe much of our sickness and discontent stems from being disconnected with nature.

When I think of what triggers me, the answer is simple: other people. I'll walk into the bush for a fortnight with my child and cross over the rocky fortress of the Waiau Pass with no problems, but I shudder to enter a room full of people I haven't met before. What will they think of me, will they judge me, welcome or reject me?

On the other hand, nature doesn't welcome or reject. It simply gets on with the glorious task of living and dying. Symbiotic relationships flourish — just look at those lichens created from algae and fungus, one providing water and minerals, and the other photosynthesising to supply a sugary food source.

I truly believe that reconnecting with our natural world, on nature's own terms, is key for our happiness, wellbeing and sense of place. The more peace and affinity we find in our natural world, the more peace we find within ourselves.

Four days after leaving the Martins Hut loo, we would reach the end of Te Araroa via the coastal trail into the windswept town of Bluff. But first we needed to walk the length of Southland's Tīhaka and Ōreti beaches.

As soon as we hit the rugged wilderness of the southern coastline, I was flooded with warm memories of wandering down Ninety Mile Beach almost six months earlier, with the excitement of beginning a big adventure lightening our steps despite our heavy packs.

It seemed like a lifetime ago, yet it had all happened so fast. I wanted to slow down, to soak in as much trail magic as I could, to gorge myself on the solitude and the emptiness and the majestic spectacle of Papatūānuku's wild places before it was all behind us. But we needed to keep moving. The sky overhead was clear, but there was a nasty southerly front due to come through that evening and we needed to push on down Tīhaka Beach if we wanted to make it to Riverton.

But my legs were heavy, and I didn't want to push on.

I wanted to stay there amidst the clumps of salt-whipped tussock and flax and watch the waves lap the shore. Nature still had so much to teach us. I realised I'd walked over 2000 kilometres across New Zealand's North and South islands, but suddenly I felt like I'd learned so little. Maybe I should have sat still longer, watching the wind blow through the tussock grass and the dying rays of sunlight caressing the high mountain sides, or stayed outside to witness the rhythms of the night.

As if reading my mind, the trail played a little trick on us — as though it were saying, you haven't got me in the bag just yet.

Just after kilometre 2952, the trail leaves the beach and climbs up a small bluff to weave around the rocky and windswept headland, but a combination of exhaustion and distraction saw us lose sight of the faded posts that marked the way, and instead, wander along a farmland through closely cropped sheep paddocks. Apart from the nervous sheep and a couple of empty farm buildings, there was no sign of civilisation, no angry Southland farmer bearing down on us with his shotgun. Once we realised our error, we decided it would be better to beg forgiveness if the need arose, and kept walking.

According to my Topomap, if we just kept walking in a straightish line, we'd eventually re-join the official trail in the right place to climb the hundred or so metres over the headland and into the back streets of Riverton. But time was no longer on our side, and as the sun dipped low to the west, we crossed yet another sheep paddock, opened and closed a salt-spray-stiffened gate, and walked to a giant deer fence that was the last obstacle between us and the trail. Shit, shit and shit. It was now almost dark, the bush beyond the fence where our path surely led was little more than a blackened smear. It would take the best part of an hour to backtrack out of the farm and take the official route, and both of us were tired and spent.

Oh well, nothing to it, let's get over that fence, I told Emilie, launching myself at the wire. It dug into my fingers with agonising sharpness, so I tried another tactic, this time, climbing up onto the wooden post, unclipping my pack, and teetering a little as I half-lifted, half-threw it over the fence. *Now give me your pack,* I said to Emilie, only then realising her little brown eyes had filled with tears and her down-turned mouth was beginning to wobble.

I can't climb over that, Mummy, it's too high for me!

Oh my little love. She'd walked so far, lashed by the wind and rain, spurred on by the promise of a bed at the Riverton Holiday Park, a hot shower and maybe an ice cream, only to be thwarted by a giant fence and held captive in the darkness.

Of course you can do it, I told her in a gentle voice. *You've crossed giant rivers, climbed over huge piles of windfall, slipped and slithered across mountains and survived the most hungriest of mud monsters. This is just a deer fence, it's just like climbing a ladder, and once we're over it, we'll turn on our head torches and go get that ice cream! Now come on, get up over that fence!* Whether it was my words of encouragement, or the incentive of a sweet treat, or her own strength and determination, she launched her little body at the fence and ten minutes later, we found the trail marker and half-ran, half-stumbled through the forest, our head torches illuminating the twisted trunks and shimmering leaves.

The next morning, we walked another 26 kilometres, fording the mouth of Waimatuku Stream, which was little more than calf-deep at low tide, and digging deep to cover the remaining 12 kilometres to a holiday park on the outskirts of Invercargill where we called it a night.

The following day, the sky was squally and grey, but apart from the occasional shower, the worst of the rain had passed over during the night. We packed away our hiking poles and walked hand in hand, happy and quiet, watching the waves and the gulls and the sky.

Our re-entry to civilisation was a sombre affair as the southern city of Invercargill spread out around us, squat grey buildings and overhead power lines replacing the lush green canopy of the bush, concrete highways instead of gurgling streams. I felt strangely detached — an observer wandering through a foreign world.

Emilie was in high spirits. It was her birthday in 10 days' time, she would be eight years old and she had big plans. It was my birthday soon too: in less than a week I'd be 37. I had plans too, and I was looking forward to my friends being part of them.

Cold winds buffeted our tired bodies as we rounded the coastline outside of Bluff and looked out over the choppy grey waters of Foveaux Straight to Rakiura/Stewart Island. I slowed down to a turtle crawl on the homeward stretch, but Emilie wasn't having a bar of that. The café on Marine Parade awaited her, as did a hot chocolate with loads of marshmallows and whatever other treats she could find in the cabinet.

Come on, Mummy! Don't be sad! Everyone has to finish the trail eventually . . . and we can go on adventures again!

I was flooded by tears of love and gratitude as I gripped my little wahine toa's warm hand tightly in mine and together we walked the final steps of Te Araroa out into the carpark at Stirling Point.

The end of a very long journey.

Epilogue

FIVE DAYS LATER, I CELEBRATED my thirty-seventh birthday in the rugged mountain ranges in Canterbury's Arthur's Pass, waking up on the side of Mount Aicken with my little mate and my big mate squeezed into the tent beside me.

Cradling my cup of instant coffee, I smiled at them both, sleepy-eyed and messy-haired, all of us happy to be back home in the mountains.

The last few days of Te Araroa had been difficult for me. Emilie buzzed with energy and excitement at the prospect of finishing our long journey, while I felt myself lingering, uncertain, wishing every step was taking us back into the silence of mountains instead of closer to the end of the trail.

The five stages of grief rolled around in my head. Denial, anger, bargaining, depression and acceptance. Had six months been long enough for me to process the grief accumulated over a lifetime? Could I finally come to terms with living with post-traumatic stress disorder? Was it a badge I could wear openly, instead of a gaping wound that ate me up inside?

It worried me that I didn't have all the answers. But if my 2200-kilometre walk across New Zealand with my little daughter had taught me anything, it was to know that I would never have all the answers to what was ahead of me.

I write these words while sitting in Danilo's living room in Dunedin, one of the many rooms we got stuck into painting and redecorating together after deciding to combine our lives and relocate to this beautiful southern city. We painted a feature wall in Resene Sunglo, a rich reddish pink that reminds me of the spectacular sunsets and eerie sunrises we often witness in the backcountry, while the kitchen has bold hints of burnt orange like the many strange and wonderful alpine plants we find above the bush line.

After so many months outdoors, it felt intensely uncomfortable to reintegrate to society with so many concrete structures, doors and walls, but the overgrown jungle of the back garden, brimming with gigantic tree ferns, five finger and kōwhai, is home to a rich array of native bird life, so instead of jumping up to make porridge and pack my sleeping bag each morning, sometimes I've been brought a cup of tea in bed where I can lie and listen to the bellbirds. But it takes work for two very independent people, each with their own separate interests, priorities, emotional wounds and personal history, to simply come together.

Over the past few months, I've found myself alone in the house while Emilie is at school and Danilo is away doing fieldwork. I'm lonely and missing my friends and connections. Emilie and I still get out as much as we can and since moving further south, we've explored parts of Fiordland, Southland, Westland and Mount Aspiring National Park, sometimes with Danilo but mostly just the two of us. We've talked about getting back on the trail this summer and completing the 900 kilometres of the North Island that we missed due to lockdowns, but to be honest, now that New Zealand's borders have re-opened and the number of trail walkers has soared, we'd prefer to spend our time exploring some of the more quiet and remote parts of our backcountry, like the wilderness of Kahurangi National Park and the rugged jungles of Fiordland and South Westland. Some international trails, such as the HexaTrek in France, have also sparked our interest.

After sending this manuscript to my editor, Emilie and I disappeared for an epic eight-day mummy–daughter adventure in the eastern regions of Kahurangi, taking a lesser-used route up over the Lookout Range, taking in the spectacular limestone outcrops of Mount Owen before descending into the narrow, whio-filled gorge of the Fyfe River.

We were befriended by inquisitive kea and charismatic weka, and watched over by quiet tomtits and chattering fantails, spending our nights huddled in that little yellow tent or snug in backcountry huts, listening to the rain on the corrugated iron roof. Tramping remains our happy place, somewhere we can laugh, sing, pretend to be fairies or pirates or whatever takes our fancy, swim naked in icy rivers and talk to the trees and the birds.

I'm so grateful to my daughter for all that she continues to teach me, for sharing her joy and wonder and allowing me to walk beside her and observe her blossoming into a beautiful, brave and self-confident young lady with one of the warmest, softest hearts I've ever had the privilege of meeting. I hope this journey inside myself will allow me to be a better mother to her and help me guide her on her own path through life.

I know now that sometimes you need to let go of your fears and doubts and embrace the glorious, terrifying free-fall and trust that you will safely land somewhere else, somewhere of your own making.

Life, like the weather, flows in strange and fascinating ways. The best we can do is be well-equipped, resilient, and flexible in the face of adversity. Removing myself from all the stressors in my previous life gave me the time and space to reset, to observe my mind and to feel the rise and fall of my dysregulated nervous system. The physical, methodical sensation of walking allowed my body to release some long-forgotten memories, pieces of the jigsaw puzzle that make up my own lived experience and help explain how my body and brain adapted to help me survive childhood adversity. Now as an adult, with all of the information in front of me, I can begin the long journey of healing my own wounds, because now I'm strong enough and safe enough to feel the depth of the pain and abandonment and terror that, as a child, was far too overwhelming to experience, let alone process in any meaningful way.

Healing is about feeling, and while it can hurt so bad, I've learned that it's better to allow the feelings to flow through me, no matter how painful or terrifying they seem, because just like the wind, they will eventually blow themselves out and a deep calm will follow. It's there inside of me, somewhere, even if I must keep searching our wild places to find it.

Acknowledgements

WRITING THIS BOOK WAS HARDER than I had ever imagined, yet somehow a necessary, cathartic and rewarding part of the healing process. After so many years of hiding behind my pain and trauma, the act of sharing my story feels like ripping off a giant Band-Aid and stepping forward into the light as a tiny, scared and vulnerable creature. But, in doing so, I have opened myself up to receive much love and compassion from friends, complete strangers and the outdoor community.

I have many people to thank for their unwavering love and support during this journey — not only the big walk on Te Araroa with Emilie by my side, but also the more lonely, private journey of writing about why a single mother would quit her job and take her seven-year-old daughter on a long walk across New Zealand.

Firstly, I'd like to thank my beautiful daughter, Emilie, for her love, enthusiasm, companionship, laughter and all the wonderful Bush Baby stories she told me during our 2200-kilometre journey. Thank you so much, Emilie. I love you to the moon and back, and you're my best tramping buddy of all time.

I'd like to thank our friends for their encouragement and support, including: Fabio Silveira, who brought his 'landlady' beers and good vibes; Ken Oliver, who drove across from Greymouth to give us surprise goodbye hugs; the beautiful ladies Melissa Hutchinson and Nadia Cannon, for joining us on a wander through the wilderness; and Danilo Hegg, who was our InReach emergency contact and a source of sage advice about weather conditions. Thank you for sharing your company, lollies, Nutella and, ultimately, your toilet paper on that long haul through Richmond Range. Special love to Smash, who stayed on in Queenstown to help me recover from concussion, and everyone who rallied around us during this challenging time.

Thank you to all the beautiful people who followed and shared our journey online, enjoyed our blogs and photos and helped us reach our fundraising goal for Federated Mountain Clubs and the Mental Health Foundation of New Zealand. Many of you reached out to encourage us directly and offered us a place to stay, a warm meal, a lift, your friendship or to share your own story. Your warmth and love lifted our hearts.

We were very fortunate to receive practical support from a number of local outdoor stores and services, including the loan of a fancy Garmin InReach from Tony Glentworth and the wonderful team at TrackMe NZ, who checked in with us to offer encouragement throughout our journey.

A big part of Te Araroa journey includes the people you share the tracks and huts with, and the wider trail angel community. Thank you to everyone who shared the trail with us, including Erin, Stew, Tom and Hils from Team 'Best Team' on the Whanganui River, and the many trail angels who offered us hospitality, in particular, Fi and Anthony from Whiowhio Hut; Geoff Ritchie from Levin; the beautiful Dani and whānau; Lydia; Anne and Russell; Greg Wilson; Barry Drummond; Deanna and whānau; and the many other people who helped make our experience so much warmer and richer, whose care and kindness helped lighten our load and bring smiles to our faces.

Thank you also to: Jan Finlayson and Dan Clearwater from Federated Mountain Clubs, for getting behind our crazy adventure and hosting a blog of our travels; Te Araroa Chief Executive Mark Weatherall, for your encouragement to walk the trail; and the many organisations, volunteers and groups, including the Backcountry Trust and Department of Conservation for your mahi in maintaining the hut and track network that New Zealanders are so blessed to have in our 'backyard', and especially to Megan 'Meegie Weegie' Dimozantos from the Backcountry Trust for the opportunity to help fix up Stanfield Hut.

A special thank-you to Timoti and Morganne who gifted us both our beautiful, magical pounamu, which I truly believe kept us safe during our long journey and helped reveal the many tiny secrets of Papatūānuku and all her incredible forest creatures. Speaking of forest creatures, Emilie was so happy to be hosted by Zealandia in Wellington, meet the team at Wildbase Recovery in Palmerston North, and be gifted a copy of Gillian Candler's wonderful *Explore & Discover* books, which she carried across Aotearoa. You've all helped to inspire a deep love of our natural world in this curious little girl.

I'm also very grateful to the amazing team at Penguin Random House New Zealand, including my beautiful publisher Rachel Eadie, project editor Olivia Win-Ricketts and kind and sensitive editor Nicola McCloy for all their hard work and for pushing me to keep going and give birth to this book — even when I really didn't want a bar of it anymore.

There are so many other people I have not named here, but please know you all have a special place in our hearts and memories.

Last of all, I want to thank you, beautiful reader, for coming on this journey with us.

The adventures continue after Te Araroa: Winter tramping in Southland's Eyre Mountains/Taka Rā Haka Conservation Park. DANILO HEGG

VICTORIA BRUCE is a keen tramper and writer. Her popular social media and blog accounts Adventures with Emilie documented her and her young daughter's journey walking New Zealand's Te Araroa trail.

Victoria is a media and communications advisor with a background in journalism and nursing. She has worked for news agencies in Australia and Southeast Asia, including the Australian Associated Press, *Myanmar Times* and Fairfax's *Sydney Morning Herald*, and held communications roles with a number of public, private and non-profit organisations.

Since completing Te Araroa, Victoria and Emilie continue to escape regularly into the wilderness. Together they love exploring Aotearoa's wild places, learning about the environment and conservation and doing their part to care for our beautiful country.

Born in New Zealand, Victoria grew up in Australia before returning to her country of birth as an adult. She currently lives in the South Island of New Zealand.

This is her first book.